The
Male Couple's Guide
to
Living Together

The Male Couple's Guide to Living Together

What Gay Men Should Know About Living with Each Other and Coping in a Straight World

Eric Marcus

PERENNIAL LIBRARY

HARPER & ROW, PUBLISHERS, New York
Cambridge, Philadelphia, San Francisco, Washington
London, Mexico City, São Paulo, Singapore, Sydney

FIRST EDITION

Copy editor: Brian Hotchkiss

Index by Elan D. Garonzik for Riofrancos & Co.

Library of Congress Cataloging-in-Publication Data

Marcus, Eric.
  The male couple's guide to living together.

  Bibliography: p.
  Includes index.
  1. Homosexual couples, Male—United States—Life
skills guides.   I. Title.
HQ76.2.U5M36   1988   306.7′622   87-14140
ISBN 0-06-055040-6   88 89 90 91 92 HC 10 9 8 7 6 5 4 3 2 1
ISBN 0-06-096143-0 (pbk.)   88 89 90 91 92 HC 10 9 8 7 6 5 4 3 2 1

For Homer

Contents

Acknowledgments

Many thanks to Toni Sciarra, editor-in-chief at Rawson Associates, Peter Donhauser, Larry Frascella, and Alan Richardson for their initial encouragement; Jane Willson, for helping me wrestle with the proposal; Posy Gering for plowing through the early drafts; Barry Owen for editing the manuscript before submission; Nancy Welles for coming up with a title; and Larry Ashmead and Margaret Wimberger at Harper & Row for their encouragement and assistance.

I'm also grateful to the experts who offered information and/or reviewed sections of the manuscript. These include Amy and Dick Ashworth; attorney Lila Bellar; Kevin Berrill; Ralph Blair, Ed.D.; James E. D'Eramo, Ph.D., Emery Hetrick, M.D.; Larry Higgins, M.D.; Dan Hirsch, Ph.D.; Jeffrey Laurence, M.D.; Eileen MacKenzie; Alice Mehling; Mark Mishkind, Ph.D.; Sister Patrice Murphy; Brent Nance; Michael Quadland, Ph.D.; Reverend Jim Sandmire; Stuart Schear; Joy Schulenberg; attorney Mark Senak; Michael Shernoff, C.S.W.; attorney Thomas Stoddard; David Wertheimer, C.S.W.; John Whalen; and Michael Wilkes, M.D.

Finally, I would especially like to acknowledge the many men and women who shared their knowledge or views on male couple relationships with me.

"Don't go into a relationship and expect things. You've got to go in and do things. You have to show your love and show your commitment. That's what will get into someone's heart and make the relationship. Then you find somebody else who's willing to put the equal into it. Then you've got a relationship."

Introduction

The Male Couple's Guide to Living Together is a straightforward, every-day guide to the social, emotional, legal, financial, professional, and familial intricacies of living life together for gay male couples. A resource book and an advice book, it is by no means complete, but an introduction to many of the issues and challenges facing the male couple.

The Male Couple's Guide is not objective. There are many points of view expressed—my own and those of others. While I often note that there are right ways and wrong ways of doing things, the specifics of each circumstance, of each couple, are different, and you will have to tailor what you read here to your fit your own circumstances and needs.

The idea for this book grew out of a dinner conversation with another young couple. Scott and I were talking with Terry and Dennis (who are introduced in Chapter 1) about who cleans house, family relationships, writing a will, getting Durable Power of Attorney, family finances, and how to cope with fear of The Dreaded Disease. It occurred to me that there was no one resource we could turn to for some of the answers we needed. Given that the four of us all worked in some aspect of publishing, it came as no surprise that we all agreed a resource book for male couples was an interesting possibility. I decided to pursue the idea, and this book is the result.

WHO WAS INTERVIEWED

The people I spoke with in the process of researching and writing this book fall into four categories: couples, single men, families of gay men in couple relationships, and experts.

To get a variety of views and experiences I set out to find couples in different parts of the country and from different walks of life. Relying mainly on my personal network, I let most of my friends, both gay and straight, know that I was looking for couples to interview and asked them to ask their friends to ask their friends to ask their friends. . . . Where I had specific need for couples with children, couples who lived in rural areas, older couples, new couples, mixed-race or mixed-religion couples, couples with drug or alcohol problems, etc., I sent out a specific call for that type of couple or contacted an appropriate gay organization.

The couples who I quote in the book live all over the country, from the rural South to southeastern Alaska, from New York City to LA. Their professions range from doctors, lawyers, and school teachers to truck drivers. Most have been together from two to fifteen years, but a few have been together as little as six months, others for over forty years. I also spoke with single men who want to be in relationships or who had been in relationships at one time.

For many parts of the book I depended on information provided by dozens of experts in various fields, including lawyers, doctors, psychologists, psychiatrists, therapists, social workers, rabbis, priests, ministers, insurance brokers, real estate brokers, financial analysts, and so forth. I also interviewed representatives from many gay organizations.

STATISTICS

I use very few statistics concerning male couples in this book because I don't believe there are statistics available that accurately reflect the varied experiences and ways of life of male couples. Although there are indeed statistics available on male couples from a handful of studies, the numbers in them vary so dramatically that I believe they may only be a reflection of the sample group chosen, and little more.

For example, as I note in Chapter 3, "Monogamy/Nonmonogamy," no two of the handful of studies that have been done on gay couples came up with the same numbers on monogamy. The numbers range from 27 percent monogamous in Mary Mendola's book, *The Mendola Report* (1980) to 5 percent monogamous in *The Male Couple* (1984).

The biggest challenge for anyone attempting to study gay couples (this book is in no way a *study* of gay couples) is finding a representative sample. It seems to me that finding a representative sample in a population that remains largely invisible is extremely difficult, if not impossible.

GENERALIZATIONS

The temptation, of course, is to draw from statistics general conclusions about gay couples. I was very tempted to make general statements based on what I learned from the men I interviewed. And for a book like this, generalizations are inevitable. But when I do make generalizations, I'm careful to note that the conclusions made are based on the information drawn from the people interviewed or are based on my personal beliefs. These generalizations are not necessarily representative of anything beyond that and are in no way meant to speak for all gay men and couples.

RESOURCES

Where appropriate, chapters end with a selective list of available resources including books and organizations; in a few instances there are discussions about how to find a professional in your area, such as a lawyer or doctor. The Appendix lists general resources.

In choosing which organizations to list, I generally restricted my choice to the most established organizations available. There are hundreds of gay organizations across the country, ranging from social and political groups, to health and recreation organizations. Unfortunately, as I discovered much to my frustration, many organizations don't respond to letters or phone calls, and others disappear even before the resource in which they are listed gets to bookstores. Some groups are started by well-meaning people on a volunteer basis who are then not able to sustain their initial effort. Others are simply an answering machine in someone's home that gives no hint whether you've reached the organization that you've set out to reach.

There are, however, established organizations that are both well meaning and well organized, and deliver valuable services to the gay community. These groups are listed throughout the book. Many are so well established that they have toll-free telephone numbers. In a couple of instances I've listed relatively new organizations, because no others were available, and the services they offer are so valuable.

Book recommendations include brief descriptions. I cannot recommend all the books listed with great enthusiasm. Where I have reservations, such as with *The Joy of Gay Sex* (the 1986 reissue shockingly fails to include information about AIDS except for an inadequate warning on one of the title pages), I state them clearly.

Not all of the books listed are written specifically for a gay audience. Many of my favorites, such as Bernie Zilbergeld's *Male Sexuality,* were written for a larger, general audience.

LANGUAGE

How do you refer to your partner? How should you refer to him? Lover? Partner? Sweetheart? Significant Other? Friend? Boyfriend? Husband? What you do is of course up to you and your ———. Interestingly, the problem isn't limited to gay couples. Every now and then an article appears in a prominent magazine or newspaper that points up the difficulty straight couples have in finding the right word or phrase to describe their lover relationships outside marriage. Boyfriend or girlfriend seems too trite. Lover sounds illicit or limiting. Friend is too vague, covivant too pretentious. One option, which was borrowed from the 1980 U.S. census, was POSSLQ (pronounced "Possel-cue"), an acronym for Persons of Opposite Sex Sharing Living Quarters.

In its column "Couplings," the *New York Times* suggested cohabitant. In a letter to the *Times,* Jacques Barzun took issue with this choice to describe the "condition of lovers living together."He asked rhetorically, "Why promote in English one more clumsy four-syllable legal term, when we have at hand the elegant 'consort'? It has adorned princes and queens, and its Latin ancestor means companion, partner, sharer of common fate—just what romance is looking for." Not a bad suggestion, but in this book I use both "lover" and "partner." I don't find either word adequate to describe my consort, friend, and sweetheart, but for want of better words I chose these two.

THE AUTHOR'S VOICE

Throughout the book, I talk about my experiences and about my relationship with Scott. I decided to add my own voice in the hope that such information would add depth to the advice offered. Some chapters, specifically Chapters 9 and 11—"Legalizing Your Relationship," and "Insurance," (respectively), are chapters that were written as Scott and I went through the process of arranging for adequate insurance and drawing up necessary legal papers.

In these instances and in others, I hope our experiences, the experiences of other couples, their families, single men, and the advice drawn from my conversations with them and the experts will be of help to you and your partner.

The
Male Couple's Guide
to
Living Together

With the exception of experts, all names have been changed. That includes my partner, whom I refer to here as Scott. He asked me not to use his real name simply because he values his privacy. I've also changed identifying details such as physical characteristics, ages, locations and professions. All medical, legal and insurance information provided is the most current available at the time of publication. For questions or advice about specific concerns, *please* consult a professional.

CHAPTER 1

Getting Started

"You never know what's going on inside you."

I always said, "I'll know him when I see him." The problem was, I saw him everywhere: mowing the lawn next door, standing in a local bar, furiously scribbling notes across the room in astronomy class, waving goodbye at a train station in Copenhagen. I knew the intoxication of a fast-beating heart—the adrenalin, the high. I was a devoted believer in the notion of "love at first sight." But after falling in and out of love at least a dozen times, I began to feel a little weary and desperate. My excited exclamations that *This is really The One* no longer washed with family and friends.

The phrases "know him when I see him" and "love at first sight" are both very common and revealing. They expose the extreme emphasis we, as human animals, place on physical attraction. What we call "falling in love" is often no more than exploring and satisfying a physical attraction—no bad thing, but hardly a guaranteed path to a long-term relationship. All the wonderful, intoxicating possibilities that attend physical infatuation usually have less to do with the man you just met than with the man you imagine him to be.

"How could I be so blind?" I used to wonder after realizing that this man I "loved" and thought I would spend my life with wasn't even someone with whom I would want to go for a walk. "What was I thinking?" I would blame my emotions. It was a conspiracy between my emotions (need for love and attention, affirmation, etc.) and my desires (physical attraction, infatuation). Together they overpowered common sense and objectivity.

When I finally met "the one," I didn't realize it until months later.

After my first meeting with Scott I remember thinking as I left his office at the magazine where he worked: nice smile, regular guy, maybe he's gay—doesn't really matter. At the time, I was in love with an unattainable blond, a younger man who was struggling with his sexuality, and not nearly ready to commit to the kind of established life I was looking for. But I was holding on to the *idea* of him. A relationship with Scott was the farthest thing from my thoughts.

Perhaps you will be one of the few who, on some enchanted evening, discovers your true love at first sight across a crowded room. It actually happens. Stuart and Paul were both 23 when they met at a local bar. That was just over six months ago. Paul is a quiet, stocky, boyish-looking curly blond. Stuart is tall, rail thin, a talker, and dark-haired.

Paul: I saw Stuart first. I thought he was laughing at me. But we worked our way over to each other. We started talking. He bought me a drink. I found out he had a gay brother and I told him I had three gay brothers. There was immediate sympatico. We spent our first night together and we've been together almost every day since.

Stuart: I've had things start this way but they've always fizzled quickly. Six months was a milestone.

Paul: I was out looking that night, but I didn't expect to buy. I also didn't expect him to come like this. I was out for different packaging, but Stuart's all I need now, all I want.

Sometimes, physical attraction is followed by the discovery that you share values, interests, and the same outlook on relationships, or, perhaps as enticing, intriguing differences. But more often, despite the example of Paul and Stuart, you discover that after the fireworks stop firing, the only thing you have in common is that you're both gay.

Our senses (of which I think there are dozens, not merely five) are heavily weighted toward the visual, what the eye sees and tells. I remember once working for a gorgeous straight man in his mid-thirties. Everybody, both male and female, gay and straight, was affected by him and attracted to him. A young woman colleague and I were talking about him one afternoon, when it became apparent that his physical beauty had affected her objectivity. At one point she told me that she found him "very charming," but wondered "what made him so charming?" Anyone could tell that she was physically attracted to him; that, while he might very well have a charming personality, the source of his charm for her was his raw, hot, hunky, perfectly glorious face, hair, skin, height, eyes, hands, way of moving—in short, the way he looked.

Physical allure, while not always the most powerful kind of attraction, is unarguably the most common. Physical attraction, whether you're single, looking for love, or firmly established in a satisfying relationship, is a fact of being alive. It's as pervasive as it is powerful.

The problem for men who want a relationship is that physical attraction distorts judgment. This isn't to argue against satisfying physical infatuation if you can. It's just that, for many people once the physical attraction is either satisfied or abandoned, the harsh light of objective reality sets in. In that uncompromising light, the once-desired object of physical attraction, that living, breathing modern-day Adonis of last week or last night, often seems woefully inadequate. He has nothing interesting to say at breakfast. He tells you how he cried at some movie you thought stupid and boring. He's uncomfortably young or too old. Upon closer inspection, he's not so gorgeous as all that. He's already involved or uncommunicative. He's emotionally unstable. He has an annoying habit of repeating himself. In short, for whatever reason or reasons of the trillions available, he is clearly not The One.

Many men I talked to tell of satisfying one physical attraction after another, but failing to find The One. They are confused and frustrated, especially because they have friends and acquaintances whose serious relationships got their start solely from a mutual physical attraction. If it can happen for men they know, why can't it happen for them. I don't know the answer. Many successful relationships have obviously gotten started through physical attraction. But I'm convinced that physical attraction, however, usually impairs objectivity. Once physical attraction is satisfied (or abandoned), objectivity begins to return. What I call "objectivity" is really the full spectrum of considerations, like intelligence, personal interests, family background, and so forth. After satisfying the physical, men who are shopping for a relationship begin to check other considerations on their lists and often find that their latest possibility just doesn't measure up.

Some, though, find that he does measure up. They find that they share common interests and goals. Or that they're intrigued by the experience, interests, friends, and tastes of the other. So, while their beginning may have been largely physical, it led to a broader long-term relationship.

For most men physical attraction is a vital contribution to the foundation of a long-term relationship, but it is not the only important one. You must decide for yourself what characteristics in a man are important to you. For example, do you want someone who is quick to express his emotions? Must he come from a similar social background? Is it necessary that he share your views about monogamy? Do you want a man who is easy going? Do you want a man who shares your commitment to family responsibilities?

Knowing what is important to you in a man isn't going to save you from disappointment following the quenching of a physical infatuation.

If you're honest with yourself, though, it may help you to size up the prospects more realistically and perhaps help you give more weight to some of those long-term qualities you've decided are important. This is a kind of discipline that isn't easy for many men, but for many others has led to successful long-term relationships.

MEETING HIM

Once you have an idea of the kind of imperfect man you're looking for, you have to find him. That can still be frustrating and painful. The crowded room across which Chet and John met five years ago was the living room of a mutual friend. And it was no accident that John was there.

Chet: I set it up. I asked friends if they knew of anyone. I didn't want to hit the streets anymore. I was frustrated with the whole thing. I called my friends Monday or Tuesday. They said they knew somebody and I suggested they plan a get-together or party. They were close friends so I trusted their opinion. I don't let things lie, so I called them right back and said "Why don't you make it this weekend?"

There's no big secret to meeting a man with whom you share some common ground. Meeting a man who is gay, single, interested in you, interesting to you, and capable of entering a lasting relationship is far more difficult. By finding a place where you share common ground, you at least increase your chances of meeting the lover you're looking for.

CLUBS, ORGANIZATIONS, AND RELIGIOUS GROUPS FOR GAY MEN
At an outdoor-activities club, running club, professional organization, square dance club, religious group, or volunteer organization specifically for gay people, you'll have the opportunity to meet other gay men in relatively bright light, in a setting that emphasizes something other than the search for sex. It's a lower-key way to meet potential partners, and it allows you to get to know other men without the pressure of being on the rack or on a date.

An ideal resource in which to find a group that interests you is the *Directory of Homosexual Organizations and Publications* (see Appendix). The directory lists social, religious, recreational, and dozens of other categories of organizations where you can pursue personal, professional, social, athletic, and cultural interests and meet men with similar interests at the same time. The directory has hundreds of listings from Missoula, Montana to Jackson, Mississippi, from Fairbanks, Alaska to Pensacola, Florida.

FRIENDS AND FAMILY

Never underestimate the resilience of a mother's love. My mother did not think it half as odd as I did when she suggested I call her friend's son who was also gay. And friends, as Chet and John discovered, are invariably more objective than you are, and may do a better job of matching you up with a potential partner than you could do on your own. Let your friends—and when appropriate, your family—know that you are available and interested in meeting a potential partner.

SCHOOL

Away at college you're thrown together with many people who have similar intellects and aspirations, if not backgrounds, and you get to see them regularly in all sorts of circumstances with many different people.

Tony and Doug met as undergrads at college:

Tony: I was 20 and Doug was 18. I started going to the gay and lesbian meetings at school and met Doug's best friend Chuck. I started going out with Chuck, but I broke up with him at the end of the school year because I knew that I was in love with Doug. But Doug didn't know I was in love with him. And I wasn't even sure he was gay.

Doug: I was not only not out, I had never dealt with being gay.

Tony: I had told all our friends, "Wow, I'm really in love with this guy," and they said, "He's the straightest guy, and you don't stand a chance." Doug had a job for the summer at school and I decided I would stay there for the chance something would happen. We were friends, but nothing happened for a long time. Then much to my surprise, on July 3, Doug asked me if I would spend the night with him and we've been together ever since.

Doug: I have tremendous powers of control—or self-deception. I had never known any men that I was really attracted to until I met Tony, even though on some level I knew I was attracted to men. Then when I met Tony I left openings six lanes wide, during the whole time that we knew each other, for him to make a move. But he didn't.

Over Christmas vacation I had decided I would bring it up with Tony, but when I got back to school he was already going out with Chuck. I didn't have any reason to think he was attracted to me. Then, that summer, after Tony broke up with Chuck, I finally got up my nerve to broach the subject.

RIGHT IN FRONT OF YOUR EYES

Keep your eyes open at the office or in the laundry room, at cultural events, weddings, etc.

When I met Scott at the office, my eyes were pretty much sealed shut. His were wide open. "I knew I was interested in him so I finally got my courage up to take him up on his offer to go on a walking tour of the city. I suggested a Saturday so we would have more time together than if we went out on a weeknight."

GAY BAR, DISCO

Not bad for finding someone with whom you can dance, talk casually, or have sex. Not quite as good for meeting a lover, but plenty of men have met long-term lovers at bars and discos "on purpose" and "by accident." If you live in a large enough city, you can probably find a bar that specializes in a particular "kind" of crowd. If you live in a small town where there are few if any alternatives, a local bar may be the one place you can meet other gay men.

In Juneau, Alaska, (total population under 20,000) for example, there is one small bar just a few blocks from downtown that is gay "at least until someone straight walks in, which is about every ten minutes," according to the bartender. It's the kind of place where high-pressure staring is impossible because, with only eight chairs and even fewer places to stand, you can't help but meet everyone there. If you live in a town smaller than Juneau, you may have to go to another town to find a gathering place.

PERSONAL ADS AND DATING SERVICES

QUALITY NOT QUANTITY, looking for that one special person who knows himself, G/W/M, 25, blond, quiet, romantic, sensitive, honest. Looking for relationship based on old-fashioned morals, lifetime commitment, trust, honesty, true love; not just sex and infatuation. You: 25–30, no drugs, non-promiscuous. I'm willing to relocate for that special person. Let's make life worth living! Send descriptive letter, photo if possible, telephone number to . . . .

The odds? Who knows? But personal ads and dating services for gay men who are looking for a lasting relationship exist across the country, from low-tech newspaper ads in the "Relationships" section of *The Advocate*, a national gay magazine, to a computer matching service in Illinois and video dating in Los Angeles.

Lloyd and Eliot, who have been together for ten years, met through an ad Lloyd placed—while he was still married—in the *Village Voice*. Lloyd was living with his wife of eleven years and two young children in Scarsdale, an affluent suburb outside of New York City. Eliot ran his own consulting firm and lived in Manhattan.

Eliot: His ad was so preposterous. He said he had a car and was willing to travel within a fifty-mile radius and was married. He told me later that he hadn't wanted to limit his options. I had been single for two years and was tired of meeting men in bars.
Lloyd: I got a letter from Eliot, and we met over lunch. I never expected

anything to develop with any man. I just figured that it was something I would have on the side.

Within four months Lloyd had asked his wife for a divorce and had moved in with Eliot.

Dating services can be found through local and national gay publications.

IS HE GAY AND SINGLE?

Gay?

When Scott took me up on my offer to go on a walking tour, he didn't know if I was gay, and while I liked him I didn't really care if he was gay. I hadn't given it more than a passing thought. He decided to solve his dilemma by telling me he was gay.

Scott: I was interested in Eric and the only way to break through the impasse— my not knowing he was gay—was to tell him that I was gay.

At the end of the day, when we were about to go our separate ways, I invited Scott up for some soda water. We talked for a while, and just before he was about to leave he took a deep breath and started to explain to me that he wanted to be friends, but there was something I should know about him. As his face turned red I realized what he was about to say and I was charmed. Having been in his position several times with friends and relatives, I knew the anxiety he was experiencing.

Scott: When I finally got out the words, "I'm gay," Eric got a big smile on his face and said "Welcome to the club!" and offered his hand for a shake.

Meeting a man in a setting with other gay people avoids the problem of having to find out if he's gay. When you meet at the office or in some other mixed circumstance you have to rely on eye contact, conversation, or other interaction to figure out if this guy you're interested in is even interested in men.

There are more- and less-direct ways of finding out if a man you're interested in is gay. You can avoid talking about it, but continue to spend time together, gathering information along the way, putting together a case until you're certain whether he is straight or gay—or until you're comfortable enough to bring up the subject. Or you can be very direct and ask the question, "Are you gay?"

Single?

The next step for Scott was to find out if I was single. We did that over lunch later that week where I explained to him about the boyfriend I had been dating on and off for several months who was in Europe for the summer, traveling with his ex-girlfriend. That proved not to be an obstacle. Within five days I was hopelessly in love. I still felt torn between my new-found love and my love overseas, but I decided that a bird in the hand was better than one in Europe.

Trying to find out if a man you've just met is married to a woman or in a relationship with a man is not always so easy. Howard, 29, has been single on and off for the past three years and has been looking not to be. He offers this warning:

> Single men have to beware of coupled men who are out experimenting or looking for a reason to get out of their current relationship. Such men often are not totally forthcoming. I've had two men lie to me. I've gotten excited, hopeful, optimistic, and had the whole rug pulled out from under me when I found out he was really in a relationship and couldn't get involved with me beyond a casual affair.
>
> Even if he wanted to get out of his relationship, I would never begin a relationship on the ashes of someone else's. It feels very unethical, and it would bode ill for our relationship if a man used me to get out of an existing relationship. It's a bad beginning, especially if he can't stand up on his own feet and leave the relationship.

DATING AND COURTSHIP

Dating

Dates are test drives. They give you and your love interest an opportunity to have a closer look, to get to know each other. An evening out at a movie, dinner, in the company of friends, gives you a chance to find out if this man you're attracted to is still attractive once you know more about him.

I remember one boyfriend I was introduced to by a mutual friend who thought the match might be interesting. We were in bed before we said hello, and didn't talk much after that date. He had two roommates with whom we often had dinner. The first time we had dinner alone—about a month and a half into the relationship—I remember sitting across the table terrified. I couldn't think of anything to say. It was then that I realized we had almost nothing in common. It was another couple of months before I would admit to myself that the "relationship" was not working.

I wish I could believe that dinner alone on that first date would have saved me from that relationship and the emotional trauma that went with it. I felt like such a fool when I realized that the relationship I was working on was not something I had ever wanted. He liked drugs, I didn't. I wanted a monogamous relationship, he didn't. That alone should have been enough to send me off in the opposite direction. It was a painful but instructive lesson.

Marshall and Craig, now both in their late 30s, met in 1980 on a date arranged by Marshall's ex-lover. They hit it off:

Craig: We started dating. Real old-fashioned dating. Basically we went to shows, movies, just walked around. I knew Marshall was very special.

Marshall: I felt the same way. One of the first things that Craig said was "I don't want to sleep with you," which I found terribly flattering.

Craig: I explained to him that I liked him a lot, that I had a good, basic, gut feeling. I told him that I wanted to do this one right and go slowly. It was really important to me that if this were going to be special that I offer Marshall something that I hadn't offered anyone else before. The only thing I could offer him was not sleeping with him, as opposed to sleeping with him, which is what I would have done with anyone else. I felt that if he realized how special this was for me, how important it was to try this, he would go along with it.

Marshall: It made a lot of sense because I had been in a lot of relationships where you go to bed and then you get to know him and realize "I'm much more emotionally involved than I want to be, and this isn't going to work out." You realize that what you have is a false intimacy.

Craig: The therapist I had been seeing suggested I try dating—getting to know the man before jumping into bed. I had gone through a series of relatively short-term relationships of less than a year and they were all unsatisfactory and I couldn't figure out why. I was very unhappy. I decided I needed some kind of guidance.

So I decided I was going to try dating and Marshall was the first. It was about three months before we got physically involved.

Marshall: I think it was sooner than that. Our actions were not as good as our intentions.

Craig: We tried.

NOT GOING TO BED ON THE FIRST DATE
There are two good practical reasons not to go to bed on the first date: (1) it's ultimately less complicated than going to bed, and (2) there are no health risks if all you do is hold hands.

In terms of ego, emotion, pride, etc., having sex means more to me, as I know it does for many men, than holding hands at the movies, or going for a walk on the beach, or a hug goodbye. Raising the stakes by getting physically involved right away can leave you with a complicated and unwanted entanglement from which it may be very difficult, embarrassing, or hurtful (for you or your date) to disengage. It can be particularly awkward if he works in the same office, belongs to the same running club, or is someone you meet at the grocery all the time. Finding out you don't really like him over a hamburger and beer is a lot less costly than making the same discovery when you're naked in bed.

Protecting your physical health is reason enough for not rushing into a sexual relationship. A man with whom you are developing a relationship/friendship is more likely to feel a sense of responsibility toward you and less likely to hold back on important health information about herpes, AIDS, or other sexually transmitted diseases. Going on a few dates before having sex gives you a chance to raise and discuss health issues, such as safer sex (see Chapter 8)—and personal history—without having to force it.

There is always the danger that your date will feel very threatened if you try to explain that you don't want to have sex right away. He may feel you're trying to put him off (which may or may not be true), or think that you don't find him attractive. All you can do is reassure him that you are indeed interested and that you just want to go slowly and get to know him better before getting into bed.

HOW TO STAY OUT OF BED ON THE FIRST, SECOND . . . DATE

Saying I wasn't going to bed on the first date was one thing. Figuring out how to do it was something else. It's especially difficult considering that I grew up at a time when the whole idea was to get into bed, or at least out of clothing, as soon as humanly possible. Getting to know a man before getting naked requires a different set of skills. You may know how to get his clothes off, but do you know how to keep his clothes on?

It took me more years than I like to admit to learn how to put on the brakes. I did know that going to bed with a man who turned out to be a disappointment left me far more miserable than discovering that I didn't like him before we became physically involved. But my need for affection and physical contact almost always overpowered the part of my brain that controls rational behavior, even when I suspected I was making a mistake. Since I found my behavior so difficult to control, I changed tactics.

I made a commitment to myself: "I won't go to bed on the first date, or the first week, first month, first few months, or until. . . ."

But that wasn't enough. I discovered that the secret to following through with a rational decision in the face of irrational passion was to put something other than clothing between me and my date. You can do that by observing a few simple dos and don'ts.

Do:

1. Meet in a public, well-lighted place—a restaurant or a well-populated park, for example.

2. Plan a date that includes getting together with other people.

3. Go to the movies.

4. Go for a walk.

5. Meet for coffee.

Don't:

1. Go to his home or your home.

2. Go anyplace where you will be entirely alone.

Avoid:

1. Using the same car. (It's an easy place to be alone. If you use his car, you have less control over how the date develops.)

Courting

Courtship is the period that starts after the first several dates, when you realize that you would like the relationship to continue, and can extend for weeks, months, and even years, depending on how fast you move.

Courtship can be as anxiety inducing as it is wonderful. "Should I call him?" "Will he call me?" "What did he mean by what he said?" "Is he holding back because he doesn't want to see me anymore, or is he still recovering from his last relationship?" "Should I ease off?" "Should I press ahead?" "What tactics should I use?" "What should I do?" All of these feelings are perfectly normal. And chances are the man you're dating is experiencing the same doubts and anxieties—even if he looks cool and collected.

Since you're just getting to know each other, it's very easy to cross your messages, misunderstand each other, or misinterpret what one another meant. Pick up the phone and call, or talk about it in person. I know that's easier said than done, especially since there is a risk— however small—of rejection, of ending the infatuation, or of "ruining it," if you make that phone call.

If the courtship is getting too intense, or it's gotten too intense and you need to ease off, arrange dates where you don't have to spend the night or even the entire day or evening together. For example, you can arrange just to meet for breakfast before work, or for coffee after work. If you have the self-confidence, you can try to explain that you just need to take things more slowly.

The safest approach is to do what feels right, and if you're uncertain, look to your friends for ideas and support. When in doubt, be yourself and hope the man you're dating will do the same. It's perfectly okay to be on good behavior when you're courting, but you don't want to present a man who isn't you, someone to whom you think your date will be more attracted than the real you. It's not only exhausting to present a fictional version of yourself, it's also impossible to do for long.

THE STUMBLING BLOCK OF BEING GAY

While there's plenty that can go wrong between two potential partners, especially during courtship, two things in particular can sink a relationship between two men, even when they have a lot in common and the right chemistry: sexuality and sexuality-related emotional problems.

When John and Chet met, John had more problems with his own sexuality than with Chet being aggressive. He remembers:

> The biggest thing for me was I work in a family business and I'm very close with my family. I didn't know how my family would react to Chet. Before Chet, I was dating a girl who wanted to be married. She was very sweet. If I were to marry, I would have married her. I almost married her because of Chet—just out of spite.
>
> I was very confused. When my family would come over I would have to pretend Chet was just a friend. I'm pretty sure they knew who he was, knew why he was there. But it made me very uncomfortable.

This crisis about his sexuality led John to call off the relationship at one point.

> I said he could stay in the house if he wanted. He went off for the weekend with a friend and I called up the girl I was supposed to marry. I didn't want to be gay.
>
> It took Chet being away for me to realize I really did love him. Anytime that I saw anything around the house that was his, I started crying. After the separation I felt that the only way we would be able to make it was by making a total commitment. I realized I loved him and I was willing to risk a lot of things that were important to me for him. My fear that my family might turn their backs on me or that it could somehow affect my position at work made it difficult. I couldn't risk those things after one week.

They weathered the crisis and John very quickly came to terms with his sexuality. But both acknowledge his problem came very close to destroying their relationship.

If you or your potential partner are experiencing sexual-identity problems that are more than you can handle together, there is plenty of outside help to be found, from peer counseling to professional therapy [see Chapter 13, "Health"]. It doesn't need to destroy your relationship. But keep in mind that it is next to impossible to be both objective counselor and boyfriend/lover. You can't be his savior, but you can point him in the direction of the right help. Then it's up to him whether or not he wants to take advantage of that help.

For gay people there are, of course, the added challenges of overcoming all the negative societal attitudes that go along with being gay, and of living with the emotional scars that can result from growing up gay. Many men have learned to hide the truth, to withdraw emotionally. Emotional distance, dishonesty, and negative self-image can leave you ill-equipped to form a lasting relationship with another man. If the experience of being gay has been damaging, it may take more than a wonderfully loving, caring partner, and time, to repair that damage.

If you choose to seek the help of a professional counselor, shop around. Get recommendations from friends. Find someone you feel you can work with, someone who you feel shares values that make sense to you. It may take several sessions with different counselors before you find one with whom you're happy.

LUCK AND FATE

After all the thinking, planning, increasing of the odds, calling friends, joining clubs, taking classes, taking risks, and seeing counselors, luck and fate still play a significant role in meeting the perfect imperfect man. If one of the editors at the office where I was working hadn't suggested that I call some guy named Scott, for freelance work, we might never have met. And if Scott hadn't gotten up his courage to accept my not-quite-serious offer to take him on a walking tour of New York, we might never have discovered we had common interests.

Sometimes luck and fate can put the man of our dreams within arm's reach. Dennis and Terry, both now in their early 30s, met at work in 1981. Terry, an art director for a national magazine, had gone on vacation. Dennis was hired to replace him.

Dennis: I walked into his office and saw movie posters and movie books and I thought to myself "I wonder if this guy is gay and if we'll become friends."

Dennis and Terry did indeed become friends. At the time, Terry was involved with a man; Dennis had a girlfriend. About a year after they met, Terry split up with his lover.

Dennis: He didn't have any place to stay, and my rent had just been doubled. I said he could move in for a couple of months while he looked for another place. It was supposed to be temporary.

Terry: I didn't really want to move in. I thought this guy is real sweet but he's too hyper and he's going to drive me crazy. So I said I would do it on a very temporary—month-to-month—basis. So I moved into the tiny room off the living room. I actively dated while I lived here for a year or so.

Dennis: He was dating and I was sublimating. I wasn't out of the closet then. I think I had just broken up with a woman when Terry moved in. When he moved in, Terry thought I was straight, which is another reason he didn't want to move in with me.

Terry: I wasn't interested in him at all. There was no repressed sexual desire at all. We got real close during the time we lived together. We had a lot of fun. We both have a tendency to be homebodies. This had become a real home—more than I ever thought. But, after a year and a half, I had an adult complex coming on: "I'm an adult; I should be living on my own. And why am I living with this straight man?" So I moved to Westchester. And I really missed him. We missed each other.

About two months after he moved out, Terry and Dennis went to the beach with friends. Both Dennis and Terry were very depressed. Terry had lost his job the day after he signed the lease on his Westchester apartment. No one knew what Dennis was depressed about. After the beach the two said goodbye to their friends and went to dinner together.

Terry: My being depressed wasn't so unusual, but his being depressed was very unusual. He was just totally glum. So we went to dinner and he asked me why I was depressed, and I told him. I didn't want to be unemployed. I just got a new apartment. I was cut off, living in Westchester. He said it was okay, that I should cancel the new lease, and come back. Then I wanted to know what was up with him. I knew he hadn't been dating for a while so I figured he was sad because he wasn't in love or something.

Dennis isn't very expressive so I knew it was going to be like Twenty Questions. He wanted it pulled out of him. My sneaking suspicion was that he was lonely. I moved out, and he hadn't dated a woman in a while. I asked if it had anything to do with sex and he said, "Yes." Okay, one down. And then I said—just to get this out of the way because I knew that his answer was going to be "No"—"Does this have anything to do with sexual orientation?" He said, "Yes." I was completely shocked.

During the time we lived together, a couple of our friends suggested that Dennis might be gay. I was always the staunchest defender of his heterosexuality. I would say "No, I live with him. He talks about women, he watches "Hart to Hart" and loves Stephanie Powers. I didn't know she was a role model. So that very night we came back here and we just talked and talked and something happened. It was very weird, and as soon as I knew he was gay I started feeling a lot of emotion. All the closeness that had been was rapidly changing. It just started happening. And the same thing happened to him. That night was the first time we had sex. It was very emotional. It wasn't just sex. It was lovemaking of the most intense kind. Three hours earlier neither of us had had that in mind at all. It's something I've never understood. You never know what's going on inside you.

It's more like the way it would happen in a small town than in Manhattan because we knew each other so long. We were very different when we first met but through our friendship we became closer to each other and more like each other. I think we influenced each other. We each picked up the best habits the other had to offer. We almost became people each of us could fall in love with. Then it was almost immediately like love.

Dennis: We woke up the next morning in love.

Dennis and Terry's story demonstrates one simple truism: You never know. So no matter how much thinking, planning, or looking you do, meeting The One may be more a matter of chance than anything else. But you also have to put yourself in situations where your chances of meeting a suitable partner will be greatest. And, if you can, you should remember that where long-term relationships are concerned, looks (physical attraction) aren't everything. Still, that is no guarantee you will find The One without a lot of struggle, or without many false starts. Good luck!

CHAPTER 2

Getting Along

"When I lived alone I didn't have to compromise
on anything. But then, I lived alone."

BEING A COUPLE

In Fantasyland you never disagree with your partner. Relationships are
endlessly passionate and harmonious. Decisions are easy because both
men in Fantasyland relationships have the same vision of what the
relationship should be. No one is ever jealous. No one is ever insecure.
No one ever feels guilty. Commitment and love are unwavering. Relationships in Fantasyland are pure, unadulterated, and always-reliable
bliss.

On the other hand, real-world relationships, while often enduringly
fulfilling, are fraught with pitfalls and usually require attention, work,
and at bottom, commitment. Tony and Doug, who met in college and
are now both in their mid-20s, started out hopelessly in love. It was a
storybook romance, complete with a leafy New England setting. But
after a few months, Doug started to wonder what he and Tony were
doing wrong:

By the end of six months, we were fighting about who would do the dishes.
It was very hard for me not to feel disappointed in our relationship because
it wasn't just like my parents', who have a very, very good marriage. I didn't
stop to think that when I was 16 they had been married for seventeen years.
It occurred to me that my mother is the world's most enthusiastic antismok-
ing campaigner, and always has been, and my father smoked until I was 12.
They must have argued about it sometime. But it's still hard not to think
sometimes, "God, why can't it be just like my parents who always seem to

get along? Why can't Tony do this thing and just agree with me? Why don't we always want the same thing?"

I don't see anything wrong with comparing our relationship to a straight model. My mistake was comparing it to one that's been going on now for twenty-five years.

As relationships go, Tony and Doug were actually getting along just fine. Realistically, you and your partner are not likely to get along like a couple of friends who have known each other for decades until you have actually been with each other for a couple of decades. True, during those delirious first weeks and months it may seem as if you know all there is to know about each other, and you may like everything you see. But, as the early passion cools, you get to know each other in the context of day-to-day living. What you regarded as cute or endearing may begin to appear as obstinate and evidence of bad judgment. You'll discover all kinds of differences: differences of opinion about how to do the dishes, what movie to see, where to spend Thanksgiving, how to balance the checkbook, what you do with free time. . . . And learning to negotiate the differences, learning to be a couple, takes time.

Every successful (that is, mutually fulfilling) relationship shares at least five features. You could say that these are the five minimum requirements of a successful relationship, so read them carefully:

1. *Commitment* to the Relationship

2. *Agreement* on the Fundamental Rules—or Code—of the Relationship

3. Willingness to *Communicate*

4. Ability to *Compromise*

5. *Acceptance* of Shortcomings

Commitment

is simple, if not easy. It means fundamentally that you and your lover have decided that being a couple—staying a couple—is the most important purpose in your lives. This implies that you are both prepared to stay together through thick and thin, on days when it's easy to feel and express love and on days when it isn't. This kind of commitment—cellular commitment; commitment in the marrow—is especially difficult for two men to achieve because many men value independence over commitment, or because they delude themselves about the necessity of commitment to the success of a relationship. Of course, it's true that in Fantasyland commitment is both simple *and* easy.

John and Chet, who met through friends and have been together for five years, believe that many men in the gay community miss the meaning of commitment in a relationship.

John: A commitment to a relationship means willingness to face each other every single day—to be able to conduct your life comfortably and to accommodate your partner even when you don't feel like it.

Commitment, however, does not mean you will feel instantly secure in your relationship and trusting of your partner. Security comes with time, and trust has to be earned. But without commitment, trust and security are difficult, if not impossible, to achieve.

Agreement

on the fundamental rules of the relationship from the start is essential whether the rules allow for sex outside the relationship every other Thursday or establish a code of monogamy. If you can't agree on the fundamentals, you're in trouble. Unless you can find a way to accommodate each other's convictions about how a relationship should be conducted, you're bound for major, on-going, relationship-threatening conflicts.

Communication

is fundamental to successful relationships because many of the daily decisions of life together fall outside the mutually agreed upon relationship code, and because the code—the rules of the relationship— changes over time. Of course, not all communication is verbal and any two people who live together long enough devise ways to communicate that don't require an exchange of words, whether they're aware of it or not.

But in this context, communication means talking to each other: telling your lover you appreciate how much effort he puts into preparing meals, arguing with him about the way the household chores fall almost exclusively on your shoulders, yelling at each other over something you disagree on, telling your partner that you love him, talking over your plans for an upcoming vacation, telling your partner that he has hurt your feelings, letting him know that your sex life is less than stellar, telling him you really don't want to spend the holidays with his family, and so forth.

Communication is not always friendly, is sometimes loud, and is often difficult, particularly for men. As noted by Bernie Zilbergeld in his book, *Male Sexuality,* "It is often said that men don't communicate, which is only partly true. Men can communicate very well about certain things, like their jobs, sports, and the state of the world. But this isn't what is meant by those who fault men; they say men don't talk about their feelings and hopes and problems. That is generally true. . . ."

That doesn't mean men can't *learn* to communicate about feelings. Communication is a skill, and like any skill, it is one you can learn. Unfortunately, it may be something you learn on the wreckage of one or more relationships. Thomas, now 28, is just a half year into a new relationship and is trying his best to apply the things he learned from a failed three-year relationship.

> I wasn't comfortable bringing things up. I didn't want to make waves in the relationship, and that eventually led to the split up. I got angry about things, I was unhappy about the relationship, but I didn't say anything. I wasn't comfortable enough with my own feelings to talk. And Larry wasn't comfortable communicating his feelings. I couldn't talk and he couldn't talk.
>
> You hear time and again that communication is the key. A simple example is something that happened with my new boyfriend. He came out to the Gay Games [in San Francisco] to see me compete. It was just a couple of months into the relationship. The first day it was just wonderful. I was very physical with him. It was so loving. I was hanging onto him and I remember thinking, "I'll bet he thinks I'm just clinging on for dear life." I figured I was clinging on too much so I decided to give him a little room. The next day I didn't hang on as much.
>
> At the end of the next day, he looked at me and said, "You know, I realize that because of your WASP background and my Jewish background that the way we grew up was a little different. I realize you need a little space and need to distance yourself sometimes and may not be as physical." I gave him a very confused look and he said, "You seemed distant today. I wanted to hold you, but I felt I couldn't because you needed your space." Nothing could have been further from the truth, so I explained to him what I had been thinking. We talked about it. If we hadn't talked, I would have gone on thinking I couldn't hang onto him as much as I wanted to and he would have gone on thinking that I needed my distance.

Communication with a lover isn't always quiet and congenial. It sometimes means raised voices and arguing. For some men arguing comes naturally. They don't need drawing out. Dennis and Terry started out with one-sided arguments, because Dennis hated to discuss things that might result in an argument. He has found Terry to be a good instructor in the art of arguing.

Dennis: He's Latin and I'm WASP. I hate confrontation. I hate arguing. I hate discussions that might get mean spirited and he loves it. He's taught me how to argue and discuss.

Terry: I think we have a good attitude toward letting it out. We don't hold in. If I see he's stiff about something, I ask him.

Dennis: We go through some steam letting.

Terry: If I'm upset about something, I get upset about *that* thing. If Dennis gets upset, he'll get upset about something crazy. He'll come home from work and find a dull pencil on the table and get upset because the pencil is dull. I know by now that that means something is up—"There's a pencil on the table and it's dull. How can that be?" Wait, something's wrong, but I know it's not the pencil. So I have to drag it out of him.

Michael and Chris, both 27, have been together since they were 19. They now argue less, and less loudly, than they used to, but they see their sometimes heated discussions and arguments as symbolic of the trust they have in each other and their relationship.

Michael: When we first got together we argued very loudly. I used to throw things. I have a temper. I like to hit walls.

Chris: You hit me once.

Michael: I was raised with a big brother. The only way to protect myself was to throw tantrums.

Chris: But it's not okay for him to hit me. We often wrestle, but in fun.

Michael: We argue a lot. We bicker constantly. We disagree about a lot of things. We don't talk about politics. We don't talk about big subjects like abortion.

Chris: Because we disagree about these things.

Michael: My mother always had this phrase: "The more they fight, the more they like." I have no fear of arguing. If you're secure in a relationship that shows in the fact that you can argue very intensely and not be afraid that the relationship will end.

Communication, however heated, should not be confused with having to talk about everything with your lover. There are days when you're not going to feel great about him. You don't have to share your fantasies about killing him. According to Bernie Zilbergeld:

Communication . . . may conflict with the equally important right to privacy. Despite what some of the therapy gurus have been preaching, there is no such thing as complete openness or honesty, nor should there be. You have the right to keep private many of your thoughts and feelings, and so does your partner. These rights should never be surrendered. Further, there are times when it is best to keep one's mouth shut. We have seen permanent damage done to a relationship when, for example, a man told his partner about an affair he had or when a woman told her partner that the conception of their child was not the "accident" he thought it was. There is no guarantee that talking is going to produce joy and goodwill. There is simply no substitute for common sense and good judgment in this or any other area. You have to consider the possible consequences of what you say. In most cases, the consideration can be brief because the consequences are not serious. Other issues are potentially more volatile, however, and you should take into account the value of discussing them.

Michael and Chris agree on the importance of selective communication.

Michael: There's a difference between the communication Chris and I call communication and the 1960s idea of communication. In the 1960s they said *communicate.* I don't believe in that—where you have to tell *all, always.* Because your mind is babbling and you don't always mean what you're thinking or you don't want to always say what you're thinking. You want privacy, even in a long-term relationship. You want to have your own mind and thoughts and sometimes you have thoughts you don't want to share. And sometimes it's better you don't share some thoughts. You may find out in the long run that you don't want to know.

Chris: But communication is number one. I find a lot of problems start when we get our wires crossed and fail to communicate clearly. The typical line is, "I thought I told you. . . ." So we try to stay in contact a lot. I call Michael every day from work. I'll call from the train station. Little things like that.

Compromise

is the fourth leg of a successful relationship. Communication is essential, but it's not enough because, without a willingness to compromise, you will be bound to a useless spiral of discussion and argument that defies resolution. A relationship should be a cooperative, not a competitive, effort. If you go into every discussion or argument with a win-or-lose attitude, one of you will inevitably lose and your relationship will suffer.

Neal and Greg have been compromising for twenty-six years and have gotten so good at it that, more often than not, it's automatic. Neal says:

First, you must understand, "compromise" is not a dirty word. The best kind of contract is where both people benefit, where one person doesn't feel like he's being taken advantage of by the other person.

Compromise does not mean that in every situation where you have differing opinions, you meet half way. Compromise often means yielding to your partner. However, if one does all the yielding, the net effect cannot be called compromise.

Tony and Doug try to meet each other halfway, but often they find there are things about which they can't reach a satisfactory compromise.

Tony: The truth of the matter is that in individual decisions there's very little compromise. But overall, who gets to make decisions changes enough so it's not that one of us always gets his way.

Doug: He got his way about how we were going to rearrange the furniture. I wanted the bed on one side of the room, he wanted it on the other. There's no way to compromise. You can't put the bed in the middle of the room.

Tony: Last summer we argued about where we were going to spend the summer. I wanted to be here in New York and he wanted to be in Connecticut. We couldn't pick a third place that would be agreeable.

Doug: I already had a job in Connecticut so there would have been no point to choosing a third place. So we spent the summer in Connecticut.

Peter and Ned have been together three years. For Peter, who is months short of his thirty-fifth birthday, twenty-five-year-old Ned is his first live-in lover. He finds some of the compromising frustrating, but better than the alternative.

> The things that we each find different in the other can be frustrating. They're the things for which we have to resort to using compromise. But the compromises help weld the relationship. He gets to see the world from my point of view sometimes and I see the world from his point of view, whether I want to or not. Because I've compromised and given in to things that Ned wanted, there are a lot of things I've done, places I've gone to, that I never would have gone to or done on my own. Mostly the things I've experienced have been good. Some not so good.
>
> When I lived alone I didn't have to compromise on anything. But then, I lived alone.

Before women's liberation took hold it was tacitly understood in a heterosexual relationship that it was the woman who made most of the compromises, the woman who made the relationship work. In any relationship, straight or gay, the relationship benefits, and it's easier, when both partners work at it. True, one partner may compromise more often than the other; a 50–50 compromise record is unlikely. But both partners must have the willingness—the disposition—to compromise based on a commitment to the relationship.

Acceptance

of who your partner is, and not who you would like him to be, will save you the trouble of trying to make him over in your image, and will save him the grief of telling you to get off his back. If your partner was not a runner when you met him, you can encourage him to join you for 5:30 A.M. runs, but you cannot force him. He may not have the body you think he could have if he worked on it. He may not dress the way you would like. If your lover tends to be jealous of the attention men give you, you may be able to help him feel less threatened, but you can't force him not to feel jealous.

If you go into the relationship expecting to change everything about your lover that you don't like, you'll learn a lot about arguing, little about compromise, and nothing about what it means to accept a partner's differences. Inevitably, you will learn from each other and change in small ways, but many of the fundamental differences will likely remain. So, as Donald and Andrew learned, you have to get used to the differences and learn not to fight about them.

Donald and Andrew are an extreme example. Andrew grew up in a well-to-do family, is a hospital administrator and wears business suits, suspenders, wire-rim glasses, and oxford shoes. Donald, a singer, has blond-tipped brown hair that stands straight up from his head. His fashion tastes run from a T-shirt and jeans to ultra-high-style designer suits. Donald grew up in an urban working-class neighborhood.

Donald: We had to get used to being different. When I hear him talk about his childhood and family experiences, it's so, so different from my own. He just said the other day, "I remember when we used to all be at home we would play badminton and croquet. Now that we have the house in the country it would be nice to get a croquet set." When I was growing up at home we played in the streets, hiding under the cars and in the garbage cans.

Andrew's family rented a beach house. We had an apartment where I shared a room with two brothers.

I guess it's no surprise that we have different attitudes.

Andrew: I like opera.

Donald: I'll take it or leave it.

Andrew: He loves Linda Ronstadt, I'll take her or leave her.

Donald: When we met, I was 22 and doing anything popular as far as clothing goes. I had an earring.

Andrew: That freaked me out.

Donald: I wore it anyway.

Andrew: He was so confident. Even to this day, like the time we went to a formal benefit dinner for AIDS.

Donald: He thinks you gotta wear a blue suit. But I have my own personal style. We usually fight it out to the point where I'll put on the blue suit to shut him up. Then once we get to where we're going, there are in fact other people there who are dressed in the way I'm usually dressed. So I yell at him that I could have worn what I wanted and been my own person and had my own personal style.

Andrew: It's really very unusual that I will try to change his style anymore.

Donald: Also, I've really toned myself down. And I've kind of spruced him up. We do an updated preppy for Andrew and I'm a toned-down trendy.

Because Fantasyland is, after all, fantasy, no lover is ever exactly as you would like him to be. You won't always agree. And because you won't always agree, you'll have to talk or argue with each other until you *can* agree. And then, you don't always get your way. But, as Greg and Neal note, it can be worth making the effort.

Greg: The problems, the disagreements, the differences of two strangers coming together are really worth working out, because the pleasures far outweigh the problems. But it's not easy to find someone with whom you can share your life.

Neal: There's nothing like having someone firmly planted in your life. I know that, no matter what, Greg is somebody I can rely on for love. And if something happened to me tomorrow and I couldn't earn a penny, I know I would be taken care of. That's one of those things you get out of a long-term relationship—getting to the point where you know you can really trust another person.

CHAPTER 3

Monogamy/Non-monogamy

"My brain knew it was ridiculous to feel insecure, or jealous, but my heart has no brains."

DEFINITIONS OF MONOGAMY AND NONMONOGAMY

Because any given term can mean so many different things to different people, no discussion on the subject of monogamy can begin without setting forth definitions.

MONOGAMY

The definition is clear and simple according to *Webster's Third New International Dictionary:* "the condition of having a single mate at any one time."

There are those who make a distinction between emotional monogamy and sexual monogamy. In other words, two men who are emotionally committed to each other exclusively are "monogamous." If they agree that they can have sex outside of the relationship, they are still "monogamous," but not sexually exclusive.

I find that definition confusing. In my book, monogamy means one emotional and sexual mate.

NONMONOGAMY (OPEN RELATIONSHIP)

Nonmonogamy is almost a euphemism. For couples, it means *one* emotional mate, but sexual involvement with other men (or women). Nonmonogamy comes in a remarkable variety of shapes and forms, from relationships where outside sex is permitted only when partners are separated for periods of more than six months to couples who invite a third man to dinner every Saturday night and ask him to stay for "dessert."

In a nonmonogamous relationship, there is an understanding between the two partners that sex is permitted outside of the relationship.

MYTH AND REALITY

Since the early days of gay liberation, the issue of monogamy has been hotly debated in the gay press, by experts, and discussed by anyone who has entered a relationship. And in that time the debate has spawned myths and misinformation that have done little to help couples make informed decisions.

The Myths

Four popular myths are:

1. There is no such thing as a monogamous male couple.

2. Monogamous male couples didn't exist before the AIDS crisis.

3. Nonmonogamy solves the problem of being attracted to other men, sexual boredom, and possessiveness.

4. Gay men have no trouble incorporating casual sex into their relationships.

Most of the handful of studies on male couples help perpetuate these myths. In *American Couples* (1983)—"A major, enlightening report on how Americans live their private lives," according to the *Philadelphia Inquirer*—authors Philip Blumstein, Ph.D. and Pepper Schwartz, Ph.D., state:

> If a gay man is monogamous, he is such a rare phenomenon, he may have difficulty making himself believed.

[and]

> Gay men can make nonmonogamy part of everyday life. They have no trouble incorporating casual sex into their relationships. Since their partner is male, they are not called on to honor the female preference for monogamy.

A variation on the myth that there is no such thing as a monogamous male couple is that monogamous male couples are rare and that even if a couple is monogamous at the outset of the relationship, it doesn't last.

According to David P. McWhirter, M.D., and Andrew M. Mattison, M.S.W., Ph.D., authors of *The Male Couple:*

> Only seven couples [out of the 156 interviewed] have a totally exclusive sexual relationship, and these men have all been together for less than five years. Stated in another way, all couples with a relationship lasting more than five years have incorporated some provision for outside sexual activity in their relationships.

That translates into 5 percent monogamous, 95 percent nonmonogamous. (Mary Mendola, in *The Mendola Report,* 1980, came up with a figure of 27 percent monogamous.) While McWhirter and Mattison may not have intended to imply that monogamy is rare and short lived, one man I interviewed said that during an argument with his boyfriend over monogamy, his boyfriend waved *The Male Couple* at him as proof that gay men didn't have monogamous relationships, so it wasn't even worth trying.

Blumstein and Schwartz don't mince words about what gay men can expect in their relationships.

> Sex outside their relationship occurs within the first two years for most gay men. But these years are like a honeymoon; as the relationship goes on, virtually all gay men have other sexual partners.

The Reality

It was clear from my discussions with male couples across the country that gay male monogamous relationships are not nearly as rare as some of the experts claim. I didn't have to look under rocks to find long-term—seventeen years, twenty-five years, forty-two years—committed monogamous couples. Whatever the actual numbers, it is safe to say there are many men in monogamous relationships and many men in nonmonogamous relationships.

Contrary to popular myth, nonmonogamy has the potential to add rather than defuse the difficulty of achieving—or coming close to achieving—and *sustaining* the ideal of a long-term loving relationship. Outside sex does not necessarily mix well with a committed emotional, loving, and sexual relationship. And to say that nonmonogamy is easy fails to consider how fragile the ego is and how great is the emotional irrationality that has to be overcome. Not that monogamy is easy; it isn't. And not that it's essential; it may not be. It's only that the popular notion that men must have access to multiple partners, and the belief that this is essential to the success of a relationship is, in fact, self-delusion.

The experts are in agreement that a nonmonogamous arrangement brings with it potential problems. In *American Couples,* authors Blumstein and Schwartz note:

> Sex outside the relationship is potentially very disruptive. It triggers people's insecurities and fears . . .
>
> Because gay men have so much casual sex, it is inevitable that some serious romance will intrude. Two strangers may have sex with every intention of keeping it impersonal, but they may be surprised to discover they like each other.
>
> . . . Although their relationships remain intact, they [the couple] are likely to make love to each other less often.

According to McWhirter and Mattison:

> Although most of the [156] couples have some degree of sexual nonexclusivity, they have not reached these arrangements by the same routes, nor has it been easy for many of them. In fact, more than 85 percent of the couples report that their greatest relationship problems center on outside relationships, sexual and nonsexual.

CHOOSING

If you're honest with yourselves, and what you and your lover honestly want is a sustained, long-term, relationship, you must *honestly* evaluate for yourselves which arrangement will contribute to your ability as a couple to *sustain* your relationship. It's possible that your sincere and realistic answer to this question will be to opt for nonmonogamy. If this is the case, you should both try to understand the possible consequences and limitations, just as you will need to try to understand the consequences and limitations of monogamy if that's the arrangement you choose.

This is not a decision you can make without talking with each other. It is not enough to simply assume that your lover has the same beliefs you do. You must discuss your beliefs, concerns, and needs in order to reach an accommodation.

Don't Make Assumptions

Plenty of couples don't discuss their options or make a choice early in their relationship, often because they have no expectation that the relationship will develop into something significant. As a result, each partner operates under his own assumptions. As long as those assumptions are compatible, that is, that you both assume the relationship is monogamous or both assume that it is nonmonogamous, you won't have major problems. Brian and Robert, both now in their early thirties, met when they were in graduate school. They didn't discuss their views on monogamy vs. nonmonogamy until Brian gave Robert gonorrhea.

Brian: We were very cold and calculating about the fact that these things don't last. We didn't have any illusions about it. So we didn't talk about the future or what kind of relationship we would have.

Robert: I don't think we ever discussed monogamy in Chicago, but it became an issue in L.A.

Brian: We were having too much sex to ever think about having sex with anyone else. In Chicago at that time it was kind of fashionable to be gay and to be coming out, but we weren't in the circle where promiscuity was big. We weren't going to the bars. We weren't going out dancing. We weren't exposed to that until we went out to L.A. Then *I* was exposed to it.

After that I started going out. I just started doing it on my own. It was very easy and very available in the neighborhood. There was a bookstore here.

Robert: I didn't know what was going on.

Brian: I did it secretly. I guess I was very brave. I got very good at it very fast. I started doing it a lot. Then I got gonorrhea and gave it to Robert. That's when we realized we had totally different world views about monogamy.

Trying to accommodate each other's differing views almost destroyed their relationship. Eventually Brian and Robert sought the help of a professional counselor.

How to Make a Choice

Since no two couples and no two men are the same, how you and your partner reach your decision will depend on many things. For example, you may base your decision on past experiences, health concerns, or on personal, political, or religious beliefs, or a desire to accommodate your partner. Or you may base your decision on a combination of these reasons.

Whether or not you and your partner share similar views, you won't be able to make a choice without talking with each other about your views, your needs, and what you think will work best to help you and your lover sustain a lasting relationship. And even after you settle on one set of rules at the start of your relationship, you may later choose to change those rules and for that you will need to talk and reach accommodation once again.

PAST EXPERIENCE

Negative experiences with monogamy or nonmonogamy, or positive experiences with either, can go a long way to helping you decide what works best for you in a committed relationship.

Peter and Ned, who have lived together in Hawaii for three years, were in complete agreement about the type of relationship they wanted.

Peter: We talked about monogamy early and decided it was okay to have sex with other men. That was what we both wanted, but we had to be honest about it.

Ned: Right off the bat. It had been a problem in relationships for me in the past—the sneaking around and the lying. The last relationship I was in I was doing that and so was the guy that I was with. I could see no sense in doing that again.

   When Peter and I got together we decided that if it was going to happen we were going to tell each other about it and if it didn't happen it was no big deal.

By the time I met Scott, I had been out for seven years. I had plenty of time to discover what did and did not work for me. When I came out at 17, I learned quickly from more experienced gay men that there were advantages to being gay. (Given that I was less than thrilled to be gay, it was nice to discover what I first thought to be advantages over unattainable heterosexuality.) Sex was easy to find. No game playing. No rules. From what I observed, and from what the men I met said, it seemed that I could find love, security, and stability in a relationship and continue to have sex with whomever I wanted, whenever I wanted. In time I learned that it wasn't quite so simple.

During my freshman year at college I was dating a very busy upper-classman. One spring Saturday night when we were supposed to attend a party together, Kevin decided he could neither spare time for the party nor spend the night with me. He told me to go to the party and, if I met a man I liked, to spend the night with him. And I did. When he found out who it was, he got very upset. "Of all the people," he said, "did it have to be Carl?" I learned Rule Number One: Make certain you know who is off limits.

I discovered that, contrary to what I had originally perceived, there were lots of rules and that, in my case at least, my emotions did not allow me to enjoy my new-found freedom anyway. That was especially true when it came to a boyfriend exercising *his* gay birthright to sex whenever, wherever, with whomever. When I found out that a boyfriend of three months' duration was having sex with two women and another man, I felt betrayed, jealous, and angry. My ego was a wreck. My self-confidence and self-esteem were badly shaken. Of course, his flings meant nothing to him, they were only physical things. Hadn't I learned from past experience that it was no threat to our relationship? That he still cared for me? That I shouldn't feel emotional about it? Sure, my brain knew it was ridiculous to feel insecure, or jealous, but my heart has no brains.

When Scott and I started our relationship, within a very short time we discussed the issue of monogamy—staying faithful to one another, not cheating, no infidelities, no fooling around. We were in agreement. We were possessive and we knew it. We cared tremendously for each other. What we had between us was very special, a quality we felt would be compromised if we were not monogamous. I knew from experience that nonmonogamy didn't suit me and that, despite its limitations, monogamy did. Scott had been out for barely a year when we met, but felt certain that a nonmonogamous relationship didn't suit him either. Not that either of us thought it would be easy.

PERSONAL/POLITICAL BELIEFS
Basing your decision on what you think you *should* do, rather than on what works best for you in practice, will work out fine if you and your partner discover that your beliefs match reality. When they don't, as was the case for Tony and Doug, you may be forced to change the rules of your relationship to accommodate the reality of your emotions.

Tony and Doug, who met in college and have been together for five years, based their decision to have a nonmonogamous relationship on personal beliefs about gay-male relationships. Because both attend different universities about an hour and a half apart, they maintain two apartments and spend at least three days away on their own each week.

Tony: We had a spoken understanding that we could see other men, but for two-and-a-half years neither of us did. Then Doug asked if he could see someone. I said, "Sure, no problem." I had read all the books and heard all the rhetoric about open couples and I thought it was a good thing—cerebrally.

The minute that he started to see this other man I went off the deep end. I couldn't deal with it at all. If I had been there and seen how harmless it was, maybe I could have handled it better, but I was here and it was happening there, and I had this picture of them being together all the time and talking about the things that I couldn't be there to talk about and eating the meals that I couldn't eat with him. I was jealous.

Doug: Mainly we talked about you.

Tony: I started to see a man here, not to get even, but to prove that I could have someone too. That I didn't need to sit in the apartment and feel lonely. That was disastrous because at least in Doug's relationship there was some genuine affection, and with mine it was just a thing to do.

Doug: But he liked you.

Tony: Yeah, too much.

Doug: That made *me* jealous. It was not a good feeling to call home and have Doug whispering on the phone because this other guy was asleep next to him. And I was annoyed at him because I thought it was a stupid thing for him to do, just to prove that he could do it. It was definitely the low point of our relationship.

Tony: It turned out ironically because we both decided that, since it wasn't working out, we should be honest and say that we didn't want to see other men and didn't want each other to see other men—to just admit we were conservative and admit what we wanted. We decided that we would get out of these relationships as quickly as possible. Doug got out of his pretty easily. Mine was much harder to disentangle. Doug had to mother me through it.

After that it was kind of a sore point between us in that we never talked about it. It was at the heart of every argument. The big argument became where were we going to spend the summer. I wanted to be in Connecticut and Doug wanted to be in New York. I was feeling "You always get your way. You always get to do what you want to do." That was just that other argument buried and coming out in a different way.

Doug: Ultimately we did break up for about twenty minutes, on the side of the road on the way to Provincetown. It was over the argument about where we were going to live that summer. Right before the exit for Cape Cod, I pulled off the road and I said, "Okay, we're going to work this out right now, because if we're breaking up I'm not going to Provincetown with you for a weekend. We're either going to put this relationship together and go to Provincetown or I'm going to Connecticut and you can do whatever you want." We put the relationship more or less back together on the side of the road and had a great weekend.

Tony: Part of it was understanding that the fight we were having was not about that but still about this monogamy question, and once we decided that, we realized there that it was something we could work out.

Doug: It became very clear that we both wanted the relationship. So it would be stupid to break up over past pique.

Tony: It was easy to make the decision. I would have been leaving him for nothing. Not that it didn't cross our minds to end the relationship anyway.

We resolved the argument about where to live that summer by staying in Connecticut and I went away for a month of that time to be by myself.

I'm kind of glad we went through it. Although I certainly wasn't glad at the time, nor would I have predicted that I ever would be. It made us articulate a lot of things that a couple should articulate. This whole issue of monogamy and possessiveness. We're better at forcing ourselves to be honest. When I come up with the knee-jerk liberal response, like "Yes, couples should be open to sex with other men," Doug knows he can say "Do you really believe that?"

This is an odd position to be in because I feel really caught between my duties as a good political gay person and my upbringing. I've read all the books and I know that one of the great things about being gay is that you don't have to be involved in possessive ownership-based relationships. Then I realized that my rhetoric and my beliefs were in conflict.

Doug: When you're gay, you're without the model that marriage provides. Married people are monogamous and that's the rule. They decide to break the rule or they follow it. We did feel kind of stupid because we felt, "Hey, we're these wild liberal, radical guys. We don't have any rules." And then we made this rule, and it's the same rule all those conservative people have.

It's hard for me to imagine how nonmonogamous relationships work, because it didn't work for us. Even when I was repeating back all the things I had been told over the previous years about why open relationships were a good thing and how they weren't a threat and how I could grow in other ways and blah, blah, blah . . . it wasn't strictly true.

I would be really interested to know what it feels like to have a nonmonogamous relationship that works. Not interested enough to try it.

Tony: Our gay-couple friends are monogamous. When they have problems it's usually that problem. One of them was flirting with someone else or seeing someone else.

Doug: We're not saying that it's right for everybody to be monogamous, but it's right for us.

The same realignment of beliefs and real life also happens in nonmonogamous relationships when couples discover that the rules they set—such as sex with other men only on vacations—don't work in practice. More on that subject later in this chapter.

HEALTH CONCERNS

AIDS has forced many men who are starting out in relationships, and those already in nonmonogamous relationships, to reassess their views about monogamy and the safety of having sex outside of a relationship. But no couple needs to feel forced into monogamy because of a fear of contracting AIDS or because of the fear of contracting other sexually transmitted diseases. Practicing safer sex (see Chapter 8) greatly reduces the possibility of catching most sexually transmitted diseases, including AIDS, from outside sexual contacts.

Accommodating/Negotiating Different Views

Because no two men are the same, you may discover that you have different views from each other's at the start of your relationship, or several years after you first start living together (as Brian and Robert did), and wind up knocking heads and going through a period of trial and error until you reach an accommodation that works for both of you, or until the relationship falls apart.

Accommodating different views may be a matter of gentle persuasion, or it can be an all out war that may require the intervention of a counselor to keep the two partners from killing their relationship. For Robert and Brian it was war.

Robert: The arguments built. They became bigger and bigger. We started knocking our heads together on the issue. He wanted one thing and I wanted another.

Brian: We really butted heads about whether I would be allowed to have sex with other men. I remember at the time, when I would go home to Chicago, I would start doing it a lot, or when he was out of town. I used to live for the times I could go out.

Robert: My position was that we should have a monogamous relationship.

Brian: That seemed ridiculous to me at the time.

Robert: What we tried to do was come up with a compromise whereby, if I weren't around or if he were out of town, then he would be free to do as he pleased. If I was in town and we were both sleeping here together at night, we should be having sex together, not with other men.

But I began to feel Brian was taking advantage of the compromise situation, actually looking for ways to create situations under which he could go out and have sex. The tension got worse and worse.

At the same time it made me question my views about monogamy because I really thought I must be the biggest stick in the mud. I must be abnormal to want a monogamous relationship and not to want to go out and have sex with other men. Lots of men probably thought that there was no place for them in the gay movement or in gay life if that's what it was all about.

Brian: That period [of nonmonogamy] lasted for a couple of years.

Robert: At least a year of your going out when I didn't even realize what was going on and then probably two more years of building to a head. Finally I said this is over and done with unless this stops.

Brian: It wasn't "It's over and done with unless. . . ." It was over. It was goodbye. And I remember thinking where would I get an apartment. But we decided it was worth it for the eight years we had, to go to see a marriage counselor.

I can't remember if at the beginning the counselor laid it out that he was pro-monogamy. He presented it as you both have problems with yourselves that you're blaming on each other and you have to work out the problems with yourself before you can come to terms with your problems as a couple. He put us in individual therapy. I realized I really had a problem with this running around.

Therapy was really incredible in showing me the value of a relationship.

To say Robert and Brian's relationship problems were cured by monogamy would be an oversimplification. Both readily acknowledge that there were other problems in their relationship, some of which were in part caused by the open relationship. Other problems were made worse by the conflicts, distancing, and decline of their sex life that resulted from Brian's sexual involvements outside of their relationship.

Dennis and Terry, who have been together for three and a half years, went into their relationship with different views about monogamy, but

Terry has come around to Dennis's view for a variety of reasons, including a desire to accommodate Dennis's strong feelings about monogamy.

Dennis: I've always been monogamous in relationships. I think you haven't.

Terry: I probably thought it wasn't necessary.

Dennis: I probably thought it was absolutely necessary.

Terry: AIDS changed my views. I came out in 1976. My background was Harvey Milk. I was used to a variety of sex and I felt you could have a long-term relationship and that, while you wouldn't have two ongoing love affairs, you could have a primary love relationship and have a little spice every now and then just because you had to—just had to do it. I had these urges.

But I've really been domesticated. There are two reasons why I believe that spice theory less. First, because of AIDS. I would never risk myself and I would never risk Dennis. I would take more chances for myself than I would ever take with Dennis. Secondly, we have a consistently gratifying sexual relationship that I didn't know was possible. Now, even if there were no such thing as AIDS, knowing how important monogamy is to Dennis, I would try to be monogamous. I would probably be successful.

Dennis: He's never said this before. We've had discussions in the past. We discussed monogamy early in the relationship. At first I don't think either of us had the time or energy to pursue anyone else.

Terry: There's always time.

Dennis: I do think at the very beginning we were infatuated with each other. I think I told Terry very early that I wasn't interested in other men. Terry would say, "Well, things are really great now, but if something comes up in the relationship where we had more interest in other men, we could get a houseboy."

Terry: I always felt that a relationship would be in an awful lot of trouble if one partner became very frustrated. If you vented that every once in a while, the relationship would be better off.

Dennis: I don't believe that at all.

Terry: That was when I thought that my sexual desires could get in the way of love. I don't feel that anymore. I'm older.

Dennis: I really feel that having sex with people outside the relationship can destroy the relationship. It doesn't serve to vent any frustration. If anything, it exacerbates the situation.

Terry: My feelings have really changed. I wouldn't feel good if I slept with someone else. There have been a couple of opportunities that Dennis doesn't know about, and I haven't taken them. I just couldn't let myself do it. I would come home and talk about it, but Dennis would rather not hear.

Dennis: If Terry slept with someone else, I would kill him. In reality I don't think we would break up.

Terry: I would probably be a little hurt. I would feel very threatened if it was someone we knew.

Dennis: I would make him pay for a while. If it happened a few times I would seriously have to reconsider the relationship. Even if it happened only once with certain men, that would be it.

But I never stop and think Terry's late three times this week and I wonder what's going on. I trust him.

Terry: Time may prove me a fool, but I trust Dennis, too.

MONOGAMY

Pros and Cons

At those moments when I'm wildly attracted to a man other than my lover, it's difficult to sing the praises of monogamy. Holding back in the face of strong attractions can be very frustrating. And when we were having some problems in our sex life, I couldn't—nor could Scott—do anything other than deal with each other and the problem. But being forced to deal with the problems in our sex life actually goes in the long-term Pro column for monogamy. Monogamy can help force you and your partner to face problems which, if ignored, can ultimately threaten the physical and emotional health of your relationship.

Monogamy has provided for Scott and me, as well as for many of the couples I interviewed, a stable context in which our relationship, our trust in one another, and our love for one another could grow and deepen. And as long as neither of us slips up, we don't have to worry about catching sexually transmitted diseases from outside sexual contacts. (Because you or your partner may already have a sexually transmitted disease, such as herpes, or may already be infected by the HIV virus—the virus believed to cause AIDS—monogamy will not necessarily eliminate all worries about passing along or contracting a sexually transmitted disease.)

Monogamy doesn't guarantee that you and your partner will love each other forever, or that you won't ever have arguments. Nor does it assure a stellar sex life, or that you won't be frustrated at times; nor is it necessarily the "natural impulse." However, committing to a monogamous relationship can help to exclude the relationship-threatening jealousy, insecurity, conflicts, and disruptions that often come with a nonmonogamous relationship. For Scott and me, and for many of the couples I interviewed, the tradeoff, while not always ideal, has been worth it.

Making It Work—Staying Monogamous

Staying monogamous begins with a commitment. It is not the kind of arrangement you can make a half-hearted attempt to maintain. Commitment can be a verbal promise between you and your lover. But in that promise, leave yourself room for future discussions. Agree that if you want to change the status of your relationship, you will discuss it first.

Staying monogamous doesn't end with making a commitment, particularly if you find monogamy something of a struggle. You still have to deal with attractions to other men. That may mean avoiding temptation, talking about attractions to other men with your lover, even seeking outside support to help you keep on the straight and narrow.

AVOID TEMPTATION

Commitment to your partner to be monogamous means doing whatever it takes to keep that commitment. If you know that you're easily tempted to fool around, avoid those circumstances or men who threaten your will power. If you go to bars, don't go alone. If you travel for business, don't go to bars, period. If your lover plans to be out of town for a few days, make certain that you fill your time alone by seeing and doing things with friends.

Even if you do your best to avoid temptations, there will always be circumstances in which you meet available men to whom you're attracted. It's moments such as these when you need to remind yourself of the commitment you made to your partner and the commitment you made to discuss with him any change in the rules of your relationship— prior to doing anything that means breaking your agreement to be monogamous.

TALK ABOUT ATTRACTIONS

If you and your lover are comfortable talking about other attractive men, do it. It doesn't hurt to acknowledge that you have attractions to other men. Those attractions are normal no matter how much you love your partner. However, if your lover gets jealous when you even look at another man, be considerate and save your discussions about the attractive man you met at the office for your friends.

SEEK HELP IF YOU NEED IT

It may take more than making a commitment to your partner to stick to an agreement to be monogamous, particularly if you've been accustomed to nonmonogamous relationships in the past.

Support can come from a professional counselor, as it did for Brian and Robert. It can come from friends or from a self-help group. It is not, however, a great idea to put your partner in the position of playing policeman. Besides the pressure and potential tensions that can result from such an arrangement, chances are that your partner is too emotionally involved in the issue to provide the objective support you may need.

Steve had been through a long-term relationship that collapsed under the pressure of a secondary relationship he was having with another man. He decided that he had a problem and needed help. "I couldn't commit to monogamy, but I wanted to." Steve believed his inability to commit to monogamy was a form of compulsive sexual behavior and sought out the help of a group specifically for sexual compulsives (see Chapter 13 for more information on sexually compulsive behavior). Steve depended on the program and the people in it for support to help him stay monogamous in his new relationship. The support was particularly important, he said, because "I didn't have any buffers. I couldn't go out and have sex everytime something went wrong in the relationship." Now when something "goes wrong," Steve turns to fellow group members for support.

Accommodating Infidelity

People make mistakes. Sometimes they slip up despite a commitment and despite the best of intentions. I'm not, however, referring to a circumstance where you intentionally break a commitment to remain monogamous because you're unhappy with your relationship (see "Breaking the Rules" at the end of this chapter).

Because there is always the risk that one or both of you will be overcome by desire or loneliness while you are separated during an extended business trip, for example, talk about that possibility and what you should do if that ever happens. Should you keep the infidelity a secret? Should you talk about it? Should you wait a year or two before bringing it up? That's up to the two of you.

And what happens if you discover your partner has been unfaithful? There is no way to predict exactly how you will react and no general advice about minimizing the damage. Even if you've agreed in advance that you won't let a mistake destroy your relationship, that is no guarantee that the fallout from a broken trust won't have a significant negative impact on your relationship.

Friends of ours have an agreement they call "The Napa Valley Pact." They both travel a lot on business and are sometimes separated for weeks at a stretch. Early in their relationship, while on a visit to the California wine country, they agreed that in the event one of them strays because of overwhelming desire or loneliness, they won't let that infidelity destroy their relationship. They're both committed to monogamy, and note that their agreement is not permission to have sex outside the relationship. The "Pact" is simply an acknowledgment that they are each capable of making a mistake, and it is a commitment not to let that mistake destroy their life together.

Scott and I have a similar agreement, but the agreement includes a promise not to let one another find out about the infidelity. It's the only circumstance where we've formally given each other permission to lie. The truth, we feel, would be too destructive to our relationship.

Knowing that I would have to keep the infidelity and resulting guilt a secret is just about enough to keep me from slipping up. I'm awful at keeping secrets and inevitably Scott would find out. He would get upset. I would get upset. We would probably argue and no doubt there would be hurt feelings on both sides for months or longer. Neither of us imagines that an infidelity would end the relationship. But we do know there would be very unpleasant consequences to deal with.

NONMONOGAMY

Pros and Cons

Monogamy for some men can be a straightjacket, or an impossibility. They may consider the restrictions and frustrations threatening to the future of their relationship. For these men, nonmonogamy can offer the freedom to pursue outside sexual interests either as a couple (three-ways) or individually.

For Peter and Ned, their decision was based on what they thought would be best for their relationship, given what they knew about themselves. As Peter says:

> Having the freedom to have sex with other men isn't a real important thing in our relationship, but it's one of the things that's stabilized it, because we both honestly know in our hearts we're not the type of people who could say that "forever after I'm not going to have sex with anybody else." For us it was realistic to be honest about that. That's something couples should talk about before they get deeply involved in their relationship. For different people the answers will be different, but it's something they need to work out.

Gary, 39, and Mitch, his 29-year-old lover, agreed to a nonmonogamous relationship when they first met three years ago. Mitch wasn't enthusiastic about the arrangement, but went along with Gary's wishes.

> *Mitch:* Gary said he had been in a difficult relationship before and could never be monogamous. He said it had to be a free relationship, that although we were committed to each other that what he did when I wasn't around didn't have any effect on the relationship. He said he would have to be free to talk to people in the bar and if they were attractive to him and attracted to him to go home with them. And as long as he came home to me, he felt that it would be okay.
>
> I had never been in a relationship like that before. I had always gotten

involved and been totally monogamous. But I thought what the hell, I'll give it a try.

Gary: I want to clarify something. I operate better without restrictions.

Mitch: He was telling me that he had to have the freedom to do as he pleased, that he probably wouldn't do it, but he had to know that he could.

There are, however, rules to be established, and there are many significant drawbacks to be considered. For example:

1. Nonmonogamy can be an emotional roller coaster that results in feelings of insecurity and instability.

2. It has the potential to intensify the difficulties some men have in making a commitment, trusting a partner, and developing a sense of intimacy.

3. Nonmonogamy can be used to distance yourself from your partner by enabling the two of you to avoid facing and working through the emotional and sexual problems that you're likely to experience in your relationship. For example, it's much easier to turn to a new and uncomplicated sexual partner than to tackle a problem you're having with the man you wake up to each morning.

4. Nonmonogamy can lead to less sexual interest in your lover.

5. It can get very complicated when outside sexual partners become emotionally involved, or if you or your lover get emotionally involved with an outside partner.

Besides the complication of Tony's outside partner's becoming emotionally involved with him, nonmonogamy for Tony and Doug led them to feel less a part of each other's lives.

Tony: I think it has to do with being excluded and wanting to feel needed. To be needed means to be the *one* who is needed, not just one of many. If that's all you are, then you might as well be just friends.

Doug: It's very hard to trust somebody completely unless you feel like he needs you completely. Need is very closely related to trust. That also started to break down between us.

When I felt depressed, I would go to this guy at school. He would make me feel better and Tony felt cut out. I would say to him, "I was really depressed and I went over there and now I feel good again." That was a hard thing for Tony. He wanted to think of himself as the other half of me, as the one I should turn to when I'm depressed and as the one who can make me feel better.

I started to feel that there were things I couldn't tell Tony because they would make him unhappy and I didn't want to fight about it. I started to constantly censor the things that came into my head. "What can I say? How will he react?"

Making It Work—Setting the Boundaries

There are couples who make make nonmonogamy work, but they make it work by spending considerable amounts of time talking about it, considering the type of arrangement that best suits them individually, and that gives them the best chance of achieving a loving, sexual, long-term relationship together. They do not, however, use outside sexual involvements to avoid problems in their relationship, or use outside sex as a substitute for sex with their lovers.

The options you consider, and the type of arrangement that best suits you and your lover, depend upon your individual circumstances. The following list of options for you to consider is a paraphrase of a list of ground rules for sex with others that McWhirter and Mattison gathered from the 156 couples in their study. Please note that this list was compiled prior to the AIDS crisis, and that when sex of any kind is discussed, you should follow safer sex guidelines (see Chapter 8):

1. Sex is allowed at such places as the baths, where having a brief sexual interchange is a mutual and unspoken understanding.

2. No sex with mutual friends.

3. Sexual encounters must not interfere with the couple's customary or planned time together.

4. Sex is permissible only when one partner is out of town.

5. Sexual encounters are always verbally shared with each other.

6. Talking about outside sex is expected, but at least forty-eight hours must pass following the sexual encounter before any discussion is permitted.

7. Outside sex is allowed only with the advance agreement of one's lover.

8. No emotional involvement with sex partners is allowed.

9. Outside sex is allowed, but only in three-ways or groups where both partners are involved.

10. Outside sex is allowed, but it is never to be discussed.

11. Outside sex is not permitted at home. If it is permitted at home, each must simultaneously be occupied with a sex partner of his own.

12. Outside sex is permitted at home in the partner's absence, but not in certain places, such as in the couple's bedroom.

13. Secondary emotional relationships with sexual friends are allowed, but the lover is not to be excluded.

McWhirter and Mattison conclude this section of their book by noting that:

> Many of these rules appear alone or in some combination. At times they may change, be dropped, or be replaced by new ones. The important point here is that, generally speaking, some framework is set for sex with others.

Once you've set rules, leave room for discussion to adjust the boundaries should you find that the original rules aren't working in practice.

Learning to Live Within the Boundaries

It's likely to take time and fine tuning of rules to adjust to a nonmonogamous relationship. Peter and Ned decided it would be "no big deal" if one of them slept with another man, and they decided they would be honest about it and tell each other whenever they slept with another man. Both decisions took some getting used to and some practice.

Ned: It was important to be honest about it. And we haven't slept with other men lately; but we have before, quite a bit at times. It's never been a problem.

Peter: It was a problem once. I was the first of the two of us to have sex with another man alone, after Ned and I got together. Initially, we had sex with other people together—threesomes. After we were more comfortable with ourselves, we started talking about, "Well, I think who you pick isn't that great," or, "He wouldn't be my first choice." We decided it would be more comfortable if we picked a man we each wanted to do it with and did it by ourselves. As long as we mentioned it, it was okay.

I did it with a real good friend of both of ours. In spite of all the verbalizing we had done about how we were going to be honest about it, I didn't know how to go about telling him that I had done it. So I didn't tell him right away, but waited three months. It bothered me all the time, because I had wanted the honesty in the relationship. Because there are so few people you can have complete trust in. When I finally told Ned, I was expecting him to be angry because I had had sex with another man. I expected him to be upset in spite of everything we had said about it not being a big deal. Of course what he got angry and hurt over was that I hadn't kept my commitment on the trust end of it—that I waited three months to say something.

Actually it was a problem more than once. The first time Ned went to bed with someone by himself, I had trouble adjusting to it since that was the first time it had ever happened to me in my life.

Ned: It didn't matter to him that he had already done the same thing.

Peter: Those were things that we talked about quickly afterward so they never had a chance to fester and grow. We each got the other's perspective. We had a chance to digest it.

It was a new experience and my logic was telling me one thing and my emotions were telling me another.

Ned: A couple of days after I did it and told Peter, he got real pissed off and told me I had no business having sex with other men because of the way it hit him. It didn't matter to him that he had already done it, and that we had talked about it from the start of the relationship. For a couple of days there, I guess he was thinking about himself.

What it comes down to is that we're now comfortable enough in our relationship with each other that, for us, this arrangement works. For other people it wouldn't. Having that freedom to go and have sex with another man if we want to is important to us. We don't make a habit of it and, in fact, all that has pretty much slowed down since the first year because we've both tested negative for the HIV antibody. We tested negative twice in tests six months apart and we want to keep it that way. We've agreed that if a situation comes up where we need to have sex with another man it would only be safer sex.

CHANGING THE RULES

Relationships change, circumstances change, people change. Men who entered relationships planning to be monogamous may not find that the arrangement suits them. Men who started a relationship agreeing to nonmonogamy may find over time that that arrangement isn't working out. That's why it's important to leave the door open to discussion about the ground rules of your relationship.

Any change in your original joint agreement has to be a mutual decision. Obviously, you can't decide alone to make your relationship monogamous; you have to make that commitment together. If you're in a committed monogamous relationship, one of you can decide to have outside sex but, unless you've both agreed to nonmonogamy, that's infidelity. This is not a matter of semantics. There is a world of difference between deciding together that it's now okay to have outside sex, and deciding on your own without the knowledge or agreement of your lover, to have outside sex.

From Monogamy to Nonmonogamy

If, at some point in your relationship, you and your partner decide monogamy is not working for you—or even if it is working—you may choose to experiment with nonmonogamy. However, if you're going to try sex outside of your relationship, wait until you feel your relationship is secure and strong enough to weather a storm, in the event that an outside excursion together or alone causes one. If you're having emotional or sexual problems with your relationship, opening up the relationship is no solution. If anything, your problems will become more serious as you put more and more distance between each other. [See Chapter 14, "On the Rocks," for more information on relationship problems.]

After the second year of their relationship and two years of monogamy by default—they never talked about it—Chet and John experimented with sex outside of their relationship. At a bar not far from where they lived, John spotted a man he found attractive and he and Chet decided to bring him home.

John: It was my idea. And we had a good time, but when I woke up the next day I was crazy.
Chet: He blamed *me.*
John: I was upset. It was an invasion. I was upset as if someone had broken into our house. I was upset by it. Chet didn't understand. He said "It's over, we don't ever have to do it again." Even though I was a part of it, I look back at it and think that our physical relationship was something that was private and sacred for us to share, and we opened it up to someone else.

They never did it again.

From Nonmonogamy to Monogamy

Some couples discover over time and through experience that nonmonogamy doesn't work for them, or decide for health reasons to end outside sexual contacts. The transition can be difficult, particularly if you and your partner have used outside sexual involvements as a safety valve—as an outlet for sexual or emotional strains, or for other problems in your relationship. One therapist who counsels male couples says that he has been seeing more and more couples who have switched to monogamy—primarily because of health concerns—who have consequently had difficulty dealing with each other and with problems in their relationship. If you're having trouble adjusting, you may want to seek the help of a professional counselor.

Gary and Mitch, who started out with a nonmongamous arrangement, initially agreed they could go out on their own whenever the other one was away on business. And sometimes they would pick up a third person and all go home together. After a while, because of jealousy and insecurity, they stopped seeing men separately, but continued picking up a third. Eventually, even that stopped.

Mitch: Every once in a while it was somebody we met in a bar. Sometimes it was a friend. Then we started seeing the problems of doing that. Men would come on to us a lot and pretend to be friends. It was the trendy thing to do; invite your friends over and go to bed. Then you find out they didn't want to be your friend, but just wanted to go to bed with you and then you didn't see them anymore.

We also got in trouble with people talking about us. Then we had a regular three-way with a guy who got a little too attached to Gary. And he was talking to our friends about what was going on.

Gary: It was a very bad situation. He had visions of being a permanent live-in three-way and that was not our intention. The problem is always that emotional involvement.

Mitch: It really complicates things unnecessarily.

Gary: I'm sure there are people who do pull it off successfully, but it was not the answer for us.

Mitch: Then we got into the health crisis which scared us terribly and that ended the whole bit.

With us it hasn't been a conscious effort to switch to monogamy. It's just the way things happened. Still, there have been times when I've been attracted to somebody that I've met and really felt the temptation to say to Gary, "Let's try this again," but then I start thinking, "Well, what if this?" and "What if that?" and it becomes too much of an intellectual decision and it's just not worth it.

Our very last time was a close call and a nice little subtle reminder that we weren't being careful. Gary got the clap.

Accommodating Broken Rules

People make mistakes in nonmonogamous relationships just as they do in monogamous relationships. And the results—the hurt, shock, disappointment—may be no different from those of a partner who discovers his lover has been unfaithful. For example, if you've agreed not to talk about your outside sexual involvements and you've agreed never to bring anyone home, and your lover discovers you making out with another man in your bedroom, you've violated your agreement and his trust and he will react accordingly.

Again, talk in advance about how you will handle broken rules. Should mistakes be kept secret? If discovered, how might you handle the circumstances? However, don't consider prior discussion an excuse to break rules.

INTENTIONALLY BREAKING THE RULES

If you, your lover, or both of you are intentionally, knowingly, calculatingly breaking the rules of your monogamous or nonmonogamous relationship, your relationship may well be in serious trouble. If you are the one breaking the rules, you need to consider why you are doing it and what that says about the future of your relationship. The same holds true if you discover your partner is breaking the rules. The rule breaking may be a symptom of greater problems in your relationship. This gets into the complicated subject of relationship problems, which is discussed in greater detail in Chapter 14, "On the Rocks."

CHAPTER 4

Moving in Together

"Different words mean different things to each of us."

Moving in together is far more involved than just picking the place to live or deciding where to put the bed. It means mixing all the habits and tastes of two individuals, from how socks should be folded to how to "define" domestic cleanliness. It requires hundreds of decisions, both tacit and negotiated: what and where to eat, who buys the groceries, what brand of dishwashing detergent to use . . . and who uses it. You have to balance the responsibilities of maintaining a household, be prepared to disagree, on occasion to argue, take a stand, give in, compromise, trade off, and adjust. Crossing the threshold and living happily ever after can be hard, but rewarding, work.

WHAT YOU SHOULD KNOW
ABOUT EACH OTHER BEFORE MOVING IN

The fantasy of falling in love over a weekend and moving in together a week or two later can be far more romantic than the reality. Even if you've known your partner for months or longer, there are bound to be a few surprises after you move in together. So, before you move in—before you even talk seriously about moving in together—get to know each other. Do you know what your partner's views are about relationships? Are your lifestyles compatible? Do you share interests that will last beyond the first few months? Does he have any habits that will make him impossible to live with? For example, will his compulsive neatness drive you nuts? Will his compulsive spending bankrupt both of you? If you discover major problems while you're still courting, it's easier to bail out if you don't already share, or plan to share, the same home.

Gary and Mitch lived out a fantasy cross-country romance, which turned out to be something less than ideal as they got to know each other and then moved in together. Gary and Mitch met in a bar in Miami, spent two weekends in Miami and one week in Seattle together, then Gary packed his things and moved West to be with Mitch. When they met, Gary, 39, had a high-level research job that he had no plans to leave, particularly since he was anticipating a major promotion. Mitch, at 29, was just spreading his wings after leaving his native South. He liked his job, and had no intention of returning to the South and his family just yet. As he says:

> It was the unrequited love. We were destined to be together but separated by something out of our control. I kind of enjoyed that. It was a big story when I was with my friends. I had this lover who was clear across the country and who knows when we would ever be together. I played the part pretty well. And my friends humored me, but they didn't take the relationship seriously.

Fate intervened. Gary's promotion went to someone else at the company.

Mitch: Gary's career came to an abrupt dead end. He was devastated. There were lots of tearful phone calls.

He had so much seniority that they couldn't get rid of him. As a consolation they offered him a transfer anywhere he wanted to go.

Gary: I asked to be transferred to Seattle.

Mitch: I was shocked. We had talked about moving in together, and now it was actually happening and I was panicking, but I don't think I let Gary know that.

In the beginning our situation was unsolvable, which made it attractive. Now there was a solution and I was scared. I thought to myself, "I don't even know this man. He is moving to Washington for me. He is giving up his life, his friends, and his home to live with me." I wasn't sure I was ready to accept that responsibility.

Gary: Most of my friends thought I was crazy. They thought I should go for an extended vacation, rather than move. That was the advice my own therapist gave me. I decided to go—on the fantasy side—for that individual search for happiness, to live happily ever after, to put a lot of things behind me.

Mitch: I don't think we ever really thought about what was gonna happen when we moved in.

Gary: I don't think people discuss the whys and wherefores of getting together. Someone comes up with the idea. Two people move in together and then they're faced with reality.

Mitch: Once the decision was made, we had to talk about how we were going to live together, what kinds of rules we were going to make about the relationship. This was going to be a real change in our lives and we hardly knew each other or what we were expecting from one another.

Gary: I think we assumed a lot.

Mitch: Shortly after Gary called to say he would be moving to Seattle we started talking about the kind of relationship we were going to build. Gary said he could never really be monogamous, that although we were committed to each other, what he did when I wasn't around didn't have any effect on the relationship.

That was totally against anything I had tried before. My attitude was, you meet somebody, you fall in love, move in together, and live happily ever after. You're totally monogamous and remove yourself from the bar scene.

Once Gary and Mitch decided they were going to move in together and talked about the "open relationship thing," they didn't talk about what the other was doing when they were apart. They continued to make arrangements for Gary's cross-country move. Mitch had to go East for a conference just before the moving date, and he arranged to meet Gary in Miami. Together they planned to drive back across the country.

Mitch: We led each other to believe that we were monks while waiting for our marriage. I had the impression, but never discussed it, that Gary wasn't seeing anybody else.

At the conference in Washington, D.C., I stayed at the home of one of the members from the organization that was sponsoring the conference, along with three other men who were attending the conference.

The first night, there we were sitting around the living room getting to know each other and I noticed a poster of Miami on the wall. So we started talking about Miami and I mentioned my lover who I was going to meet in a week. And our host, Kyle, said, "Well, I was just down there a couple of weeks ago on vacation."

Kyle talked about all the fun he had and said that he'd met this real hot guy and they had spent the night together. Somehow it came up that this guy lived in the same suburb as my lover. And I said, "What a coincidence, my lover lives there, too. His name is Gary." And Kyle said, "Well, this guy I met is named Gary, too." The coincidence was incredible.

Gary: It was a panic. It was like getting caught with your pants down.

Mitch: I was totally disillusioned. I thought, "This guy is an asshole. He's just using me to get someplace." I started thinking, "I don't even know this guy and here I am, I'm going to bring him into my home."

It was several difficult phone calls and days before Mitch felt convinced to continue with their plan to move in together. But that was not the end of their discoveries that they were very, very different from one another.

DECIDING WHETHER OR NOT TO LIVE TOGETHER

Not long ago, two men living together was not quite so easy as it is today—not that it has become all that much easier in some parts of the country. Each man kept his own house or apartment because, according to one middle-aged man, "You just didn't think of living together." Why not? The usual reasons: fear of how the neighbors would react, what the families would think, and how such an arrangement would play at the office. While many gay men now commonly expect to share a home with a life partner, concern about the reaction of neighbors, family, friends, and employers is still part of the discussion about the type of living arrangements, if not a central issue in the decision to move in together.

Although it *is* easier today to make the decision to move in together, there are still reasons why some men don't, or at least delay such a move. These include a desire for independence, career or education necessities, and caution.

For example, George, 35, and Guy, 50, have been a couple for four years and don't live together. Guy is retired and lives ten minutes away from George, who is a mail carrier for the federal government. George lives in a house that he renovated with Guy's help. It is on a quiet, modest street in Minneapolis, Minnesota. He likes the independence of owning his own home. While Guy is interested in their living together, he's not pushing, especially since he lives so close by, sees George every day, and spends several nights a week with him. George considers living together a possibility somewhere down the line, but for now finishing the renovation of his house is a much higher priority.

If you do decide to live together, how long should you wait before moving into the same house or apartment? The simple rule of thumb is to wait until you *both* feel comfortable about the decision. If you have strong doubts about the future of the relationship, it's best to wait until those doubts diminish before setting up house. The couples I spoke with who live together waited, on average, a few months to a year or more before moving in together. One alternative if you're moving into a new lover's apartment or house is to do what several couples I spoke with have done: keep your old apartment as an option during the first few months you live together. When you feel more confident about the future of the relationship, you can give it up.

CHOOSING A PLACE TO LIVE

Before you get down to who gets the big closet and where to hang the family pictures, you have to decide where to live. There are generally three options: your place, his place, or a new place. Your decision will of course depend on your living arrangements at the time you and your partner meet, and what the two of you need and can afford.

His Place or My Place

Peter and Ned waited only two months before Ned moved into Peter's two-bedroom rental apartment in Hawaii. Peter, 35, is a newspaper reporter. Ned, who is ten years younger, is a social worker. At the time they met, Ned was sharing an apartment with a roommate. His roommate held the lease. Peter lived alone in a two-bedroom apartment. The obvious choice was for Ned to move into Peter's place.

Ned: I tried to be real hesitant, insisting that we weren't going to move in as soon as we did.

Peter: I was unrelenting that I wanted us to move in together. I was very ready for a relationship.

Ned: I had already spent quite a bit of time over at Peter's and had my own bedroom picked out and had quite a bit of my stuff over there . . .

Peter: . . . and had already decided what furniture had to go where . . .

Ned: . . . and what had to be replaced. We ended up using the second bedroom for storage. But I did want separate bedrooms.

Peter got his wish for Ned to move in, but not entirely because of his pushing. Once Ned mentioned to his roommate that he might eventually move in with Peter, his roommate pressured him to move so he could find a new long-term roommate.

Ned: It was a little rough at first when we moved in together. There weren't any problems, which was part of the problem. Neither of us was willing to make an issue out of anything.

Peter had never had a relationship before and had never had to cope with living with anyone before.

Peter: I always preferred living by myself. I had a lot of independence and not much experience in compromise.

Before Ned moved in I pictured eternal bliss—that things would be happy and contented. I had no perception of all the compromise that goes into a relationship.

Ned: We were on the same wavelength for such a long time. We used to wonder when we would have our first major argument.

Peter: It took longer than normal, because by the time little things finally started frustrating us, we had gone so long without any waves neither of us wanted to be the first to start an argument.

Finding a New Place

If your respective living arrangements prevent either of you from moving into the other's apartment or house, or if you both prefer to get a fresh start in a new house or apartment, you should consider many things before choosing a new home, including:

1. What can I afford?

2. What can he afford?

3. What can we afford?

4. Will we rent or buy?

5. What are my priorities (e.g., light, space, separate bedrooms)?

6. What are his priorities (e.g., budget, abundant sunlight, one large bedroom)?

7. What are our priorities?

8. Will one of us need space to work at home?

9. Do we each want our own work area or room?

10. Will we have a lot of overnight guests?

11. Are we willing to tackle a handyman's special?

12. Do we need an extra room in anticipation of caring for an elderly parent?

13. Do we need an extra bedroom so that it looks as if we're roommates and not a gay couple?

14. Do we each want our own bedroom because we want our own bedroom?

15. Is it important to live in a neighborhood where there are other gay people?

Ideally, you'll have time to discuss your priorities and have the chance to look for a new place together. If that's not possible, make certain you talk at length about what your priorities are; otherwise, you may be unpleasantly surprised by what your partner chooses without having you there to help decide. That's what happened with Gary and Mitch.

Once Gary decided to move from Miami to Seattle to be with Mitch (their conflicting views on monogamy notwithstanding), he and Mitch had to decide on living arrangements. At the time, Mitch had a small, sparsely furnished, "bachelor's" apartment in Seattle. Gary had a house filled with traditional furniture, in an affluent section in Miami. So they had no choice but to find a new place to live that could accommodate both of them and Gary's furniture. Unfortunately for Gary and Mitch, they didn't talk much about the kind of place they would both be satisfied with.

Mitch: First we talked about Gary trying to get a place of his own and living separately for a while, while we dated and got to know each other. But Gary was adamant about living together, so I had to give up my "dump," as Gary called it, and find a place we could share.

Gary: If I was going to make the commitment to move out here, then it was going to be all or nothing. I thought we should move in together and give it a try. That's what I was coming out here to do.

Mitch: Because Gary was in Miami, I had to look for a place by myself. I had to go with what my idea was of what Gary and I could live in together and what we could afford. I had to go on assumptions of what Gary would like. That was really a shot in the dark.

Gary: I was disappointed when I saw the apartment. After my house, the apartment was confining, but I didn't tell Mitch how I felt.

Stuart and Paul are both 23 and lived just a few blocks from each other in Brooklyn when they met. They both lived in apartments with several roommates and had no choice but to look for a new and affordable apartment. Because they apartment hunted together, talked at length about their priorities, and knew each other a little better than did Mitch and Gary, they were able to settle on an apartment that they both liked. Stuart and Paul had never been involved in a long-term relationship before they met each other in a gay bar that caters to young professionals. They started talking about living together four months after they met.

Stuart: I think that I initiated that conversation about living together. We were in very temporary living situations. We knew we would have to move at about the same time.

Paul: And we were together practically every day.

Stuart: Four, five days out of seven. I was thinking, "What if I have to move to Staten Island and Paul has to live in the Bronx? Then we can't see each other so often because it's too damn difficult. And one of us will wind up always spending time at the other's apartment and it would be a waste of rent . . ."

Paul: . . . and time.

Stuart: Paul was a little hesitant about the idea, while recognizing the practicality. It was a big step.

Paul: It was a big deal and it wasn't a big deal.

Stuart: It was the first time that each of us was going to move into a place of our own. Previous to that we each shared someone else's apartment.

It was going to be a big step in any case. The fact we were going to do it together just made it all that much bigger.

Paul's biggest concern was that his parents would realize he was gay if he moved into a one-bedroom apartment with another man. Three of Paul's brothers are gay.

Paul: Here I am moving in with a guy—my brother Shawn moved in with Jim seven years ago and my brother David moved in with Glen five years ago, here I am moving in with Stuart, and my youngest brother is a gay activist. I was afraid that my parents were going to jump off a cliff. I was trying to play it down as much as possible, trying to find a two-bedroom place, which was impossible to find in our price range.

Stuart: Besides family worries, we were also very aware and concerned about dealing with brokers and agents as a gay couple. One broker made a comment, "Well, you know a lot of people see two guys and they don't really want to rent." We quickly got a sense that the neighborhoods we were looking at were not going to be easy neighborhoods for us to live in.

Through a newspaper advertisement, Stuart and Paul eventually found an apartment in an owner-occupied row house, in a neighborhood where being gay was not an issue.

Straight Neighborhood/Gay Neighborhood

In some cities you can choose to live in a predominantly gay neighborhood. Given a choice, whether you live in a predominantly gay neighborhood or one that is basically straight depends on what you and your partner find more comfortable. Or, your choice may simply be a matter of where you find the best apartment or house at the best price.

Whether or not there is a choice, the bottom line is (according to one gay broker in Portland, Oregon) that: "Most couples simply want to know if they will be accepted in a neighborhood that they find appealing."

In a predominantly gay neighborhood you won't have to worry about being accepted. In a predominantly straight neighborhood, especially a neighborhood where you are the only gay couple, acceptance may take some time. It was a few years before Chet and John were accepted by their neighbors.

Chet and John love the suburban/rural neighborhood where they live. When they started going out, Chet had an apartment in a nearby city and John was renting the house they now own. Their decision to buy the house evolved over time, and had a lot to do with their mutual desire to live in the same type of setting in which they were raised. They weren't concerned about the fact they were the only gay couple in the neighborhood.

Chet and John now spend most of their weekends on ladders with hammer and nails, renovating the house. They get along well with their neighbors, but when they first moved in together they came home on a few occasions to unwelcome messages spray painted on their front door. "And kids would ride by and call John names when he was working in the garden," said Chet. They were upset by the incidents but never considered moving.

What do you do? Chet and John simply cleaned their front door and went on as usual. They called the police about one neighborhood boy who continued to harass them even after they asked him to stay away from their property. "The police turned it around and made it sound as if I was trying to seduce the kid," said Chet, who was less than satisfied with the police response. "I knew enough *not* to give the police my name before discussing the problem."

After their negative experience with the police, Chet and John decided to keep a low profile ("No kissing goodbye on the front step, which we didn't do before the problems started") and continued to upgrade their property and house. In time, Chet and John got to know their neighbors, who recognized that they were having a positive impact on the area. The work they've done on their house has inspired other neighbors to scrape peeling paint, replace front doors, and improve landscaping. "Now we all watch out for each other's homes."

Buying/Renting a House or Apartment

When you first move in together, whether you buy or rent depends on many factors, not the least of which is what your present living circumstances are. Whatever your situation when you first move in together, the best approach is a simple one in combination with common sense. If you're moving into a new place together, it's easiest to rent. If you must buy, one of you should do the buying, or you should make the purchase as Tenants in Common. (See Chapter 9, "Legalizing Your Relationship," for more information on buying or renting a home.) A joint purchase may make sense if you've known each other for a long time before deciding to move in together, and you both feel confident about the future of the relationship. The simplest approach when one of you already owns a home and your new lover is moving in is to have him pay a part of the monthly costs. Later, if you choose, you can transfer part ownership to your lover, or sell him an interest in the property.

For most of the couples I spoke with, the joint purchase of a home or apartment is something they did after at least a year or more of living together. If one partner already owned a home, it wasn't until the couple moved to a new home or purchased a second home that the purchase was made jointly. Buying a home for many of the couples was more than just a financial arrangement. It was also an important step in their relationship.

Gary and Mitch bought their condominium apartment two years after they moved in together. For both of them, but particularly for Gary, the purchase was an important symbol.

Mitch: Gary had owned several houses by the time we met. Part of his idea of a relationship was to own a home together. I was terrified by it. I looked at what our mortgage would cost us over thirty years and it was mind boggling. I fought it.

Gary: This was a big commitment.

Mitch: Gary needed the security of us being invested together.

Gary: There aren't many ways that we can represent our relationship, so own-ing a home is one. We have joint tenancy. It represents a foundation, having roots, being part of a community in which we live.

Mitch: The apartment is also a physical tie in the relationship.

Gary: For Mitch at least, it symbolized that I wasn't going anywhere.

Before you commit yourself to any major joint investment or sign a lease, be certain to consult Chapter 9, "Legalizing Your Relationship," for the legal guidelines you should follow when purchasing or renting property together.

RENTING AN APARTMENT IN AN OWNER-OCCUPIED BUILDING

Unless you live in an owner-occupied building where the owner clearly has no problem with gay people, you can run into several problems. An in-house landlord is more likely to discover that you're a gay couple. If he does and has a problem with gay people, he could ask you to leave. In certain localities, you're protected by law from being evicted, but in most you're not. Even if your landlord chooses not to evict you, living in a building with a hostile landlord can be uncomfortable at best.

Worrying about keeping your secret from the landlord can also add tension to home life. You may feel reluctant to have friends over, you may not feel free to speak loudly, or make love loudly.

If you have a choice, avoid renting an apartment in an owner-occu-pied building unless you are certain you are welcome, or you're certain you're willing to put up with the potential hassles.

Moving to a New City or Town

At some point during your relationship you may be faced with a move to another city or state. Whether you're moving to increase your career options, because of a job transfer, or just for a change of scenery, there are many factors to consider in choosing where to live.

Hugh and Arthur are both in their 40's. Hugh is an engineer, Arthur a psychiatrist. When Hugh and Arthur decided to relocate from Virginia to Austin, Texas, their prime consideration was improved career opportunities for Arthur and comparable opportunities for Hugh, but they also considered a number of other things. Following is the list of priorities Hugh and Arthur drew up when they first started their search for a new place to live.

1. Job possibilities

2. A state without sodomy laws

3. Moderate climate

4. Cultural activities

5. Some gay community

To find a place that met their requirements, Hugh and Arthur started by speaking to friends in their respective professions to find out which cities would offer wide career opportunities. They also consulted the *Places Rated Almanac* (see "Resources" at the end of this chapter).

Hugh and Arthur were both fairly extensively involved in gay political and health organizations in Virginia and expected to continue their involvement in their new home city. The *Gayellow Pages* helped them to determine what kinds of organized gay life existed in the cities on their list. They made phone calls to gay organizations in each city, and when visiting a city stopped in at local gay bars and asked what gay life was like in that town.

Moving involves countless decisions, and these mean compromise. Disagreements are unavoidable as you deal with movers, real estate brokers, lawyers, landlords, etc. If you're leaving friends and family behind and are changing jobs as well, the pressure on the two of you can increase dramatically as you depend more on each other for support. If you're already having trouble communicating or reaching mutually acceptable decisions, putting yourselves in a situation that requires lots of decision making will only increase your problems.

Before moving across town, or across the country, Hugh and Arthur offer this warning: "If you have problems in your relationship it's much better to solve them first and then move. When you move you just take the problems with you. If a relationship is not stable, the worst thing you can do is move. It only adds to existing pressures and conflicts. And it takes a pretty stable couple to take the considerable pressures of moving."

The Value of a Real Estate Broker

Whether you're looking for your first joint rental apartment to move into, or you're relocating and want to buy a house in another part of the country, you may want to seek out the help of a professional—particularly one who is accustomed to dealing with gay couples. In most parts of the country, brokers can be very helpful.

A gay broker, or a straight broker who is accustomed to working with gay couples, can provide a link into the local gay community and can answer many of the apartment or house-hunting questions you will have: Are there any neighborhoods in this town where it would be difficult for a gay couple to live? Is there a gay neighborhood? Which of the local banks offers joint financing to two unrelated men? Can you put me in touch with a gay lawyer? etc.

One way to find a gay or gay-friendly broker is through Realty Referrals (see "Resources" for this chapter), a company that provides referrals to gay and gay-sensitive real estate brokers nationwide. Christopher is a broker in St. Louis who is gay and is listed with Realty Referrals: "I see the clients I get through Realty Referrals as a group I feel very well prepared to serve. I'm going to be more understanding of their concerns. And they can be straightforward with me about those concerns."

When Hugh and Arthur were planning their move from Virginia to Texas, they sought the help of a gay realtor.

Hugh: I tried to find a gay realtor through the *Gayellow Pages,* but I wasn't able to get through to anybody in Austin who could lead me to one. So I called some real estate companies and said, "Do you have people who specialize in gay couples?" Some said, "Oh, no," and hung up, and one said "I don't really know of anyone, but let me check." Someone else got on the phone and said he wasn't gay, but "I have no problems working with gay people."

SETTING UP, FIXING UP, AND RENOVATING YOUR SHARED HOME

Adjusting to a Shared Home and Shared Decisions

If you're used to living alone and making all the decisions about how your home looks, it may be difficult to get used to sharing decisions—

particularly if your new lover is moving into your already furnished apartment or house. It's usually easier if you're moving into a new place together, but even then there can be problems about deciding which place to rent or buy and who gets to decide what color to paint the living room, where to put the couch, etc.

Before Ned moved in, Peter had lived all of his adult life on his own, which made for a difficult transition from a single-person household to one that is shared. Peter found he had to work hard to overcome his natural inclination to treat his new partner as something less than an equal. This was especially difficult for Peter, because his money was behind the decision to purchase the new home he and Ned planned to share.

Just a few months after Ned moved in with him, Peter decided to go ahead with plans to sell a nearby plot of land and invest the money in a house or condo that he and Ned would share. Because he was buying the new place with his own money, Peter didn't think that choosing the new place would have to be a joint decision, but he quickly discovered Ned had strong opinions.

Ned: I didn't want anything to do with it. I didn't like the condo Peter chose because it was like living in an apartment.

Peter: He thought we could wait the next year or two until we saw something we both liked, because we weren't paying much rent. Whereas I had decided I wanted to move into something I owned even if it was not up to my expectations. I just wanted to get out of where I was.

So I told Ned, "I don't care, it's my money and I'll do what I want."

Ned: I was pretty pissed off.

Peter: I think you were hurt too. As soon as I said it, I instantly knew I had said something wrong by just looking at his face. Almost immediately I knew what I had done. It hurt Ned that I was still thinking in terms of mine and his, and not ours. I wanted to make the decision without his input.

Ned: I just knew from right then I would have to smack this boy around some.

Peter: I apologized to him about it.

Ned: But I pretty much gave up on fighting the condo. I knew how important it was to him and it did make more sense to pay into equity instead of paying rent.

By treating your partner as less than an equal, whether by making a major decision such as buying a house, or simply deciding where to hang your map of Alaska, you almost guarantee his resentment. During a period of adjustment, which for Peter and Ned lasted several months, some resentment is to be expected, but unresolved resentment can undermine a relationship. So if you're inclined to be overbearing and territorial, pay attention to it and try to keep it under control.

At first, Gary and Mitch almost killed each other over who got to decide what. When they finally arrived in Seattle after a grueling cross-country trip, they found their new apartment was still empty, except for Mitch's dismantled waterbed and his books. The moving truck had been delayed and was still in Miami with all of Gary's furniture. It arrived while Mitch was away on a week-long business trip.

Mitch: When I got back, it was all set up. Gary is very traditional in his tastes, so he set up the apartment a lot like his home in Miami. I walked in without having had any say in how it was done and did a slow burn.

I felt like, this is my house too and I'm going to have some say in how this is done. But I didn't say anything. I was almost too sensitive to what Gary had to sacrifice to get here. I had to be nice to him and tolerate this. So I didn't say anything for a while, but finally I blew up.

Gary: It was over the waterbed. I had a nice traditional Mediterranean bedroom suite and he wanted to set up the waterbed.

Mitch: The bed represented *me*. He had done all this stuff without asking me and when it came to the bed I stood firm. I told Gary, "We're going to put together this waterbed and we're going to sleep in it come hell or high water."

Ultimately, after many discussions and arguments, Mitch got his way with the waterbed, a framed print of a pink flamingo, and purple-framed poster, but only after Mitch gave in on the "tacky" living room chairs (they've since been reupholstered to mutual satisfaction). To avoid future major battles over their differing tastes, Gary and Mitch divided their two-bedroom apartment by room. Gary was to be responsible for decorating the living room and dining room. Mitch got the master bedroom and bathroom. They shared responsibility for the second bedroom which they used as a den.

Time together has also helped. Now, even in rooms where each has his own jurisdiction, Gary and Mitch make joint purchases and find they can usually reach a compromise. The pink flamingo print has been replaced by something more subdued, but the waterbed and purple-framed poster are still sore points for Gary. Gary said (with a smile) that he hopes an earthquake one day knocks the purple-framed poster from the wall and has fantasies about slicing up the waterbed.

Gary: I think the bed is extremely unattractive and is a royal pain to make. I'm a meticulous housekeeper, so I like nice crisp corners on a bed. That's impossible with a waterbed. I refuse to make the bed.

Peter and Ned didn't divide up their apartment between them, but they decided on a two-bedroom apartment; in part, so that each could have a room where there was no need to compromise on anything.

Peter: If you have one room that's identified as your bedroom, you don't have to compromise on decor. The living room is a compromise, but you can have your bedroom the way you want—if you want, with your clothes strewn all over. It's like a teenager and his parents' house.

Ned: My bedroom is my own space.

Peter: Also, Ned likes to say, "Go to your room."

Ned: Yeah.

Peter: We use his bedroom most of the time because he doesn't like mine. He doesn't like the mattress. It's pretty lumpy. And despite the fact Ned is a country boy, he's pretty picky.

Veto Power

Since it's unlikely that any two people will agree on absolutely everything, at least for the first decade or two they're together, it's best to have a system to deal with differences. Dividing up your home by room is one approach. Separate bedrooms is another. But often there isn't enough room to set aside more than a desk area as "his" or "my" territory, and inevitably you will need to compromise. That's where veto power comes in handy.

Scott and I fell into using veto power early in our relationship. We discuss any major purchase or furniture rearrangement that will affect the house in advance. We each have the right to veto the other's request concerning a piece of furniture, paint color, room arrangement, etc. We've never discussed how many vetoes we each have, but it's understood that they are to be used sparingly and only if compromise is impossible. For example, when we moved into our new apartment, Scott preferred that I not put up any of my father's paintings, which are, I admit, a little outlandish and depressing, but nonetheless important to me. He could have vetoed all of them, but instead said okay to a couple of the paintings under the condition that I said okay to displaying a couple of his *objets trouvé* (junk) on the bookshelves and that I hang the paintings in the hall where they weren't too conspicuous.

The beauty of the veto system is that it allows each of you to make proposals, however ridiculous. And you don't have to be deadly serious about the negotiations, so it can be fun to make proposals back and forth. The veto system assumes that you're reasonable, so if one or both of you is stubborn and not open to give-and-take or compromise, the veto system won't work.

Michael and Chris use the veto approach, which doesn't necessarily eliminate arguments. As soon as we started discussing how they fixed up their apartment, Michael, an architect, and Chris, a law student, began arguing. The two 27-year olds live in a modest one-bedroom railroad flat on the first floor of a small row house. Their apartment reflects Michael's keen interest in design as well as Chris's moderating influence.

Chris: Michael comes up with these ideas and then he has to run them by me
and I have veto power. But usually Michael has a good argument.

Michael: He says that I usually have my way.

Chris: When it comes to decorating the house he gets his way most of the time.

Michael: That's not true.

Chris: My taste is in my mouth.

Michael: It's a little bit of martyrdom.

Chris: He'll come to me and say I want to change the kitchen and do this.
. . . And I say the landlady will never approve it. But I'll say yes to part of the
plan, but I'll also say you can't do everything you want to do. We usually reach
a compromise.

Michael: I like color, so I picked out a bright aqua green for the kitchen. He
said to me that it was too bright, so we compromised on a milder color. He
does have a lot of input.

Chris: Originally I would have preferred to have everything white.

Renovating Your House or Apartment

If you plan to do major renovation work on your home, it will intensify
whatever difficulties you have reaching an agreement concerning any
aspect of fixing up your home.

Marshall and Craig have been renovating an 18th-century house that
they bought two years ago after giving up a condo apartment. Marshall,
an architectural-history buff, has been doing most of the work himself.
It gives them plenty to argue about.

Craig: It's really a communication thing. Even after six years together we have
trouble trying to understand what the other means.

Marshall: Different words mean different things to each of us. I think it's
because we come from different places in the country and because of training. I have just enough art training to be dangerous. I also tend to be very
visual; he is not. That's a real problem when we talk colors—in terms of how
I describe how it's going to look. He has a different perception of how it's
going to look.

Craig: Often it doesn't matter to me. One thing we have trouble with is Marshall believing me when I say I don't care. He'll say, "We have a very important decision to make," and I'll say "You know, I don't have an opinion either
way, so you pick what you want and that will be fine." Marshall feels I'm not
telling the truth and somehow I really do have an opinion and if he picks the
wrong thing that I'll be upset.

I may come home and say, "Oh, that's different than I thought it would be."
He interprets that to mean "You did it wrong, you didn't pick what I wanted."
My comment has no weight behind it. And he'll get upset and say "Well, I
asked you what you wanted."

When asked if he has learned to better interpret what Craig means,
Marshall answers that he wishes he could say yes and notes that under-

standing what Craig is saying is still one of the problems in their relationship. The new house served to increase, by many times, the number of misunderstandings.

Marshall: Our lawyer says that people can live in an apartment and never talk. But they move into a house and suddenly there are all these decisions that you have to make. And the thing about decisions is that you have to make them before you can come to conclusions. And to come to conclusions you have to talk. And a lot of couples, when they start talking, realize they don't like each other!

MANAGING THE HOUSEHOLD—COOKING, CLEANING, AND SHOPPING

Most couples manage to get around differences in their views about money, clothes, religion, and politics, but differences of opinion over cleanliness and the grocery shopping can lead to murder. It may take a little while for the problems to surface, but in time they will, and you and your partner will have to work out a system with which you both can live. For some couples, responsibilities will fall comfortably and almost automatically into place. For others, it may take time, arguments, and a lot of work.

If you find that after a couple of years you and your partner are still having serious arguments about who takes out the garbage and who does the laundry or dusting, then it's time to ask yourselves if the problem isn't more complicated than dividing up the chores. It's easy for dissatisfaction with other aspects of a relationship to spill over into everyday routines.

Housework

Because such necessities as scrubbing the toilet and washing the dishes are not the first things that come to mind when you move in together— especially if you're feeling the passion of a new relationship—balancing household chores and distributing responsibility may take some time and trial and error. If you believe there is only one right way to do things, the adjustment can be particularly difficult.

After their first full week of living together, Gary decided it was time to clean.

Mitch: We both had just gotten home after a long hard week. It was 6:00 on Friday night and Gary said that's when we do the housework. I was very disgruntled, but I went along with it because I thought, fine, we'll do this once.

So we start scrubbing the floors and the bathrooms and vacuuming and dusting. When we talk about clean, it wasn't just superficial, it was over the picture frames and take all the books out of the bookshelves and dust behind.

Gary: I'm Midwestern, Bohemian German. We were taught to live very clean. Mitch had the living habits of a pig.

Mitch: I appreciate a clean place, but what I didn't like was being forced to participate. In my single life, Friday night meant taking a nap and getting ready to go out. I so resented him telling me to get the mop and bucket. And he resented my resisting that.

Then I discovered he wanted to clean every Friday night. Finally it blew up one day in a session with our therapist.

Gary and Mitch came up with an alternative approach to cleaning. They've hired someone to come in once every two weeks to do the heavy cleaning and divided up the remaining tasks.

Gary: I do most of the extra cleaning that doesn't get done every other week. I find it relaxing.

Mitch: And I show Gary that I appreciate it by commenting and praising his work. I also clean the bathroom. I've learned to clean up right after I use the bathroom.

Gary: He still will not dust.

Mitch: For me, dusting can wait several months.

Gary: When we visited with his folks, I know why. His mother does not dust. I love her dearly, but she needs to dust. The hardest thing is when you're staying with your in-laws and your mother-in-law has your partner's habits. It was hard not to say, "Claire, can I have a dust cloth."

You may not recognize that you and your partner disagree about how clean your home should be kept or how the chores should get done until after the honeymoon—the weeks, or months during which your partner can do no wrong. What do you do when the dew dries from your eyes and you find yourself doing all of the housework, or find the sink piled high with dishes, or you're just not happy about how things are—or are not—getting done? *Talk about it.* Talking is often difficult, but it will be next to impossible to change anything without talking about it. And as I discovered, dropping hints will get you almost nowhere.

During the first year Scott and I lived together, I was a student. I had more free time. I didn't mind doing the housework, and wound up doing all of it. Scott's job was demanding, and when he had free time, he didn't use it to clean house. Everything was fine until after I went back to work full time. I told Scott, after several weeks of trying to keep up with everything, "I just don't have the time to do it all." I wasn't diplomatic when I raised the subject. I usually waited until I was pissed off and overwhelmed by the frustration of trying to do everything, and then got angry. That's not the time to have a rational discussion. You can be far more effective over a quiet dinner.

In fact, at first I didn't directly raise the subject. I just started making slightly hostile remarks every now and then about Scott not pitching in enough, but he never took the hint.

After several discussions, much frustration, and trial and error, we worked out a system we both feel comfortable with. I do the vacuuming and dusting, Scott is responsible for cleaning the kitchen and bathroom. I'm in charge of the dry cleaning and shirts. Scott does the laundry. We try not to be dogmatic about chores, so if one of us is under a lot of pressure at work the other may volunteer to handle a chore he isn't normally responsible for.

We don't keep a list of who is responsible for what chore at what time. We're not nearly that organized. Nor do we rotate chores. You may find either of these alternatives appealing if it works for you.

Once you divide up the chores, you have to learn not to intefere, even if you think you can do it better or get it done faster. I once (maybe twice) made the mistake of trying to tell Scott how to do the laundry. Realistically, he's a grown man, putting quarters in a machine doesn't require a keen intellect. After annoying him to death, he offered to let me do the laundry. That worked. I no longer interfere.

If you like being in charge and think no one can do anything better than you can, or you're not willing to live with how your partner handles a chore, you may get stuck doing things you don't want to do. Gary hates doing the laundry. "It's the thing I least like to do, but if I wait for Mitch to do it, both of us will be wearing our holeyest underwear by the time he gets around to doing it. That doesn't bother him, but it makes me crazy." Gary could do his own laundry and let Mitch do *his* own, but it would still make Gary crazy to think that Mitch was walking around in holey underwear.

Shopping, Cooking, and Deciding What to Eat

Differences in background and conflicting views about the ways in which things should be done also affect how you shop, the ways in which you cook, and what you eat. As with housework, discovering each other's differences, and strengths and weaknesses, will cause you to have to work out systems to accommodate those strengths and weaknesses, and to learn to accept differences that won't go away.

For example, Donald and Andrew, who have lived together for five years, had their first and biggest fight over food shopping several months into their relationship. They almost came to blows over the purchase of a melon.

Andrew: We have two different personalities. I'm very choosy. When you go to a store and pick something out, you just don't pick it out, you look and see, question the salesman, see what's going on. Donald will just walk in and take something off the shelf. That's what he did with the melon.

Donald: Andrew went crazy. It was our first serious argument. I was so angry. Consequently I haven't bought a melon in a long time. Andrew's not real satisfied with my shopping techniques. I don't like to grocery shop. I just get it and get out. Andrew really likes to comb the place.

Within a very short time Andrew took over the shopping responsibilities. The rest of their household chores fell into place along the lines of their own likes and dislikes and their abilities. According to Andrew, "We both understand there are certain things we do better, so we've fallen into a lot of that stuff."

Doug and Tony don't have major arguments about who does the shopping or the cooking because Doug does almost all of the shopping and cooking. But he does try to get Tony to pitch in. The method he describes in the dialogue that follows is one that several men I met have found effective in getting their partners to pitch in with cooking.

Tony: I hate to cook.

Doug: Tony can cook, but he doesn't unless I make him help cook. Actually I don't care all that much if he doesn't cook, but I can't stand having him sit on the sofa doing this Italian male thing, and watch me cook the way his father sits in the kitchen and watches his mother cook and his grandfather sits in the kitchen and watches his grandmother cook.

So at first I made him stand there and peel carrots or just hand me things. But if you have to stand there telling him to peel the eggs, cut up the eggs, put the eggs in the tuna fish, not only will you be in each other's way constantly, but you will also feel like what we refer to as the "kitchen commandant." The most effective way to get your partner involved is to make him responsible for the soup, dessert, or even the main course.

John is also not very happy doing all the cooking, but Chet has no interest whatsoever in pitching in, so he and Chet worked out a different compromise.

John: I like coming home and the two of us having dinner. I hate ordering out. I hate the whole conception of ordering food out or eating pizza. That bothers me. But I've compromised because there are nights I just don't want to cook.

Chet: Our compromise is that one or two nights a week my job is to go out and get that stuff.

There are also all sorts of systems you can use for cleaning up after dinner. The one I like is simple. The one who cooks gets to leave all the pots, pans, and dirty dishes for the other to clean up. I do most of the cooking, so Scott does most of the cleaning up. Scott's lucky because I'm neat. When he cooks dinner for two, he leaves the kitchen looking as if he's prepared dinner for twenty. (I do have to give him some credit: When he prepares an occasional dinner for guests, he proves himself to be a superb chef. Except for turkey, he is by far the better cook.)

Michael and Tony, the architect and law student, have a different system that has a built-in guarantee to encourage relatively neat cooking habits. Whoever makes dinner also cleans up. Both like to cook, so they shop together and trade off cooking responsibilities every other night, except on weekends when they prepare dinner together or go to the homes of relatives for dinner.

One final anecdote on the subject of living with each other's differences around the house: As you've probably guessed by now, Gary and Mitch, whom I've featured extensively in this chapter, are very, very different from one another. But during their three years together, they've managed to work out a lot of their differences to each other's satisfaction. This includes their cooking styles and eating habits, about which they've had some of their worst arguments. I hope the following dialogue, and their experience, proves instructive in the art of kitchen diplomacy.

Mitch: At first, we started cooking together. Granted, I'm a messy cook. I pull out every pan, bowl, and spoon. With Gary, everything goes in one pan and you clean up as you go, and the kitchen stays spotless. I throw flour all over the place, and if I don't like something, I'll start over in another bowl. We got in a lot of heated arguments.

Gary: Mitch is from the South, so no matter what you're having for dinner, biscuits are involved. He gets out this pastry cloth and the rolling pin and the first item on the recipe is, "Throw flour around the room." I remember standing in the kitchen the first time and he literally threw flour around the room.

Mitch: I resented having to explain everything to him.

Gary: He was in his glory.

Mitch: As soon as he started complaining, I would just kill the conversation, not cook, and go in the other room and sulk.

Gary: We have such different backgrounds and we came into the relationship with a lot of our parents in us. Your family and the environment in which you were raised is part of you. This was terribly frustrating for me.

Mitch: Because of our different backgrounds, we also argued about what we should eat. I'm from the South and we fry everything, and eat bread and potatoes with every meal. Gary would tell me, "You can't have two starches with your meal. If you're gonna have potatoes, you can't have biscuits." I went along with it because he's such a nag sometimes.

I really resented someone telling me that after twenty-five years I couldn't have two starches with my meal.

Gary: That was a few years ago. I don't think we're still as outspoken about what

the other one eats. I've also learned to stay out of the kitchen while Mitch
is cooking.

Mitch: On those rare occasions when he wanders in, I don't hesitate to tell him
to get out. The difference between now and a couple of years ago is that now
he won't throw a fit when I tell him to get out. But I'll never forget the last
time he couldn't resist interfering.

Gary: I was in the living room and could see the reflection of the kitchen in the
glass door of the china cabinet. We've since moved it. Mitch put some cheese
in the food processor and blew it all over the kitchen.

Mitch: The bowl was too short, but I figured I'd get all the cheese back into the
bowl when I was finished.

Gary: There was cheese hanging all over the kitchen. But I knew enough by
then to leave the kitchen and let Mitch clean it up. Not that it didn't upset
me. I just knew better than to say anything.

RESOURCES

Finding a Real Estate Broker

In cities where Realty Referrals does not list real estate brokers, you can try to
find a broker through the *Gayellow Pages* (see Appendix). Even if there is no
broker listed for the city to which you are moving, you can call a local gay
organization or local chapter of a national gay organization and ask if they can
refer you to a gay broker.

Organizations

Realty Referrals, PO Box 14221, Portland, OR 97214, 503–239–5051

> This free service lists brokers nationwide, but has very few listings for
> brokers in the South, and none in some Southern states, such as Mississippi
> and Arkansas. (Realty Referrals gets a percentage of the sales commission
> from the broker you work with if the broker makes a sale or if you sign a
> lease.)

Books

Places Rated Almanac: Your Guide to Finding the Best Places to Live in America, by Richard Boyer and David Savageau. Rand McNally & Co., 10 East 53rd
Street, New York, NY 10022

> *Places Rated* describes 277 metropolitan areas throughout the country.
> Metropolitan areas are ranked and compared for climate, housing, educa-
> tion, health, recreation, the arts, transportation, prosperity, and crime.

CHAPTER 5

It's Tough on Family

*"My first reaction was disbelief. I wanted
him dead. And I told him so."*

Most gay men—most human beings—desire close relationships with
their families, whether their parents, siblings, grandparents, or extended family. They want to remain a part of their families, want to be
loved by them and to be included in family gatherings; and they want
their relationship with their partner to be acknowledged and supported. Close family relations aren't always possible, but more often
than not, it seems, the absence of strong family bonds has little to do
with the fact that one member of the family is gay.

There are probably as many reasons for remoteness within a family
as there are families. Being gay doesn't have to be one of them. But by
hiding your homosexuality and your partner from your family, you
guarantee a degree of remoteness. Coming out to your family, however,
does not ensure that family life will be perfect. Family life is never
perfect. But, if you stay in the closet and hide your relationship, there's
no chance of having your family's involvement and support. You may
not want their involvement or support. That's up to you.

Coming out to family members, and teaching them to respond to you
and your partner as a couple, can be extremely difficult experiences.
Given that your parents and families are likely to know almost nothing
about homosexuality and gay relationships, except for what they've
read in the newspapers or have seen on television, you will have to be
a patient and persistent educator. But if you value involvement with
your parents, siblings, and extended family and you value their support,
the effort—the struggle—will be worth it.

Just a short note to those of you who have not yet accepted your own homosexuality or come out of the closet, even to your closest friends. Coming out, to your family in particular, may seem impossible, beyond your wildest nightmare, not for you, not in your situation. Believe it or not, almost every gay man, from every walk of life, who lives an open or partly open gay life has felt what you feel. For many, if not most, gay men, it *is* possible to come out to friends, co-workers, even family. Life can be better than one characterized by suffering under the burden of half-truths, deception, and self-degradation. You deserve better. But the process begins with your own acceptance of who you are, what you are. You can't expect those closest to you to accept and understand you if you don't yourself. (See Chapter 13, "Health," for information on how to find someone you can talk to if you're having conflicts about your sexuality.)

COMING OUT TO YOUR PARENTS

If your objective is to integrate your relationship with your lover into family life, you will first probably have to let your family, your parents in particular, know that you are gay. If you're already out to your parents, but your partner is not out to his parents, you can be supportive of him, providing encouragement to tell his parents, but you can't force him. The decision must be his own, just as the decision to tell *your* parents is *your* own. Ideally, as with all challenges you face individually and as a couple, you will both be able draw support and strength from each other. And the strength you draw from your relationship may be just what you both need to confront the challenge of coming out to your parents.

Assuming your parents don't yet know that you are gay and you are deciding if and/or how you will tell them, there is much for you to consider. Because no two families are alike, you have to review the guidelines discussed in this section and tailor them to your specific circumstances. For example, you have to decide: Can you sit down with your parents and talk openly about your homosexuality? Should you tell them in a letter? Should you ask one of your siblings to break the news? Should you tell just one parent and not the other? Should you let your parents know about your homosexuality by dropping hints or simply by introducing your lover and letting them put to-gether the evidence? Or should you keep your homosexuality and your relationship a secret?

When David, 28, decided it was time to tell his parents about his being gay, he decided to tell them both in person at the same time. He had grown tired of hiding the truth, and found himself pulling further

and further away from his family, particularly in the months since his
lover had moved in. David had had a close relationship with his parents,
four brothers and sister and wanted it back. Before talking with his
parents, who are in their late 40s, he first sought the advice of his
siblings, who encouraged him to break the news and reassured him they
would be supportive. David felt fairly certain he would not be rejected
by his parents but, nonetheless, he feared their reactions. With the
support of his partner and the self-confidence that came out of his new
relationship, David felt he could handle those reactions, however harsh.

It took me years to get up enough courage to tell them, and months of
pushing from my lover. But finally I made a date to see them at their apartment.

I started by telling them how upset I was at the growing distance between
us. We had been a close family and over the past two years I'd really avoided
my parents.

Then I just told them "I'm gay." My mother took my hand and started to
sob. "Where did I go wrong?" she asked me between the tears. Mind you,
my parents are sophisticated people. Then my father suggested it was because he competed with me for my mother's love. They both agreed that I'd
never be happy, that I'd be alone all my life, and could die from AIDS.

"But Mom, Dad, I'm happier than I've ever been," I told them. No response. My father asked, "Well, who's hungry?" as I headed for the bathroom
and closed the door behind me. Then I heard my mother let out a wail and
she ran up the stairs to her bedroom. I splashed some water on my face and
headed back into the living room for the next round. My mother was still
upstairs crying. Dad was on the couch reading a menu from a Chinese
restaurant. "What'll it be," he asked, "spareribs or roast duck?"

That was about six months ago. My father just called the other day to set
up a date so we can talk about "it." My mother and I have spoken about it
a few times and I know they've both spoken with my siblings. In our first
conversation after that night she asked if I had someone "special." I told her
about Lew, but I didn't tell her we were living together. I was taking it step
by step. Like a good Jewish parent, my mother asked, "Is he Jewish?" That
was a very good sign.

Whatever approach you decide to take, whether you talk to your
parents directly or let them figure out the situation on their own, do not
make the mistake of expecting your parents to understand your homosexuality, or even accept it quickly. In time most parents will begin to
at least accept, if not understand. Acceptance based on love, however,
is infinitely more important than understanding. Think of it this way:
You can't completely understand your parents either. But you can give
them the same things you expect them to give you—acceptance, if not
understanding.

Questions to Consider Before Coming Out to Your Parents

If you decide to come out to your parents by speaking directly to them, before you make plans to tell them that you're gay, there are at least thirteen questions that you should ask yourself—questions you can talk over with your partner. Most of the following questions were drawn from "Coming Out to Your Parents," a pamphlet published by the Philadelphia chapter of Parents and Friends of Lesbians and Gays (see "Resources" at the end of this chapter).

1. *Are you sure that you're gay?*
   Odds are, if you have a lover and have gotten to the point of thinking about telling your parents that you're gay, you are. The reason you have to consider this question is that it is one your parents are likely to ask. So be absolutely sure of yourself, sure enough that you can answer the question with confidence: "Yes, I'm gay and that's not going to change."

2. *Do you feel okay about being gay?*
   Struggling with depression and guilt about being gay doesn't go well with projecting a positive self-image to grief-stricken parents. You'll need every ounce of positive energy in order to tell your parents. If you haven't accepted yourself, you can't expect your parents to accept you. They will sense your ambivalence, and quite possibly will latch on to that as a sign that your homosexuality is a passing thing.

3. *What kind of relationship do you have with your parents?*
   How you tell your parents has a lot to do with your relationship with them. If you've gotten along well with your parents and talked about your personal life to some degree and you know they love you and you love them, sitting down with them for a face-to-face discussion may be perfectly appropriate and natural. And chances are that your parents will be able to deal with the news in a positive way eventually. If you've never talked with your parents about anything personal and your relationship has been distant, a face-to-face discussion about anything more intimate that the state of the world may be something neither you nor your parents can handle. A letter, or unspoken understanding, may feel more appropriate.

4. *What are their moral/societal views?*
   Carefully consider the kind of parents you have and have answers ready for *their* specific concerns. If your parents tend to see social issues in clear terms of good/bad or holy/sinful, you may anticipate that they'll have serious problems dealing with your sexuality. If,

however, they've demonstrated a degree of flexibility when dealing with other changing societal matters, you may be able to anticipate a willingness to work this through with you.

There are most definitely families with rigid religious/moralistic views that may never accept a homosexual child. For these families, even great love for a child may not be enough to overcome strictly held beliefs. And, in such a case, you may be better off not telling them.

5. *Do your parents hold the purse strings?*
If you are still financially dependent on your parents and/or live at home, and if you think it may be possible for your parents to withdraw college finances or throw you out of the house, it may be a good idea to wait until they don't have this to hold over you.

6. *What's doing on the home front?*
Given a choice, consider the timing. If your mother has just lost her job, your father's going in for triple bypass, and your grandfather just died, you might wait until things quiet down. Also consider your own home front. If you and your partner are having serious troubles with your relationship, it's probably a good idea to wait until *your* home front stabilizes.

7. *What are your motives for telling them?*
Be sure that you're telling your parents because you love them and want to improve your relationship with them. It's also okay to want to tell them to get a load off of your shoulders. But don't do it in anger, to get back at them for something you're upset about.

8. *Do you have a shoulder to lean on?*
In case your parents react negatively, can you depend on your partner, friends, or an outside group for emotional support? In particular, talk over your plans with your partner before you break the news.

9. *How much do you know about homosexuality?*
It's the rare parent who knows much about homosexuality. By reading up on the subject and anticipating their specific questions, you'll be able to help them with informed and well-thought-out answers on AIDS, promiscuity, grandchildren—whatever you think their concerns will be. You have to be the educator, whether or not you like it.

10. *Do you have handy resources?*
Have available at least one of the following: a book written specifically for parents of gay children, a contact from the local or national Parents and Friends of Lesbians and Gays organization, the name

of a nongay counselor who you know can deal fairly with gay issues. If you recommend a counselor, be very certain that the counselor you choose has no homophobic tendencies.

11. *Can you be patient?*
Whether or not you are patient, parents usually require time and patience to deal with the information you're about to share with them. It may take from six months to two years just to deal with the information and years more before they're comfortable with it. If you think that is a long time, remember how long it took you to accept your own sexuality.

12. *What's the worst that could happen?*
One way to minimize your own apprehension and fear is realistically to think through the worst possible ways in which your parents could react.

13. *Is this something you have decided to do?*
Coming out to your parents may not be the best thing for you, no matter how much pressure your partner or friends may be putting on you. Don't give in to pressure if you're not sure you will be better off by telling your parents.

The Dos and Don'ts of Telling Your Parents That You're Gay

If, after considering the previous thirteen questions, you decide you're prepared to come out to your parents, there are universal dos and don'ts of breaking the news:

Do:

1. If you tell them in person, set aside a special time to get together. Choose someplace private—someplace where they will not feel compelled to put on a front. While no time is a good time to deliver this news, some times are better than others. Choose a moment when you know your parents will have time to ask questions and to recover from the initial shock.

2. Get to your point quickly. You can preface the critical word or phrase with a sentence or two about love, but don't beat around the bush for too long or you'll force them to guess.

3. Start by telling your parents that the reason that you're talking to them is because you love them. Be sure they understand that, if you didn't feel this way, it wouldn't be necessary to share something like this with them; that if you kept something like this to yourself you

would only build walls; that you can't build a good family relationship on secrets; that if you didn't tell them, they would never know who you are.

4. Assume the role of a parent. You need to be educator, handholder, reassurer. You may not like playing parent with your own parents, but it's likely that you will have to.

5. Be firm. Your parents may suggest that what you've just told them is a phase, or they may suggest you seek counseling or see a psychiatrist who can "cure" you. Concentrate on convincing your parents that your sexuality is innate, fixed, not a choice or changeable if only you wanted to or tried hard enough. Do not give them false hope that things may change in the future.

6. Explain that you are no different than before they knew this about you. You know you are no different, but your parents may need to hear this from you.

7. Emphasize the emotional, full-person nature of attraction, sex is an element, but not the only component of being gay.

8. Soften your language. If you know your parents can't handle hearing the word gay or homosexual, you can say that you're attracted to men instead of women. They'll get your point. The same holds for other words (such as lover) or phrases that may be frightening to your parents.

9. Use positive examples. If your parents have welcomed any of your friends into their home who they knew or didn't know were homosexual—someone they liked—use one of those friends as a positive example.

10. Pursue gently, and keep the lines of communication open. If, after you break the news, your parents have made it clear that they've heard enough, the dialogue doesn't have to stop. You can still tell them you love them, or show that you love them. Over time, very cautiously let them know some of the things that you do related to your sexuality (e.g., that you run with a gay running club). Your straight friends can serve as particularly good role models for your parents. Some parents are amazed to discover that your straight friends, or the parents of friends, accept you without apparent difficulties. This can help accelerate their acceptance. Just don't let them drift away.

The same holds true of parents who fail to raise the topic at all after your initial discussion. Give them a few weeks. If they still say nothing, the ball is in your court and it's up to you to raise the subject, but gently. It isn't enough to tell them once and let it go at that.

Don't:

1. Don't tell them as you're racing out of the house. It simply isn't fair to drop this kind of information if you're on your way back to school or heading half way around the world the next morning. It may be painful, but you have to be prepared to see it through.

2. Don't tell them in anger. It may feel good for a split second to use the fact that you're gay against them, but it's simply common sense not to use your sexuality as ammunition in an argument, whether it's the first time you're discussing it or in later conversations.

3. Don't assume that your parents know anything about homosexuality. Their knowledge will likely be nonexistent or of a stereotyping nature, so be prepared with the most basic information about homosexuality and about AIDS.

4. Don't force material on them. Let them know it's available if they want it. Don't surprise them by sending information anonymously in the mail. Don't just leave a book or pamphlet in their house for them to find without letting them know you are going to leave it.

5. Don't bring up your boyfriend unless they ask. Just dealing with you initially will be difficult enough. But if they ask, tell them. Otherwise, wait for a later discussion. You have time.

When Circumstances Aren't Ideal

It isn't always possible to plan a quiet evening of carefully thought out discussion. If an unsuspecting parent arrives home from work early while you're making out with your boyfriend in the living room, the problem you face is damage control rather than careful planning. Also, suspicious parents aren't beyond searching a child's room, steaming letters open, or listening in on phone conversations. Whether or not it's their right to do so, it does happen. There's also the point-blank question: "Are you gay?"

Chris's mother wasn't quite so direct, but Chris understood her question. He and Michael, who have been together for eight years, were both living at home and attending the same local college. They were both 19, in love, and in the closet. Both come from conservative blue-collar families.

We were in the kitchen. Mom was sitting on the floor pinning up my pants— she was hemming them. We were just talking. I don't remember about what.

I can't recall now, but we got onto the subject of Michael. We had been spending a lot of time together since we had met at school a few months before.

Mom looked up at me and asked, "So what's going on between you and Michael?" My heart stopped. "Do you really want to know?" I asked. She said yes. If she hadn't said yes, I don't know if I would have ever told her. But she did and I told her. "I'm gay and Michael is my boyfriend." She started crying. I started crying. We both sat on the floor crying.

The next day Michael came home with me after school as he often did and we went up to my room. As soon as we got up to my room, my mother called from the kitchen and told us to come downstairs right away. Michael and I were no longer allowed to be alone together in my room.

The house rule had always been, "No girls in your room." Now that she knew we were gay, the same principle applied: no fooling around under her roof.

Once you've been found out or confronted, try to avoid lying. That is, of course, unless you live at home and have reason to believe that you will be thrown out of the house, or if you're financially dependent on your parents and suspect they will use that financial dependence as a weapon. Otherwise, you just have to dust yourself off and do the best you can, whether or not you're ready to talk about it.

Your parents will probably want to know why you were hiding your homosexuality from them (which is a question they may have even if they weren't the ones to bring up the subject). There are several valid reasons you can give them for not telling them before their discovery, including: "I didn't yet feel comfortable discussing the subject with you"; "I was afraid of your reaction"; "I didn't want to hurt you."

There is every reason to be angry with your parents if they've gone through your mail or your room. That's a separate issue of privacy. But save that for after you deal with the gay issue.

If the Worst Happens

The sad reality is that some parents reject their gay child outright or use sexual orientation as a staging area for constant warfare. If that happens to you, don't give up and don't react to their rejection with anger or hostility, which will get you nowhere.

The following is the story of one young man who came to a Parents and Friends of Lesbians and Gays meeting seeking advice on how to deal with his family, as told by one of the parents attending the meeting:

This young man was from the Bible Belt. He came to meetings and read letters that he received from his mother in which she told him that she would rather he be a murderer or rapist than be gay. She didn't want him to come home. And we kept encouraging him to just keep talking to her, to keep sending her letters and making phone calls, and to send her some brochures and books. Eventually she came to accept him and now invites him home. I wouldn't say she's openly happy about what he is, but being from where she is, she's come an awfully long way. She accepts and loves her son again.

The key is to keep the doors of communication open. Don't give up because your parents say horrible things, no matter how cruel. If it's at all possible and bearable, and it matters enough to you, keep trying. Which isn't to say your relationship with your parents will improve. It may not. But most often, some kind of accommodation is possible. If you're not certain what approach to take with your parents, seek the advice of your local chapter of Parents and Friends of Lesbians and Gays.

HOW PARENTS REACT TO A GAY CHILD

Whatever the reaction of your parents, you can count on one thing: No matter how open minded they are, no matter that half of their friends are gay, no matter that your brother is gay and your parents are actively involved in protecting gay civil rights, the odds are that they are going to be upset. There is just no getting around it. But anticipating how they will react can help. At least you won't be surprised and you can prepare to address their reactions, perhaps ease their pain; and you can prepare yourself emotionally. You can ask your partner for an extra ten minutes of hugs before heading out to have that long-put-off meeting with your parents, go for an extra-long run, or just take a couple of deep breaths.

What most parents experience when they learn that their child is gay is something akin to experiencing a death. This may sound extreme, but the child they thought they knew is gone (or seems to be gone), or their expectations, dreams, aspirations have died, or they grieve for the grandchildren they believe they will never have.

Some parents react to the news that a son is gay with immediate loving support, if not understanding. For other parents, while love for a child is never withdrawn, the loving support takes time to emerge, and for a long time they may find it impossible to discuss the subject.

Their Emotions

Parents can—are likely to—react to your news with a full range of emotions, including shock, tears, anger, denial, disappointment, guilt, embarrassment, love, or any combination.

SHOCK
Shock is a normal reaction and can last ten minutes, a week, or more. Most often it wears off in a few days.

TEARS
Even if you don't cry yourself, don't be surprised if one or both of your parents do.

DENIAL
A parent may not acknowledge what you've just said, or may downplay its significance by suggesting that it's just "a passing phase," or that it can be "fixed." It's simply a natural defense mechanism indicating that they've heard as much as they can handle for the moment.

ANGER/HOSTILITY
This could result from many feelings including a sense of betrayal, that you had lied to them, that you hadn't told them sooner, that you are something they consider unimaginable. In some cases the anger may even be a result of a parent's own deeply repressed homosexuality.

When Alex first broke the news to his mother, Karen, she went into a rage. Karen, a widow who teaches high school, remembers that she surprised her then 27-year-old son by the depth of her anger. "My first reaction was disbelief. I wanted him dead. And I told him so. As far as I was concerned he was dead. He was out of my life." In the years since then, Karen and her son have grown close once again.

DISAPPOINTMENT
All parents have hopes and aspirations for their children, whether or not they ever express those dreams to their children; and such ideas are more likely to include a wife and children (their grandchildren) than a homosexual son and his lover.

For Elaine, overcoming disappointment was her toughest hurdle.

The most difficult thing for me was abandoning this dream that I had of my family. I used to think about having these four sons who would some day come home with four wives. I used to have pictures of it in my mind. And that was very hard to give up. To realize that it wasn't going to be. I thought surely I would be surrounded by grandchildren by now. I was married when I was 18. I figured I had a head start. I loved being a parent and I really anticipated being a grandparent.

Two of Elaine's sons are gay, the other two are in relationships with women, are not married, and have no children.

GUILT

Most parents feel responsible for their children, whether their children are 5 years old or 50. Because their son is gay, they obviously did something wrong—like spanked him too often, didn't force him to play baseball, forced him to play baseball, let him play with his sister too often. Fathers may question whether they were good enough role models. Mothers may wonder if they were too overbearing.

Single parents are especially vulnerable to guilt, believing that a child's homosexuality is a result of the single-parent home, the trauma of a divorce, death of a parent, or lack of attention.

Even when parents are convinced that they're not responsible, the emotional, irrational guilt is likely to linger. Only time can erase it.

EMBARRASSMENT AND FEAR

When you step out of the closet, your parents suddenly take your place. They may feel as worried as you did when you started coming out. They may ask you not to tell anyone else in the family, or their friends, or the neighbors. They may feel isolated. They may feel they have no one to talk to, that their friends will judge them and think less of them as parents, that their colleagues will reject them, that they could lose their jobs.

In the three years since Alex first told her that he was gay, Karen has told several of her friends and a handful of colleagues, all of whom have been very supportive. But she is very fearful of what her other colleagues would think and she is afraid how her students would react if they knew.

> Hardly a day goes by when one of the other teachers doesn't come bouncing in to school talking about a new grandchild. "Don't worry, this will happen to you soon," they tell me. I used to run out to the bathroom and cry. Others say, "The worst thing that could happen would be if my child were a homosexual."
>
> I don't want their pity or rejection. I know I shouldn't feel this way. I should grow up, but that's how I feel.
>
> And I'm terrified of having my students find out. Almost every day they call each other "fag." Of course I feel compelled to scold them. If only they knew.

LOVE

Even if your parents are in shock, are disappointed, or angry, they may still respond by simply telling you that they still love you.

Fathers vs. Mothers

Parents are individuals. One may react differently from the other. While it's difficult to say that fathers are more likely to react one way and mothers another, it is not so difficult to look at how a father's expectations differ from those of a mother.

Richard Ashworth, a lawyer and president of the New York chapter of Parents and Friends of Lesbians and Gays, is the father of two gay sons and one straight son. He offers a concise explanation. Fundamentally, he doesn't believe fathers differ from mothers in how they react, but

> . . . fathers do have different expectations for their children. We train males to be macho. So being a "he-man" is a very important thing. Fathers may expect to live their lack of success in that area through their children. I think you may find more disappointment in a father at first. I don't think you find that as much in a mother. Mothers don't have those expectations.

If you're concerned that your father may react more negatively than your mother, you may choose to talk to your mother first. If you decide to tell one parent before the other, who you choose to talk to first depends upon the kind of relationship you have with each of your parents. In this case, as in many of the decisions you have to make when deciding if and how you will tell your parents, common sense and careful judgment play important roles.

COMING OUT TO YOUR SIBLINGS AND GRANDPARENTS

For the most part, the same principles already discussed apply to how to break the news to your siblings and grandparents, but there are differences.

For some men it's easier to talk with a sibling than with a parent, and siblings are more likely to be accepting. But for others, it may be more difficult, especially if you have a competitive relationship with a sibling, or if your sibling idealizes you, which is not at all unusual if your brother or sister is several years younger.

Grandparents can be more accepting and dispassionate than parents, because often their expectations for you are not as monumental as they were for their own children, and they won't feel guilt.

But from your family's perspective, while it may be okay to tell the world that you're gay, they may be irrational when it comes to grandparents. "Your grandparents are elderly, fragile." "You'll break their hearts." "They haven't long to live; why upset them?" "You can tell anyone you want, but for God's sake *don't* tell the grandparents!"

I haven't yet told my grandparents. I feel just a little foolish, particularly given this book, but I never really relished the thought of "breaking their hearts" and besides, I promised various family members not to tell "The Grandparents." Now I feel somewhat trapped by nearly a decade of half-truths and white lies and find myself wishing that I hadn't taken family advice. But there is no underestimating family pressure, particularly when family advice says not to do something you find easy to put off indefinitely.

If you decide to tell your grandparents, check with your parents first, but remember that the final decision is yours. This is something your parents may want to do themselves. Remember, your grandparents are their parents. They may ask you to wait until they themselves feel comfortable with your homosexuality before involving their own parents. On the flip side, if *you* don't want your grandparents to know yet, make that clear to your parents.

Bob, who raised four sons with his wife Elaine, waited until a couple of years after his son told him that he was gay to tell his own parents, both in their early 80s at the time, that he had a gay son. He characterizes his parents as truly accepting, "but they didn't quite understand."

> I went to visit them at home. I told them I had something I wanted to talk to them about. My mother asked, "Is there anything wrong?" "No," I said, "just sit down. I want to have a conversation. You know all those Sundays when you wanted to come visit or you wanted Elaine and me to come here and I said I had business appointments? We never had business appointments. Elaine and I are members of an organization and we have meetings to go to. The name of the organization is Parents of Gays." I stopped at that point. There was no reaction. So I asked, "Do you know what gay is, Mom?" And my mother looked at me. "Sure, that's when a guy likes a guy." And I added, "Yeah, and when a girl likes a girl." "Oh," she said, "the girls do it too?"
>
> So I proceded to explain homosexuality. They said, "That's fine." And I said, "The reason we go to the meetings is that one of our sons is gay." My mother said, "Oh, we've known that for a long time." I looked at them and my mouth fell open in awe. So I asked her which of my sons they thought was gay. And they said Danny. I said, "You happen to be right, but what made you think Danny was gay?" "Well," my mother said, "when he talks his voice squeaks and he uses his hands a lot when he talks." I said, "Mom, that has nothing to do with being gay." I explained a bit more and at some point they commented, "They're entitled to everything in life just like everyone else."

INTRODUCING YOUR PARTNER OR "SPECIAL FRIEND"

If parents know relatively little about homosexuality, they're likely to know even less about homosexual relationships. Given what they have read—or have not read—in the press, or have seen on television, they may not know that long-term relationships between two men are even a possibility.

You have to assume then, that they know nothing and will respond accordingly. If you expect your family to respond to you and your partner in the same way they would have treated you and the wife they probably still wish you would marry, you will be disappointed. For Marshall and Craig, acknowledgement of their relationship came from Marshall's parents in the form of a check to be used toward a down payment on their new house.

Marshall: The check from my parents was as close as they will ever get to saying, "It's okay." Sixties rhetoric wouldn't have accepted that as sufficient. But I'm happy with that. Why do I need them to say, "Yes, it's wonderful that you're gay and have a lover."

Craig: Both families have given us money for the house. Once you get into a situation of buying a house, boy, you're really in tight with your parents because they know what you're going through.

What you can expect at first is that your parents and family may not quite know how to handle your relationship. Ordinarily, when a son falls in love, expectations tend toward a wedding, a daughter-in-law, a baby, and a station wagon. When there are two men, they don't know what to expect or how to react. How do they live? Does each play a specific role (Who's the wife. . . .)? Is my son's partner just one in a series? Do I treat his partner like a son-in-law? This lack of understanding, for which you should avoid blaming your parents, can easily lead to misunderstandings. You may perceive their actions to be inconsiderate or unloving, while they may not realize they've done anything wrong.

For example, when your parents first learn of your relationship, they are not likely to include your partner in invitations to family events or gatherings. This may have nothing to do with how much they love you or even how much they care for your partner. Depending on the circumstances and your family, their failure to invite your lover may be an oversight—they didn't realize that they should include him—or it may be a conscious decision made because they can't yet handle having the rest of the family and/or friends know that their son is gay. Either way, it's best to clear up a possible misunderstanding by gently asking them why they haven't included your partner. If it's an unintentional oversight, you can explain to your parents why it's important to you that they include your partner—that he is to be thought of as a son-in-law and not a roommate, for example. If the exclusion is intentional and a result of their difficulty dealing with your sexuality and/or relationship, it may be best to live with their decision until they have a chance to grow accustomed to your being gay and to your partner. That can be several months, a year, or longer. How long you wait is up to you. But there will likely come a time when you are no longer willing to overlook the exclusion of your lover from family invitations.

Even twenty-four years into his relationship with Greg, Neal found he had to explain to one of his cousins the facts of his life with Greg. For most of the years they've been a couple, family invitations have almost always been addressed to both Neal and Greg. Then, two years ago, Neal's cousin was getting married and sent Neal an invitation that didn't include Greg. If you're faced with such an invitation, you have three basic choices. You can accept the invitation and go alone. You can decline the invitation with the hope that your parents or relatives will get the message. Or you can contact whoever extended the invitation and set the record straight—that you are a couple and all invitations are to be addressed to the two of you. For Neal, the time had long since passed for patience or gentle words, which had been his approach on a couple of occasions over the years.

> My family has known about our relationship for eighteen years. My reaction was that I go nowhere without Greg. This particular time I wrote a letter and put it very bluntly: "Greg and I come as a package deal. You certainly would not do this if Bret were a wife" . . . so forth and so on.

Because each circumstance and family is different, there is no way to generalize about how to handle an invitation that excludes your lover, or how to respond to a remark that reveals your family doesn't understand your relationship, except to say that you will probably have to play the role of educator, that you should do your best to be gentle with your family, and expect that the process of learning may take many, many years.

Of the many couples with whom I spoke, the approach that Michael and Chris took with their families seems to represent the most middle-of-the-road and pragmatic approach. They've given their families a lot of time to adjust, they don't confront their parents about the fact they're a male couple, and they have what they consider realistic expectations based on who their parents are. According to Chris,

> We both come from very conservative families. We can't expect them to take us in as a married couple. Everyone knows the intensity of our relationship. We try to make them more comfortable by not being physical in front of them. It's tough enough on them that they have to accept the fact that neither of us will marry a woman.

Using this gentle approach, Michael and Chris have, over the eight years they've been a couple, become more and more a part of each other's family, so much so that invitations to family events are now always extended to both. Some say "bring your friend," others, "your partner," and others invite Michael or Chris by name. When they join their families for vacations, it's expected they will share a room together. To most of their siblings' children, they are Uncle Michael and Uncle Chris.

Taking a patient, understanding, and perhaps charitable approach to integrating your partner and your relationship into your family life may tax your patience to the limit. But that's the short-term price for better long-term family relations.

One thing not to forget, but one that I do not cover here in detail, is that whether or not your partner gets along with your parents may be more of an in-law issue than a gay issue. Do your parents and partner get along? Do they like his personality? Do they approve of him? Does he like their personalities? How they feel about him may have nothing to do with your and his sexuality.

For Ken, 32, who lives in Florida with his lover of a year, homosexuality had nothing to do with how his parents felt about Louis. Ken's parents are less than enthusiastic about the fact their son is gay, but they've accepted him and were friendly with Ken's previous partner of six years.

My parents reacted very negatively to Louis because they had certain expectations of me and who I should be involved with and he didn't live up to those expectations. It has nothing to do with being gay and has everything to do with national origin. Louis is from Puerto Rico. Their reaction is based on prejudice and ignorance because they never even gave themselves the opportunity to get to know him. My last lover was also Hispanic, but he came from a diplomatic family. So they felt he had the right social standing, even if he wasn't what they would have preferred.

I just thought they would be taken aback slightly. I never suspected that it would lead to a break. I don't speak to my family members at all and they don't call me. I think it's the first time my parents have reacted this intensely toward any of their children in regard to whatever we've done with our lives. My eldest brother had been addicted to heroin and they had a difficult time accepting that but my father put him through detoxification and they pulled him under their wings and protected him. But that was different. They helped him as long as he did the things they wanted. I didn't do what they wanted. In fact, they thought my decision to live with Louis was radical.

Introducing Your Partner Before Your Parents Know That You're Gay

Before you let your parents know that you're gay, you can introduce them to your lover. In fact, it's probably a good idea. As far as your parents know, he's your roommate. By introducing him, they will have a chance to meet him and, with any luck, grow to like him independently of the homosexuality issue. This may make it easier for them when you let them know at a later date that you're gay. At that time you can then explain that the familiar friend they've grown to like is in fact the man with whom you share your life.

The secret is to stick to the truth as much as possible, so that when the time comes to tell the whole truth, it's more a matter of what you didn't say than trying to explain half-truths. In other words, if you live together, avoid lying about it—unless you're afraid that will tip them off to your homosexuality before you want to discuss it. Or if you take vacations with your lover, avoid substituting another friend or adding a couple of women to the story. Also, avoid dropping hints about the nature of your relationship with your partner, unless you want them to figure it out; dropping hints can be cruel and confusing for parents.

The major drawback to this approach is that once they learn exactly who he is, they may feel an added sense of betrayal. But that may be outweighed by the fact they have already grown to care for him.

This is the approach Michael chose to use with Chris. He never actually told his parents that Chris was his lover or that he was gay.

> From my parents' perspective, Chris started out as my buddy. Over time, they realized that Chris was more than just a buddy and by that time they liked him, so they had to accept him.

Your other choice is to hide the existence of your lover entirely. If your parents live far away and rarely visit, that may not be very difficult logistically, especially if you and your lover maintain separate phones. But there's an emotional price to pay in your relationship with your parents and possibly with your lover as well. You will be excluding your parents from a major part of your life and excluding your lover from your extended family life.

Introducing Your Partner After Your Parents Know That You're Gay

While there is no one way to introduce your partner to your parents for the first time, and no one way to make him a part of your family, the "Dos and Don'ts" guidelines in this section can help make the introduction of your partner less uncomfortable for your parents, for him, and for you. This section is specifically for those of you who haven't brought a partner home before and/or for those of you whose families are still unused to dealing with a homosexual son and his partner.

Before you decide how you will introduce your partner to your parents, it helps to anticipate how they will react. It's always best not to be surprised and to be carefully prepared with answers to their questions. Your partner can mean several different things to your parents (besides the fact he is your chosen partner), depending upon their perspective and how comfortable and knowledgeable they are about homosexuality. If they had been hoping beyond hope that your being gay would go away, the introduction of your partner will most likely represent confirmation of their worst fears—that it won't. They may view your partner as a corruptor. They could blame your homosexuality on him, especially if he is older than you. If you are the older partner, they may accuse you of being the corruptor. On the flip side, they may be relieved that you have only one man in your life, especially given the popular image of gay men and your parents' likely, and reasonable, concern about AIDS.

With this perspective in mind, the following is a list of general "Dos and Don'ts" for you to consider when introducing your partner to your parents and bringing him into your family's life.

Do:

1. For the first introduction, meet on neutral ground: a restaurant, a park, your parents' house. Do not, repeat, *do not* arrange the first get together in your one-bedroom (one-bed) apartment. Parents have difficulty with that one bed. After the first or second visit on neutral ground, you can then consider whether you want to have them over to the home you share with your partner.

For Bob and Elaine, on their first visit to the one-bedroom apartment their son shared with his lover at college, seeing that single bed was awfully difficult.

Bob: What made us uncomfortable was the bedroom. When we saw the one big bed in there I immediately had a terrible sensation. Elaine felt the same way. I suddenly visualized, as a lot of parents do, what goes on in that bed. We had to get out.
Elaine: We had to cut the visit short. I remember asking Bob, "Why did we come?" We weren't ready for that yet.
Bob: I subsequently recognized that a lot of parents do this. I think it's something that all parents have to come to terms with, to recognize that what their children do in the bedroom is their business. We realized we don't do this with our son and his girlfriend.

At some point your parents will have to make it over the "one bed" hurdle. But there's plenty of time to show them your bedroom.

2. Invite a close friend (or friends) to join you for the first dinner or lunch with your parents and partner, if you feel you and/or your parents

would be more comfortable. Just check with your parents in advance and choose friends they know well and respect. Or you can invite supportive siblings to join you. This may be more comfortable for your parents, who may be feeling tense about a one-on-one with your partner.

3. Assume the parental role and assume they know nothing about gay relationships. You will likely have to teach or guide your parents as to how to respond to your relationship. If they act in a way that you find unacceptable, let them know.

For example, if you and your partner go to a movie with your parents and they offer to pay for your ticket, but don't offer to pay for your partner's ticket, let them know that that's unacceptable. Don't confront them at the ticket window at the movie theater. Save that conversation for a private phone call, or when you're with your parents alone. The easiest comparison to use when trying to explain why they should make the offer to both of you is to point out that, if you were married to a woman, they would never consider paying for your ticket with the expectation that your spouse would pay for her own.

4. Go slow, be patient, and don't cram your relationship down their throats. Accepting your partner and your relationship will probably take time. Acceptance isn't automatic. The longer your partner is part of your life, the more accustomed to that relationship your parents and family will become.

It's sometimes difficult to tell just how accepting your family has become until you're faced with a situation that you think will test their limits. Seven years after Chris and Michael first moved in together, it looked as if Michael's family Christmas schedule would allow him to attend Chris's family's Christmas Eve gathering, a "family only" event. Chris was very reluctant to ask his mother if it was okay to bring Michael, especially given some of the things she had said in the past about hiding Chris's relationship with Michael from the extended family. "I was worried about approaching my mother," said Chris. "I thought the first thing she was going to say was, 'What's your grandmother going to think?' But she said, 'Fine, just tell your uncle to set an extra place.' I was surprised. Seven years ago she would have forbidden it."

5. Have something to focus on when you and your partner visit with your parents other than the fact they're visiting with your partner.

Helping with the yardwork, or with a special project, or preparing a meal can help break the ice and make everyone more comfortable.

6. Invite your parents to go out with you. And when you think your parents can handle it, invite them to your home. You may expect your parents to extend invitations, but you may not think to extend an invitation to them. Seeing you together and/or in a home setting will give them a chance to get to know your partner and to see your relationship work. By having them and other family members visit your home, they can see how much you have in common with them.

7. Do what couples do. When you think your parents can handle it, send birthday or holiday cards and include both of your names. Include news of your partner in conversations with your parents, even when they don't ask. Send regards to your parents from your partner when you're finishing up a phone call or have your partner get on the phone to say hello.

Don't:

1. If your parents have never met your partner before, don't just drop in with your partner one afternoon unannounced. Give your parents warning. First let them know that you have a partner and then arrange a meeting. If they say they're not ready to meet your partner, respect that. It may hurt in the short run, but there is time.

2. Don't introduce your partner as your "lover." If you've got a chip on your shoulder and feel your parents ought to be able to handle the word, give it up. You'll only be making trouble for yourself. To parents, "lover" equals sex. It doesn't bring to mind two people sharing their lives, commitment, or loving companionship. It brings to mind sex. And in the case of you and your lover, it brings to mind two men having sex. Your parents will have to deal with those images at some point, but certainly when you first let them know you have someone special in your life and for some time after that, you don't have to give them a verbal cue, such as the word "lover." Try "friend." "Friend" is an easily digestible euphemism. Or, as several of the parents I interviewed suggested, you might try "special friend."

The bottom line is to make this as easy for your parents as possible. If using a euphemism makes it easier for them (or for you), use it.

3. Don't be physical with your partner when you're with your parents, particularly in public. Remember, you're concerned with what is best for the long term and what makes your parents most comfortable.

On those occasions when you're with your partner's parents, I offer one point of advice:

1. Be a great son-in-law. Be careful, because there is a very fine line between being a great son-in-law and overdoing it. So use common sense. Even if you're not terribly fond of your partner's parents, you can be thoughtful. If your in-laws are in the kitchen preparing dinner, get up your courage, go in, and offer your help. Ask them about themselves. If you're nervous at first, that's only natural. They're probably nervous too.

Staying with the Parents

Staying over at your parents' home with your partner for the first time can be awkward. Again it raises questions and dilemmas for your parents. What do they do with you? You're a couple, but you're not married. Should they put you in separate rooms? But you're a couple and you'll never be married (legally anyway), so why put you in separate rooms? For you it raises the question of what, if anything, to do if your parents put you in separate rooms. I suggest you stay in separate rooms. There is nothing to be gained from pushing the issue.

If, by the third or fourth visit, they're still putting you in separate rooms, and you find the arrangement intolerable (which would be reasonable), it's time to raise the issue. If you can't reach an agreement with your parents, motels are a better alternative than ultimatums.

Siblings and Grandparents

The same principles outlined in this section for parents apply to grandparents and siblings when your goal is to gently integrate your partner into family life.

One exception: when it comes time to deal with your siblings' kids, at least when they're old enough to ask questions, first discuss with your siblings how you will handle the questions your nieces and nephews ask. If nothing else, it's a courtesy. And if they have strong opinions, it gives you a chance to discuss their opinions and yours before involving the nieces and nephews.

RESOURCES

Organizations

The Federation of Parents and Friends of Lesbians and Gays

This organization has chapters in eighty cities across North America and Europe. These self-help groups are composed of people who have accepted their children's and friends' homosexuality, and are trying to help other people do the same. The organization is a resource both for parents and friends of lesbians, gay men and for gay children who have questions about how to handle their parents.

Parents have the opportunity to meet and share experiences with other parents who have been through the same shock of learning that a child is gay. They also have the opportunity to meet gays and lesbians other than their own children.

For gay children with specific questions about their own circumstances, speaking with other parents who are supportive and understanding can be both helpful and comforting.

To find the chapter closest to where you live, check your local phone book, the *Gayellow Pages,* call a local gay help line, or call or write one of the following regional chapters of Parents and Friends of Lesbians and Gays:

PO Box 24565, Los Angeles, CA 90024, 213–472–8952

PO Box 553, Lenox Hill Station, NY 10021, 914–793–5198

PO Box 20308, Denver, CO 80220, 303–333–0286

PO Box 3533, Silver Spring, MD 20901, 301–439–FLAG

Books and Pamphlets

"Coming Out to Your Parents." Published by the Philadelphia Parents and Friends of Lesbians and Gays.

A free copy of this pamphlet is available from the Philadelphia chapter if you send a self-addressed stamped, standard business (No. 10) envelope to: Philadelphia Parents FLAG, PO Box 15711, Philadelphia, PA 19103, 215–572–1833

For information about pamphlets available from other chapters of Parents and Friends of Lesbians and Gays, contact your local chapter of Parents and Friends of Lesbians and Gays.

Are You Still My Mother—Are You Still My Family, by Gloria Guss Back, 1985. Warner Books, 666 Fifth Avenue, New York, NY 10103

Written by a parent, this book takes parents through the phases of shock, anger, and guilt. It also includes sections about how to treat a child's lover, what leading therapists have to say, and how the clergy views homosexuality.

Coming Out to Parents—A Two-Way Survival Guide for Lesbian and Gay Men and Their Parents, by Mary V. Borhek, 1983. The Pilgrim Press, 132 West 31st Street, New York, NY 10001

This book explores both sides of coming out, from the misgivings gay children have about telling their parents to what parents feel when they learn that their child is gay.

My Son Eric—A Mother Struggles to Accept Her Gay Son and Discovers Herself,
by Mary V. Borhek, 1979. The Pilgrim Press, 132 West 31st Street, New York,
NY 10001

> In a narrative format, Mary Borhek traces her experience, from first hear-
> ing the news that her son was gay to meeting her son's friend to dealing
> with the religious conflicts about homosexuality.

Now That You Know, by B. Fairchild and N. Hayward, 1979. Harcourt Brace
Jovanovich, 545 Fifth Avenue, New York, NY 10017

> Using anecdotes and balanced common sense, the authors take parents by
> the hand through the basics. The book discusses "What is Gay," and in-
> cludes sections on couples, religion and homosexuality, and Parents of
> Gays.

*Beyond Acceptance: Parents of Lesbians and Gays Talk About Their Experi-
ences,* by Carolyn Welch Griffin, Marian J. Wirth, and Arthur G. Wirth, 1986.
Prentice-Hall, Route 9W, Englewood Cliffs, NJ 07632

> *Beyond Acceptance* covers every issue concerning a homosexual child,
> from first finding out to thoughts on how to deal with the rest of the family.
> Anecdotes are used throughout.

Consenting Adult, by Laura Z. Hobson, 1975. Warner Books, 666 Fifth Avenue,
New York, NY 10103

> *Consenting Adult* is a novel about a mother, a son, and their struggles with
> homosexuality and each other.

Parents Matter, by Ann Muller, 1987. The Naiad Press, Inc., P.O. Box 10543,
Tallahassee, FL 32302

> Using anecdotes from interviews with more than 100 sons, daughters, and
> parents, Ann Muller discusses issues of critical importance to gay children
> in dealing with their parents.

CHAPTER 6

Parenting

*"I love children, but I used to love them more
when I was younger."*

Many gay men like children; like being around children; like the thought of having children of their own. Some, of course, already have children, whether from a previous marriage or heterosexual relationship, through adoption, or by arrangement with a woman—possibly a single friend who also wanted a child. This chapter explores those options as well as the decision-making process that all couples go through when it comes to the subject of children.

DECIDING

Assuming you and your partner aren't already caring for a child (or children), fantasizing about fatherhood and raising a family with your partner can be a lot of fun. But actually deciding to do something about it means having to go well beyond the fantasy to consider all the complexities of finding or producing a child and then raising that child. Ending your speculation about parenthood at the fantasy stage means coming to terms with the likelihood that you and your partner will never be full-time parents. That does not, however, mean you can never act on your parenting instincts (more on this topic is included in the "Alternatives to Having Your Own Children" section later in this chapter).

Scott and I talked about the possibility of children early on. We haven't pursued the idea beyond the fantasy stage for different reasons. He's great with kids. But he's a firm believer that children should have both an active, present mother and an active, present father. He realizes that that's a difficult ideal, even for most straight couples, but he feels that it's the ideal parents should strive for. I don't feel as strongly about the necessity for a child to have both a mother and a father; but then I don't have a strong desire to be a parent—at least not a desire that is strong enough for me to consider trying to find a way to have a child. Even if I ardently desired a child, because Scott doesn't want one and I want to stay in a relationship with Scott, the decision would have to be against our parenthood.

If having a child is something you and your partner are seriously considering, there are at least seven important questions to ask yourselves:

1. Do you *both* want a child (children)?

2. Are you fully aware of the financial, emotional, and time commitments required to rear a child? Or is your desire for children romanticized? And, are you willing to make that investment for the next twenty-two or more years?

3. Are you prepared for the social dislocation of being a gay couple with children? In other words, as a gay couple with children, you may be perceived as somewhat out of place by people in both the straight and gay worlds.

4. What about the child? Are you prepared to deal with the potential impact of two gay parents on your child?

5. Which of you will be the "real" (biological or adoptive) father? Only one of you can have legal custody. This can cause giant problems if you separate or if the legal parent dies.

6. Will your natural families—parents, grandparents, siblings and their spouses—support your decision, or will your child be deprived of the experience of an extended family? In the absence of support from your natural families, will you have a network of friends and neighbors to replace them?

7. If you decide to father a child with a woman, whether or not you raise the child together, can you realistically assess the potential for custody conflicts with the mother?

Michael and Chris, the conservative young couple who met eight years ago, when they were college students, started talking about having children when they first met. Today they are as undecided as they were then.

Michael: Having children is part of married life. But as time goes on . . .
Chris: You kind of like your freedom.
Michael: I have a more mature attitude toward children now. Up until last
   week I was saying the only reason to have children would be if it were the
   best thing for the child. For example, providing a home for a child who
   people are reluctant to adopt.

   Then my friend Randy said to me—her sister works in a placement agency
   for special kids—that that's the worst reason to adopt a child. She said we
   would always have this feeling that the child owes us something. She said we
   should also consider the selfish reasons—because we want a child to enrich
   our lives, for example. It has to be a mutual thing. You do something for them;
   they do something for you.

   We've always said it was something we would do way down the line. We
   would both have to be very financially secure. Now I'm worried that too long
   down the road you get too settled in your ways and then I don't know if
   children fit.

   I love children, but I used to love them more when I was younger.
Chris: The balance still tips toward wanting children. But I've gotten used to
   not living my life around that constant responsibility. You get busy.

   I'm still convinced that adoption of a special child will be the best way to
   go. So many children need a home and loving parents. There's no reason for
   artificial insemination. That's just ego. If we have a home to provide, we
   should offer it.

Ned, 25, and Peter, 35, the couple in Hawaii, have thought about
having children, but have pretty much ruled out children of their own.
Over the past few years they've taken care of a friend's baby at least
once a week. This has given them a close-up look at what's involved in
caring for young children.

Ned: That's kind of slowed me down about having one of my own. I love the
   kid, and if we end up moving it will be a real problem for me to get over not
   spending time with him, but a baby is such a big commitment and I like to
   travel and go when I want to go.
Peter: Taking care of the baby I discovered that I like kids, but that I'm not
   really comfortable at their level.
Ned: It's not a big worry now. Not like it was when I was in my early twenties
   and deciding that yeah, I'm definitely gay and I'm going to stay that way. Not
   having kids bothered me a lot then.

Like Peter and Ned, most gay men choose not to bring children into
their relationships permanently. The childless couples I interviewed
were very clear about their reasons for not having children. For example: "We don't want the responsibility"; "It's not fair to a child to
intentionally bring it into a family of two gay men"; "It's too complica-

ted to actually have a child"; "My lover doesn't want them"; "We don't feel our relationship is stable enough to handle it."

Donald and Andrew are in agreement about not having children. But for Andrew, the realization that he will probably never have children saddens him.

Andrew: Emotionally it's very difficult for me. I'm a child psychologist by training. At one time I had my own patients—primarily trauma care and amputees. All through college I taught retarded children. It's always been told to me that I have an extraordinary ability to communicate with children. I love children. When I first met Donald I was helping raise a newborn.

But Donald's not child-oriented at all. He likes kids as a lot of adults do, "Well, that kid's really cute. As long as they stay cute, fine." So in our relationship I don't think kids would work.

Donald: When I first came out, the biggest thing for me to get over was that I was not going to be a father. Then I got over it. And now I'm really over it. I've discovered I have no real desire to be a father. I see what it takes.

When pressed, Andrew acknowledges that Donald is not entirely responsible for their decision not to pursue offspring: "I'm also selfish."

Chet and John don't plan ever to have children, for philosophical reasons:

Chet: People were put on this earth to do certain things. A man and a woman were put on this earth to create other beings. That's how it should be.

John: With my nephew, I'm listed as his guardian. If we were forced into it, we would do it. But I would never voluntarily bring a child into this situation— two gay parents. I don't think it's fair to a child.

Chet: It's not the way it was meant to be. Why throw a child into a relationship between two people of the same sex? As far as being right, I think a child should have the option of being raised by a father and a mother.

John: Besides which, I don't think we would want that kind of commitment. We don't even want a dog. Maybe we're selfish.

ALTERNATIVES TO HAVING YOUR OWN CHILDREN

The fact that most gay men neither have, nor expect to have their own children doesn't mean that gay men don't want children to be a part of their lives. Gay men, as couples or individuals, may experience very human, and frequently deeply felt, paternal affection for children in a number of ways: getting involved with children professionally or as a volunteer, being involved in the lives of the children of siblings and friends, foster parenting, or "adopting" a young adult.

Professional or Volunteer Work

There is a range of possibilities from volunteering as a Big Brother to working with children in day care, but there can be a couple of major hitches—the perceptions some people have of gay men who want to spend time with children, and some Big Brother organizations, for example, aren't enthusiastic about having gay volunteers. Catholic Big Brothers will accept applications from gay men but according to an official at Catholic Big Brothers in New York City, "We don't encourage gay men to apply."

How people might react if they found out that he's gay has kept Andrew from doing volunteer work since he stopped working with children professionally. A decade ago he volunteered to be a Big Brother, but he's reluctant to do that work again, especially in the small town where he and Donald plan to move. He fears they will misinterpret his interest in children. He's not eager to put himself in danger by getting into that kind of circumstance.

Children of Friends and Family

Marshall and Craig, who live in a neighborhood where gay couples are not a rare sight, don't do formal volunteer work, but instead spend a lot of time with neighbors' children. They've become a local "drop-off center" for neighborhood kids.

Craig: Marshall baby-sits all the time. And the neighbors are very trusting.
Marshall: I grew up in a large family. I miss having kids. Now every Christmas I have a children's Christmas party. In this neighborhood you have a lot of parents who are so busy being parents they don't have time to meet other people. It's my excuse to get the parents together to get the kids together.

Informal Adoption

Greg and Neal, both in their fifties, have been together for twenty-six years, and while they aren't terribly interested in small children, they've been involved in the lives of two young gay men. They helped one of Neal's former students through college with both financial and emotional support. At the moment they have a 27-year-old gay man with AIDS living in their home. "We do fall into a parental thing with Joey. But it's not a burden. We have the greatest luxury of all because we can give when we want to."

Godfather and Legal Guardian

You can't decide to become the godfather or legal guardian of a child, but you can accept that responsibility if it's offered. In the case of being named legal guardian for a child in the event something happens to that child's parents, talk it over with your lover first before saying yes. Should you be called upon to care for that child, your lover will be affected as well.

Recently a dear friend called and said she was thinking about listing me as the legal guardian of her child should something happen to her and her husband. She wanted to know if it was okay if she decided to list me. "Uncle" Eric was a little surprised, but looking through some pictures that were taken of me holding the baby when he was just a few weeks old, my inclination was to say yes. Scott and I talked it over. He was strongly opposed for two reasons. He doesn't want the responsibility and expects we would face a family fight should, God forbid, anything happen to my friend and her husband. My friend and I have yet to complete our conversation on the subject.

Foster Parenting

Another alternative to not having your own children is foster parenting—taking care of children who, for the short term, lack a permanent home. However appealing this may seem, be aware that children who are removed from their homes often bring with them serious emotional difficulties.

In some parts of the country, social service agencies may make an effort to place a gay teenager in gay foster homes. But in other parts of the country, being gay may prevent you from being foster parents altogether. According to Joy Schulenburg, in *Gay Parenting:* "The criteria for being licensed as a foster home vary from jurisdiction to jurisdiction. Sexual orientation may be a prohibiting factor or it may be considered totally irrelevant. Some states may not accept you if they know that you are gay, but they will never ask you directly and it becomes an issue only if you or someone else informs them."

HAVING CHILDREN

By far, most gay fathers became such in previous marriages or heterosexual relationships. (See the next section, "Bringing Children from a Previous Relationship.") However, there are men who have adopted children, those who have fathered and raised a child jointly with a woman friend, and men who have arranged for a woman to have their child and then raised the child on their own or with their lover. There are many possible arrangements, but any of these methods of having a child is enormously complicated. This subject demands far more attention than the few paragraphs that follow. If you are serious about having a child of your own, you should read Hayden Curry and Denis Clifford's *A Legal Guide for Lesbian and Gay Couples*, (found in the "Resources" section of Chapter 9), and Joy Schulenburg's *Gay Parenting*, listed in the "Resources" section at the end of this chapter.

Finding Role Models

Despite the rarity among male couples of adoption, co-parenting (having a child with a woman and raising it together), or the use of a surrogate mother (a woman who will bear your child, so that you can then raise it on your own or with your lover), there are men out there who have done it. You don't have to pursue these methods of having a child as if you're the absolute first male couple to do it. The best way to learn about the trials and tribulations of having a child by one of these methods is to talk to another couple who has done it. Obviously it will be easier to find such couples in New York City or San Francisco than in Little Rock, Arkansas.

It may not be easy to find men or male couples who have chosen to have children, but you can start your search by asking friends if they know of any. You can also call a local gay fathers organization (see "Resources"). Be sure to specify that you're interested in talking to fathers whose children are not from a previous heterosexual relationship. Even if you don't find what you're looking for, you will at least be able to explore the issue of male couples raising children with couples who are raising children from a prior marriage or relationship.

Adoption

"The idea of adoption is more common than the actuality," says Joy Schulenburg, author of *Gay Parenting*. "Among openly gay couples it's extremely difficult. I know a number of openly gay couples who have applied and been rejected. Among more closeted men, adoption is more common, but they have to be very discreet about their homosexuality." But, while it's more common among couples who choose to hide their homosexuality and their relationship, adoption for male couples is still rare. Schulenburg estimates that between 500 and 1,000 male couples in the United States have successfully adopted a child and, of that number, 90 percent are "very closeted."

If you decide to pursue adoption, you need expert legal advice from a lawyer who knows what the adoption agencies and courts in your area are like. The Lesbian Rights Project, listed in the "Resources" section of this chapter, and the legal organizations listed in the "Resources" section of Chapter 9 can help you get started in your search for expert legal help. Besides providing legal advice, an experienced lawyer will be able to advise you as to what, if any, changes you are likely to have to make in your lives (such as hiding your relationship and homosexuality) to get through the public or private adoption process.

Bear in mind that, as a gay couple, you may face additional problems even if you successfully adopt. First, just as in any custody case, your custody of the adopted child can be challenged at any time. If you and your lover keep your homosexuality a secret during the adoption process, that can mean having to spend much of your life being very closeted and living in fear of being discovered. Discovery could result in the removal of the adopted child from your custody. And, because only one of you can legally adopt the child, if you split up with your lover you could find yourself in untested legal waters, in the middle of a precedent-setting custody battle.

When Richard, a 35-year-old office manager from upstate New York, decided he wanted to adopt a child, he had no interest in setting precedents other than being one of the first, if not the first, openly gay men to adopt a child in the New York area. Richard began researching the subject of adoption by reading every article he could get his hands on. "I was inspired to pursue adoption after reading an article about a change in New York State adoption guidelines that stated that adoption agencies could no longer discriminate against someone who was gay." Through the local gay helpline, Richard contacted a social worker who had experience with adoptions. She recommended an organization that helped prospective adoptive parents get through the complex adoption system.

Richard's lover of twelve years, Ed, then 44, didn't object to Richard's pursuit of the adoption. "He said it was okay, so I plunged ahead." Ed later admitted that the only reason he said it was okay was because he figured no agency would allow a gay man to adopt.

After going to two different agencies and telling everyone he knew that he was interested in adopting, Richard found an agency that stated specifically in its literature that it did not discriminate against gay people. After going through a home study and interviews, during which Richard did not hide the fact he was gay and involved with another man, a 6-year-old boy became available for adoption. Several months of short visits were followed by six months when the boy, Billy, lived with Richard and Ed, after which the adoption was formalized.

Billy, Richard, and Ed did not live happily ever after. During the year that Billy came to live with Ed and Richard, Richard's relationship with Ed, which had been seriously troubled for many years, fell apart and they eventually separated. Ed is now suing Richard, the legal adoptive father, for custody. The battle is as ugly as any custody case can get, with Ed filing charges that Richard sexually abused Billy. The case is pending in court.

The Law

Because of the lack of case law involving a custody battle between two men over an adoptive child, the outcome of Richard and Ed's dispute is uncertain. Richard's experience points to the biggest drawback concerning adoption, or any of the other possible choices open to two men who want children. Only one of you—you or your partner—can be the legal father, and you are not generally recognized in the eyes of the law as a couple. Two single men cannot adopt, or be the legal biological father, of the same child. This can get particularly complicated if, as in the case of Richard and Ed, your relationship ends, or the legal father dies.

All of these methods of having children should include detailed contracts between you and your lover concerning financial arrangements and contingencies in the event of a breakup of the relationship or death of the legal parent. In addition, if there are surrogate or co-parents involved, you need contracts with them as well. A note of caution concerning these contracts: Because the law is still relatively undefined for most of these arrangements, private contracts may not be recognized in a court of law.

There is a simple lesson to be learned from the experience of Richard and Ed. If your relationship is not on solid ground, do not add a child to the equation. Besides the negative impact of an unstable relationship or custody battle on the child, you'll just be asking for more relationship trouble, and in the case of adoption, you may hurt the chances of other gay couples who follow to successfully adopt.

For more information on the concerns of couples, single gay men, or married gay men with children, who are about to enter a custody battle, consult the "Resources" at the end of this chapter.

BRINGING CHILDREN FROM A PREVIOUS RELATIONSHIP

By far, most male couples who have children, bring them from a prior marriage or heterosexual relationship of one or both partners, and the issues arising from such situations are enormously complicated and involved. After reading this section, I recommend consulting additional sources of information—the "Resources" section of this chapter will get you started—before making any decisions concerning your children, your lover, and what to tell your children.

This section touches on two of the major issues that concern couples who have children living with them on a regular (custodial) basis and those who have children living with them on weekends, holidays, and/ or summer vacations (noncustodial): how to tell the children about their father's homosexuality; and whether and to what extent to integrate their lover into the children's lives.

Along the way I've heard many horror stories about vindictive wives, rejecting children, and custody battles more outrageous than the most exaggerated television melodrama. On the other hand, I've interviewed couples who have lived quietly and quite happily with their children for years. One older male couple said they can hardly keep track of all the grandchildren that race through their house on weekends and holidays.

The two couples, Larry and Thomas, and Lloyd and Eliot, whom I use as examples to demonstrate the points made in this section, are not extremes, and their experiences are mixed. Their stories simply illustrate how two different couples have dealt with unfamiliar and often frightening circumstances.

Coming Out to Your Children

Because each circumstance, each couple, and each child is different, how and what you tell your child about your relationship will depend on many things including, of course, the age of the child. However, there are several general recommendations that apply to most circumstances. The following list is drawn from Joy Schulenburg's *Gay Parenting:*

1. Come to terms with your own gayness first. Parents who consistently demonstrated shame or confusion about their sexual identity consistently reported problems with negative reactions from their children.

2. Don't wait until your children know or suspect that you are gay to discuss it with them. Tell them as soon as you think they are old enough to understand, preferably before age 12, when peer pressure and attitudes can overshadow parental input.

3. Don't "confess"; inform. In other words, don't make a big deal out of it by overwhelming them with a revelation. Setting up a big confession scene only creates pressure for everyone.

4. Let your children know that this doesn't change your relationship to, or feelings for, them.

5. Be prepared to answer questions.

6. Utilize available supports, such as support groups for gay parents and their children.

7. Stay calm.

Larry, 44, had been divorced for several years and had custody of his son and daughter, then 10 and 14, when he met Thomas, who is 28. After their first date, Larry asked Thomas to "come home and meet my children." Thomas agreed to meet them, but was concerned about what he would say. "I hadn't talked to anyone under five feet in years." Thomas had also been married, but never had children because "I knew I was gay and would one day be divorcing." Larry had never discussed his homosexuality with his children and had never had a live-in male lover.

The first meeting with Larry's son and daughter went well, as did the relationship between Larry and Thomas. From their first date, Larry and Thomas spent every night together. Larry didn't want to leave his children at home alone, so he and Thomas spent weeknights at Larry's apartment and weekends, when his children were with their mother, at Thomas's apartment. Larry had not yet told his children that he was gay even though he was sharing his bedroom with Thomas, who says:

> I felt very strange about it. I would be there in the morning when they got up. That was a period of anxiety. I was afraid the kids were thinking I turned their father queer, that I corrupted Daddy. I was afraid that I would feel hatred from them. I didn't want to cause a split in their family.

If your intention is to hide your relationship from your children, for whatever reason, this is not the way to go about doing it. If your intention is to get your kids to start asking questions, you can just about guarantee they will start asking questions of some kind if you have a man staying with you in your bedroom and you haven't already provided an explanation.

Children are not stupid and they're usually surprisingly perceptive. If they live with you full-time and a lover moves in, beyond the age of 2 or 3 your children will want to know why there is a man sharing your bedroom. Beyond a certain age, they are likely to guess that you are gay and the man sharing your bedroom is your lover. If the children are infrequent, scheduled visitors, you will likely be able to hide your relationship from them by keeping a two-bedroom apartment and living as roommates when the kids are in town. But, according to Joy Schulenburg:

> If the kids come and go randomly or spend much overnight time, however, the musical-bedrooms game becomes awkward and frustrating. Once again

resentment arises as the lover is sent to her or his room because the children are visiting. And young minds put subtle clues together with amazing accuracy. The forgotten bedroom slipper, the wrong brand of cigarettes on a bedside table—these things are noted.

To be sure, subterfuge is warranted in some situations. Where there is a custody dispute, for example.

As a responsible parent you owe it to your children to talk with them before your lover moves in with you. In addition, if you act as if what you are doing is something that should be hidden, is shameful, or not talked about, your children will take their cue from those actions. If you are straightforward and matter of fact, they will react accordingly. According to Schulenburg:

> Those who had the most positive experiences were overwhelmingly emphatic about one thing: Be comfortable with yourself as a person. Be secure in your own beliefs and accepting of your own sexuality, and your children will be able to accept it also, for then they will be able to base their judgments on a positive model.

If you're having trouble finding a way to broach the subject and are uncertain about how to phrase answers to the questions they are likely to have, find other men who have been through the same experience. There are many men who belong to gay fathers organizations who will be glad to speak with you.

After several weeks of living together, and a few discussions between them, Larry and Thomas decided it was time for Larry to have a talk with his children. They had begun to ask questions such as, "Doesn't Thomas have an apartment of his own?"

On an evening when Thomas was out, Larry brought it up. Larry told them there was something uncomfortable he wanted to talk to them about. A strained silence followed. Then his son, Warren, said "I think I know what you're going to talk about." Larry, seizing upon the opportunity, said, "Well, what do you think it is?" But Warren adroitly put the ball back in Larry's court and said, "Well, it's uncomfortable for me to talk about, too." More strained silence followed.

Then finally Warren said, "Does it have something to do with what's in your night table drawer?" There was a tube of KY lubricant in the drawer along with a copy of *The Advocate* (a national gay magazine). Larry said, "Yes, I think we all know what we're talking about here. It's time to say the word." Larry explained that he was gay and the conversation flowed easily from there. The children had already suspected their father was gay and were just waiting for him to tell them.

When Eliot, 50, and Lloyd, 48, who have been together for ten years,

met through a newspaper advertisement, Lloyd was married and had
two children—a son, 12, and an 8-year-old daughter. Several months
after meeting Eliot, Lloyd left his wife and children and their suburban
home and moved in with Eliot. Lloyd's first inclination was to get a
place of his own:

> I wanted to have a separate apartment so that it would be a cover for my
> family and my kids. I needed a place of my own for the kids to stay when they
> were with me.

Eliot insisted that Lloyd move in with him, admitting now that he was
"remarkably insensitive." Lloyd decided that if it was important to Eliot
that they live together, he would agree. The day his children left for
summer camp, Lloyd packed his bags and moved in with Eliot.

Once the kids came home from camp, and Lloyd and his wife had
explained to them that they were getting divorced they began spending one day a week with their father. Lloyd did not yet think it was time
to tell them about his relationship with Eliot and it was another six
months before Lloyd and Eliot moved to an apartment that was large
enough for the two children to stay overnight.

Eliot met Lloyd's children, Veronica and Damien, for the first time
when he accompanied Lloyd to the suburbs for a visit. He recalls:

> We went out for hamburgers. I remember sitting opposite Veronica. She was
> having a Coke or something and took the paper off the straw and wadded
> it up, put it in her mouth, and spit the wad at me through the straw. It hit
> me right in the eye. I was incensed. I can go to white heat pretty fast.
>
> I glowered at her and she looked at me and said, "What are you gonna do,
> cry?" I halfway liked her then.
>
> I come from a "gestapo" household. The children were seen and not heard.
> In Lloyd's household, the kids did exactly as they pleased. I was appalled by
> their behavior.

When Lloyd and Eliot moved into their new two-bedroom apartment, the children started staying overnight. One of the bedrooms was
a den with a daybed. When the children came to visit, Lloyd slept in
the den, Eliot slept in the bedroom, and the kids slept in the living
room. It was an arrangement Lloyd felt was necessary to keep his kids
and his own parents from finding out he was gay.

It was four years after he began living with Eliot that Lloyd talked
to his children about being gay and his relationship with Eliot. By that
time Lloyd and Eliot had moved to another apartment with only one
bedroom, which they shared even every other weekend when Lloyd's
children stayed with them. Lloyd figured his kids would eventually pick

up on things and bring up the subject themselves, which Veronica did one night over dinner:

> I went to visit them, and we went out to dinner for Japanese food. We just finished ordering. And Veronica, who was fourteen at the time, in this loud voice asks, "Are you gay?" Everyone in the restaurant went silent. I was in total shock. When I didn't answer, she repeated her question. So I told her we would talk about it later. Damien ignored the whole thing.

When they got back to the house, Lloyd spoke with Veronica assuring her that he loved her and that his homosexuality had nothing to do with their relationship. It was several days before she would speak to him. Sometime later he spoke to Damien. According to Lloyd, it's never been a serious issue, in part because his wife has always been very supportive of him.

About a year before Lloyd's daughter asked "the question," Lloyd had started to attend meetings for gay fathers, where he heard about other men's experiences:

> One of the interesting things that came out in the discussions was that in almost all cases when the kids found out, it was okay. This was their father, he was gay. They would have some problems, but would eventually come around. That was reassuring, but it didn't make it easy as far as when the time came to tell the kids.
>
> I also found out that the younger the children, the easier it was. Especially before they were teens and dealing with their own sexuality and were more aware about sexual things and had peer pressure. When they're younger, they're more accepting of things. They're not even so sure what gay is. They just want to know that their father is still their father. But no one has it easy.

Your Lover's Role

There is at least one fundamental rule about your lover's role in your children's lives: You and your lover must define it. For example, will your lover share the financial burden? Will he be involved in disciplining the children? and so forth.

According to Joy Schulenburg, there is also a fundamental *requirement* for father, children, and lover when integrating a lover into a family—patience. "Each party involved must allow time for children and lover to grow accustomed to one another; then perhaps, genuine affection may follow."

Larry and Thomas never talked about how involved Thomas would be in raising Larry's two children. Thomas considers that to have been a major mistake:

We never sat down and discussed how I should relate to them in terms of discipline or telling them to do things, which in retrospect would have been a good idea.

I didn't know if I could tell them to do something or if I should ask Larry to ask them to do something, like pick up after themselves. Finally I just started to do it. If there were any serious disciplinary situations, Larry handled them.

During the next two years, Larry and Thomas and the two children shared their lives. The kids convinced Thomas to lobby their father on their behalf to make a trip to Disneyland, no easy task because he hates California:

There was Americana cast in plastic, and all of these couples with all their children and there Larry and I were with our two children. Gradually I was beginning to feel more and more a part of the family.

At about the two-year mark, Larry and Thomas were attending a gay fathers' meeting at which Thomas was engaged in a conversation with a man who also lived with a lover and his lover's children.

I said, in a joking way, "Bert, how are your children?" And Bert told me how the three children were doing. And I said, "Our children are just fine." Larry overheard me.

When we got home, Larry said, "Don't you ever call them 'our children' again. They are *my* children. I've raised them. You *just* came onto the scene. They are *my* children. They are not *ours.*"

Even talking about it now, I am nonplussed. I was so overwhelmed, because I had tried so hard to make them my family. I felt we were bonding as a family and then to have that slapped in my face. That just left me devastated.

That to me was the beginning of the end of the relationship, because he then set up the children as coming between us two. It was no longer a circular family relationship.

I knew they were not my children. If he had just calmly said that he was uncomfortable with me using the word "ours" because he had seven years of raising them alone, I would have understood.

But my defenses went up after that. I told him that I had felt I was a part of the family and to attack me like that left me devastated. I never got an apology. I began to see him devoting more of his attention to them than to me. I knew the children came first, but I didn't like being made to feel less important. I began to resent some of the things he was doing for the children and not for me. I felt that way because they were now "his" children.

Despite my intense feelings for the children I began to distance myself from them. And that was unfortunate for the children and for me.

Two years later, Thomas moved out. It is too simple to say that this is the whole story. Larry has his own perspective on what happened, a perspective in which the children don't play a part. Nonetheless, Thomas looks back on the confrontation with Larry about "his" children as the beginning of the end of their relationship. Thomas offers this advice from his experience:

> My advice to other couples with children is to talk about that issue of how are you going to relate with the children. How are you, the lover, going to be a part of this family? And while they're not "our" children, how are we going to set this relationship up so that the children do not become a divisive issue?

Eliot never had to become very involved with Lloyd's children, in part because he only saw them on occasional visits.

Eliot: I don't know if it has to do with my lack of interest or what. The children are a little alien to me, the way they've been brought up. I just don't know how to deal with them. I made the best effort, in my view, to make them feel at home in my home. But it didn't develop much beyond that. It never developed into any sort of warmth between us.

Lloyd: I never made a big point of insisting that Eliot be involved with the kids. If he wanted to, he could participate. I knew he wasn't interested. Sometimes Eliot would come to the movies with us. I never pushed it. If he wanted to come, fine. You can't force a relationship between your children and your lover. If you don't feel like doing it, don't do it.

Things never quite clicked between Eliot and Lloyd's children. He acknowledges that they have never been close. Lloyd still sees his children regularly, but they rarely stop by or stay overnight at the apartment he shares with Eliot.

RESOURCES

Organizations

Gay and Lesbian Parents Coalition International, Box 50360, Washington, DC 20004, 703-548-3238

> The Coalition is an international parents organization that provides general information and information on parents/fathers groups in your area. Many of the groups provide support for the children of gay parents and for the parents' partners as well.

Lesbian Rights Project, 1370 Mission Street, 3rd floor, San Francisco, CA 94103, 415-621-0674

If you have questions about adoption or need a referral to a lawyer who has experience handling gay adoption cases, the Lesbian Rights Project can help you. The Project is "the only nonprofit public interest law firm in the country that deals with all matters of sexual-orientation discrimination." The Project's emphasis is on serving lesbians, but provides assistance to gay men as well. As well as referrals, services include free informal legal advice, technical assistance to lawyers, and community education.

Books

Gay Fathers: Some of Their Stories, Experiences and Advice, 1981. Gay Fathers of Toronto, PO Box 187, Station F, Toronto, Ontario, Canada M4Y 2L5, 416–364–4164 (M–F, 7–10 P.M., or leave message)

Gay Fathers will go out of print in 1987, but Gay Fathers of Toronto is working on a follow-up, as yet untitled, book that will be organized around the major issues that affect gay fathers.

Jenny Lives with Eric and Martin, by Susanne Bosche, 1981, Translated from the Danish by Louis Mackay, 1983. Gay Men's Press, PO Box 247, London N15 6RW, England

Photostory for young children of gay parents about Jenny, who is 5 years old and lives with her father, Martin, and his partner, Eric.

Whose Child Cries: Children of Gay Parents Talk About Their Lives, by Joe Gantz, 1983. Jalmar Press, 45 Hitching Post Drive, Bldg. 2, Rolling Hills Estates, CA 90274

Stories of children from the ages of 7 to 19. Interviews include other family members as well.

Gay Parenting: A Complete Guide for Gay Men and Lesbians with Children, by Joy Schulenburg, 1985. Anchor Press/Doubleday, 673 Fifth Avenue, New York, NY 10022

While not as complete a guide as the subtitle suggests, this book covers many of the issues concerning parenting. Extensive resource listings are included.

CHAPTER 7

Work and Play

*"If you give people an indication of how to react,
they will react in that way."*

WORK

Work is a fact of life. With the exception of an insignificantly small number of people, everyone works, whether it's in an office, at home taking care of children, delivering the mail, in a classroom, at home at a typewriter or computer, behind the wheel of a truck, or in an operating room. Work is a source of sustenance, often pleasure; but frequently work is a source anxiety and agitation as well.

Most work problems that couples, both straight and gay, face are universal, such as confronting different attitudes toward work, fitting your commitment to work into your commitment to your relationship, accommodating each other's work schedules, making decisions concerning job transfers, learning to work together in a joint business, and coping with competition over earning power and job status.

Some problems, such as competition and dealing with the complexities of a job transfer, are heightened for male couples. And one—coming out or staying in the closet on the job—is a problem that only gay people face. Although all gay people must face this issue, it is often a more pressing problem for gay couples.

Differing Attitudes Toward Work

Work means different things to each person. It can represent self-esteem, self-respect, independence, accomplishment, a place in the world, and a significant anchor for your relationship. Therefore, it may not always be immediately apparent why your partner is reacting to a work-related situation in a way that you might not. If you work long and hard, thinking that's just how life is, you may be shocked to discover that your partner is resentful that all you do is work. If your self-esteem and identity are not tied up with your work, your job being simply a way to earn money, you may have a hard time understanding when your partner is devastated by the loss of his job.

Remember that you are each different and, as in many other circumstances, you will not necessarily think or react in the same ways to similar situations. The best you can do is not to dismiss what your partner thinks as wrong or ridiculous. Try to be understanding of his point of view.

Fitting Work into Your Relationship

Different men place different priorities on their work. For some, work and career come first, and they think nothing of spending the weekend as well as the week at work. For others the relationship comes first and they expect their weekends to be spent doing things together. Still others' priorities switch back and forth at different points in their lives. Invariably, you and your lover will not always have the same priorities and at different times your work will have a significant impact on the amount of time you spend together.

But what if your views on the importance of work are dramatically different? What if work is your first priority and the relationship is your partner's first priority? If you want to stay together and not repeat the same arguments day after day, you will have to reach some sort of mutual accommodation. I can't repeat it enough: Accommodation—compromise based on commitment—means that neither of you will be completely satisfied all the time. Such a situation in relationships is called "success." Even after reaching an accommodation, such as cutting back on overtime or changing shifts, you may still work more than your partner wants you to, and from your point of view he may still put too much emphasis on the relationship and not enough emphasis on career.

Work life is rarely static, so you will have to make adjustments at home as the conditions of your work change. If you know changes are coming that will affect your relationship, warn your lover. And if those changes involve making a choice, talk over your options with your lover before making a decision. For example, if you're facing a job change that is likely to have an impact on the time you have together, or one that affects the condition you'll probably arrive home in after an average seventy-hour week, talk over that job change with your lover before you make it.

Whenever Terry and Dennis, who are both in their early thirties, consider a job change, they discuss how the new job will fit into their relationship, among other things.

Dennis: Every time we make changes in our jobs, we sit down and ask, "Why are you taking a job like this? Where is it going to take you? How will that new job affect our relationship?"

Terry: We're both in agreement that if it got to the point in our careers where our job was detrimental to our relationship, we would leave that job.

Dealing with a Transfer or Voluntary Relocation

For any couple in which both partners work, a job transfer or voluntary relocation involves moving two careers, a fair amount of uncertainty, and invariably some tense moments. Before you make *any* decision, talk over your options with each other.

Hugh had been in his job as an engineer for just two years when his partner, Arthur, finished his medical residency at a local hospital in Virginia. Arthur was encouraged to look elsewhere for a permanent placement. Hugh says:

Trying to synchronize two careers is very, very difficult. Even though we've tried to pick a place where there will be opportunities for both of us, we won't know until we both find new jobs. And while there's a high probability that I'll find a comparable job in Austin, Texas, I don't know what the probability will bring. I have a lot of anxiety about how that will work out.

Despite all of his anxieties, Hugh suggested that he and Arthur move to further Arthur's career—in part because of uncertainty about the future of his own job:

At any point I could have said I will not move, and he would have stayed. But when we weighed the uncertain future of my job here with the potential opportunities for Arthur in Texas, we decided the hassles of moving would be well worth the potential good rewards.

When it comes to a transfer, male couples are at a disadvantage. When a couple is straight, the transferring company often makes employment arrangements or provides assistance to the spouse of the partner who is being transferred. If nothing else, they are understanding. For a male couple, company assistance for a partner in the search for a new job is very rare. For men who are in the closet at work, for all the company knows there is no "significant other" about whom to be concerned. As a male couple, you will have to rely on your own resources.

Work-Related Separations

At some point during your careers you may face a job opportunity that requires being separated for several months or more. Before making the decision to accept that offer, discuss what impact that separation could have with your partner. For example, is your relationship secure enough to handle such a separation? If you're a monogamous couple, should you reassess your commitment to monogamy if the separation will be long-term?

Andrew and Donald live in Philadelphia. For Andrew, what started as a commitment of a few days a week in Atlanta over several months, turned into a full-time job in Atlanta that lasted close to a year-and-a-half, a financial opportunity he said he couldn't pass up. Donald wishes he had.

Andrew: It didn't work out that well. It worked well for me. But it was hard on Donald. For me it was business. It was seven days a week, twenty-four hours a day. My life was the project. Because of the way it happened, we really never had a chance to talk about it. Before I knew it I was in Atlanta full-time.

Donald: And here I was in my ivory tower. I went down twice a month, but I still hardly saw him because he was always at work.

All I did for a year-and-a-half was sit here and whine and cry about wanting him to be back.

Andrew: It made us a lot of money. It seemed worth it to me. But it wasn't worth it to Donald.

Donald: With all that, I wouldn't do it again.

While they were separated, and despite their commitment to remain monogamous, Andrew and Donald each had a one-night stand, which upset them both, they said, and increased the emotional cost of being apart.

Supporting an Out-of-Work Partner Financially and Emotionally

Unemployment can be devastating. One advantage of being a couple is having a partner on whom to depend for both financial and emotional support if faced with the loss of a job. But not every man is comfortable depending on his partner, even for a short period of time. Whether your out-of-work lover is fiercely independent or relatively comfortable turning to you for support, the best you can do is to be understanding of his circumstances and be as supportive as you know how.

Working Together in the Same Business

Before you decide to plunge into a joint business venture, there are several basic questions you should ask yourselves:

1. Do we both really want to do this?

2. Are we good at communicating with one another?

3. Are we team players?

4. Can we criticize one another professionally without taking it personally?

5. Can we avoid letting problems in our relationship affect our work, and vice versa?

6. Can we bear to be around each other all the time?

7. Have we ever successfully worked together on a small project, like painting the apartment, planting a garden, writing an article, etc.?

Even if you can honestly answer yes to the above questions, it may be difficult to predict how you will react when you actually work together professionally. For some couples, working together can be extremely rewarding. But it's not for everyone.

Scott and I have tried a few small projects together. The idea seemed exciting—being involved in the same things, sharing the same concerns, being together all the time, sharing a by-line. Because we both write and have worked as editors, working together seemed natural, inevitable. But once again, the fantasy proved to be much more appealing than the reality. We both find that it doesn't always work very well. I invariably wind up managing the project and having to set deadlines. He resists the deadlines. I get angry, he gets resentful, and then I snipe at him. If I snipe enough, he'll snipe back. We've learned to edit each other's writing without killing each other, but professional criticism from Scott makes me very uncomfortable. On the other hand, we are learning how to work together. Scott has learned to be less harsh in the manner of his criticism, and I'm trying not to be so sensitive.

Dealing with Competition

While the idea of competing with a lover in terms of job status and financial standing seems absurd to some couples—"We're a team, why should we compete? If he makes more money, great! We both benefit"—to others, it seems as integral a part of everyday life as getting up in the morning.

As men, society teaches us to compete with other men. That may be productive at the office, but competing with the man you love and live with is not. You may not feel competition is a bad thing, but when two people compete, almost invariably someone comes in second. Someone loses. That can lead to resentment and anger on both sides—from the partner who loses and from the partner who is disappointed that his partner is unable to successfully compete. In either case you both lose.

Many of the men I interviewed said they prefer to earn as much or more than their partner. As long as both partners earn the same amount, there usually is no problem. But if both prefer to earn more than the other, and one actually does earn more than the other, feelings of resentment, jealousy, and inadequacy can be the result. In addition, the partner who earns more may be inclined to feel that, as the greater wage earner, he can have more weight in any decisions that concern money (see Chapter 10).

Financial competition is not the only type of job competition. For Greg and Neal, status also figured in the equation.

Neal: I found myself in a very glamorous life because of Greg's work in the theater industry. I was a school teacher and Greg was a glamorous agent. My responses to this situation weren't based on money, but the inequality of our status. I never wanted to be seen as Greg's "young number."

Greg: There's a five-year age difference. I don't think there was that danger.

Neal: That's how I saw it. That was a motivating factor for me to establish myself in my own right. It was as hard for me as it was for my sister-in-law, who had to establish that she was more than an extension of her husband.

Greg: It's hard for the other person too. I found that it used to upset me. I was always very proud of Neal, that he was a teacher. I found it embarrassing that he wasn't forthcoming about what he did.

Neal: I began to feel better about my work when I got additional degrees, started writing, and I grew up.

The first step in trying to understand and deal with damaging competition is to recognize that that's what's going on. You may be so accustomed to competing with each other that you don't even know you're doing it. Or the competition may be one-sided, as it was for Neal, and you may have a hard time recognizing what your partner's up to. If your lover makes a comment about how well he's doing at work in comparison to you, call him on it. Let him know that competitive remarks only succeed in hurting you or making you feel resentful of his successes. When your partner seems not to be enthusiastic about your successes or is unenthusiastic about his own successes, ask him why. Perhaps he feels he has to compete and that his accomplishments are not significant in comparison to yours. In any case, do your best to be understanding of your partner's perspective and talk about it.

The One-Career Couple (by Choice)

Many couples find themselves in a circumstance where only one partner is earning a living at one time or another. Most often, and without exception among the couples I interviewed, this is a temporary arrangement to enable one partner to go back to school, start a business, or take a break to explore new job opportunities. Don't be surprised at the appearance of some anxieties about depending on one partner to provide financial support for the relationship. Craig encouraged Marshall to leave his job and start his own business, something Marshall had wanted to do for a long time. Marshall left his job, but reluctantly. He's uncomfortable depending upon Craig to pull in the majority of their income.

Marshall: I would never have been able to develop my career if he weren't doing as well financially as he is doing. But I have a problem with the arrangement. I come from a very self-sufficient background. I have difficulty not being entirely self-sufficient.

Craig: Marshall fretted because when he left his job he was at home all the time working on the house and working on starting the business. He didn't see the work he was doing on the house as work. I saw it as work because if he wasn't doing it we would have had to pay someone to do it.

You may consider drawing up a contract (see Chapter 9, "Legalizing Your Relationship") to spell out exactly what kind of arrangement you have made (for example, "I'll support you through school if you later support me through school," or "I'll spend X hours renovating the house in exchange for X financial support"). A written agreement may ease the anxiety of not feeling independent for the partner who is taking time off from earning income. For the partner who is providing the financial support, a written agreement can help ease the possible fear that his partner might not honor their verbal agreement.

Coming Out/Staying in the Closet

Whether to be out or how much to be out of the closet at work often becomes more pressing for gay men once they've entered serious long-term relationships. Once you're in a relationship, it's natural to feel a greater need to live your life more openly if you've been closeted at work. After all, a good relationship is an achievement, and it confers a certain standing among other adults. That your spouse is a man rather than a woman doesn't change the desire for acknowledgement and acceptance. But often this wish is tempered by caution, and sometimes that caution is pragmatic. Sometimes it's less necessary than you think. In any case, there are basically three ways for you to deal with integrating your sexuality, relationship, and work. You can be completely out, selectively out, or completely closeted. Each has it's upside and downside, and only you can decide which circumstance best suits you. And you and your partner may not agree what is best. If you decide to come out at work—completely or selectively—you will also have to decide how you will do so.

COMPLETELY OUT

The primary advantage to being out of the closet on your job is not having to worry about hiding anything. You can be yourself. You can talk about what you really did over the weekend and with whom. You don't have to be afraid to make friends. But, depending upon your circumstances, there can be risks. At worst, you could lose your job, miss a promotion, your employees or boss could think less of you, you could be ostracized, and you may have to deal with the hostility of straight co-workers or of gay co-workers or supervisors who are in the closet. Hostile closeted gay people can be your worst enemies.

Indeed, some of these things can happen and do happen, but much depends on the kind of job you have, where you live, and how you handle the situation. Often, just the fear of possible rejection or discrimination will keep you from considering being open at your job.

John's fear of what would happen if his co-workers at his family's landscaping company found out about his homosexuality almost torpedoed his relationship with Chet. At work he supervises several employees and he couldn't imagine how his relationship with Chet would fit in with his work relationships. John was afraid that his family would reject him and his employees would no longer respect his authority. John's anxiety turned out to be a waste of energy because no one had a problem—at least not that he knew of.

But not every story has a happy ending. There is plenty of discrimination in the world. The military routinely gives gay people who are "found out" the boot. There are simply some jobs where work and gay do not mix well, or at all.

SELECTIVELY OUT

There are job situations in which it is not a good idea for it to be known generally that you are gay and have a lover. Being "selectively out" gives you some of the freedom of being completely out, and some of the advantages—protecting your job—as well as the disadvantages of being completely in the closet, such as having to keep secrets and censor conversations.

Ned works in child care and is careful about what he says and to whom.

> Everyone at work knows Peter exists, but I'm not sure what they think. Some of them know that Peter and I are lovers. The others I'm really not sure and don't care. The people I know best and care about know, or I'm sure have figured it out.
>
> Because of my work I haven't been as up-front as I would like to be. I really don't think there would be any problem. I worry more about the parents of the children raising a lot of shit than the management. I think there are some parents who would raise quite a fuss about it. This is not a liberal town.

COMPLETELY CLOSETED
Staying completely in the closet greatly reduces the risk of having to deal with hostile co-workers, or losing a promotion, or getting fired.

But there's no guarantee that you won't be found out and the price of locking yourself in the closet can be high. Staying in the closet has several drawbacks: You have to live with the fear of being found out; it's difficult if not impossible to develop close personal relationships with co-workers; you may be forced to lie about your life; certainly you will have to constantly censor your conversations about what you did for the weekend or what's happening in your life. Such distance suits some people just fine. But, should your lover become seriously ill or die, for example, you can find yourself in a difficult position trying to explain why you have to take time off, and you also won't have the support or understanding of the people you work for and work with.

Wayne, 35, lost his lover of ten years to AIDS. His company has very liberal "bereavement" benefits, which include two weeks paid leave when an immediate family member or spouse dies. Wayne's relationship with his lover didn't fall into the designated categories and he decided not to raise the issue with his boss. So he called in sick so he could attend the funeral, and went back to work the next day.

Wayne was caught in a tight spot because he was afraid he would lose his job if his boss knew he was gay and that his lover had died from AIDS. Wayne did what he felt he had to, to keep his job.

DIFFERENT APPROACHES TO COMING OUT AT WORK
What approach you decide to take if you decide to be selectively or completely out at your job depends on at least two factors: your particular work circumstances and how you prefer to let people know that you're gay. But essentially, coming out styles are of two kinds—gentle and aggressive.

Michael and Chris, who have taken a nonconfrontational, matter-of-fact approach to letting their parents know about their relationship, have taken a similar approach to letting their co-workers know that they're gay. Both would characterize themselves and their families as conservative, and both have worked in professions many would not consider hospitable to openly gay people. Michael works for a prominent big-city architecture firm. Chris worked for a large computer software company in a suburban office park, and is now a third-year law student. They are both completely uninvolved in gay politics, have never marched in a Gay Pride parade, and do not read gay newspapers or publications (with the exception of an occasional skin magazine). However, they firmly believe in not hiding who they are or their long-term relationship from their colleagues. Their approach is pragmatic and makes a lot of sense. It is an approach that many of us are in a position to emulate.

Michael: I didn't go around saying I was gay. I just talked about Chris—my roommate—with intensity. I just took the attitude that there is this man I care for and who I live with. No one can feel uncomfortable about that. Now if they want to put two and two together and make me gay, then they can do that. And then they can talk about Chris like he's my husband or whatever, but if they don't want to put two and two together they have the option of not doing that.

It's the mystery people love to solve. They get a feeling of accomplishment when they figure it out. And you've switched the burden from you trying to push it on them to them trying to get it out of you.

And if being gay didn't fit into the company's attitude of what I should be, I never said, "Lookit, I'm gay," as if to say I'm gay and you have to accept me. I'm just living with this man who I care for. Then I got close to other people in the office and when they would talk about their husbands or their wives, or when gay colleagues would talk about their lovers, I talked about Chris. I was always very open.

Chris: It was the same thing at my office. It didn't happen as quickly and maybe not as completely. I worked in the suburbs with people who had never thought they would have close friends who were gay, and suddenly they found they were friends with me, and I'm gay. I brought Michael to the company picnic twice. I don't think it was as comfortable as when we went to his office picnic where many of his associates brought friends. At my company picnic it was all families.

Michael: Dances are very tricky. If it's a formal business party like a dance, you have to bring a woman. I think of that as bringing an "escort." It's not that she is someone I'm having a relationship with. I always make that clear.

Two years ago, Chris left his job and returned to school to get his law degree. It meant starting the process of easing out of the closet all over

again. As Chris's partner, Michael felt a little more bold this time
around.

Michael: I went to Chris's law review banquet. And I was really very proud to
do it. This was a dinner party and everybody was to bring his or her spouse.
We were the only gay couple there. I really felt very good.

Chris: I had reservations. I just thought it would be a terrible evening. I think
I had reservations because we're not really close with that many people on
law review.

Michael: I think I noticed some people who were uncomfortable. There was
one stupid ass who was rude to us—and he was gay! And it was boring,
primarily because we were a couple. If Chris was alone he would have min-
gled more.

One very common challenge Chris and Michael encountered was
coming up with a word with which to introduce each other. For the
time being they've settled on "friend," but they've tried other words.

Chris: When Michael took me to his architecture school graduation dinner
party he introduced me as his "comrade" to all his professors. Everyone
thought we were communists or something. It was embarrassing. By the end
of the night I convinced him it was inappropriate.

Michael: I would love to use "husband."

Chris: I don't like husband because what am I then, your wife? "Spouse" is nice.

When Chris starts looking for a law job he intends to be cautious.

Chris: I have to put up a front at least in the beginning if I want a job. That
does not mean I plan to lie.

Michael: You want to be hired on your merits.

Chris: People will come to know that I'm good at what I do. Then they will
come to respect me and get to know the personal side. When I have to go
to formal dinners, I'll get an escort.

Easing out of the closet does not suit everyone. Ralph, 29, a lawyer
in Boston, wanted to be certain that his sexuality would not be an issue
before he accepted his job.

I didn't want to accept my job without letting them know I'm gay. I wanted
to clear the air before I accepted the position. If there was going to be a
problem, I was going to look elsewhere. I wanted them to realize who they
were getting before they hired me. When I spoke with the hiring partner,
he was very gruff. I walked into his office and asked him if I could close the
door, which was unusual at the firm. I told him I sensed there was a good
chance they would offer me a job. I told him I thought they should know
something about my personal life before they hired me, that I was gay.

He asked me why I thought it was important to tell him that. I told him I didn't want it to come out later and then be a problem. He looked at me and said that was just his problem. He was gay and had always kept it a secret.

The cornerstone of both of these approaches is never to hide anything. If you don't lie from the start, then you have no backtracking to worry about. But these approaches are not for everyone. First of all you have to be very confident about who you are and what you are. And having a supportive partner goes a long way to provide the security you may need to overcome the fear of the potential consequences of coming out. If your partner is not supportive or is dead set against your coming out, then you may find honesty a more difficult approach.

One final anecdote comes from lovers who have been out at work for nearly twenty years. Both are in high-profile jobs, one is a senior "corner office" executive for a major corporation, the other is a senior official of a major international cultural institution. They've lived together for seventeen years and have always been open in their jobs about their relationship. They often accompany one another on business trips. Their comment on the subject is brief: "If you give people an indication of how to react, they will react in that way."

In other words, if you hide/lie, or act as if you and your relationship are shameful, the people you work with will often take the cue and treat you accordingly. If you are matter-of-fact, proud of who you are and of your relationship, the cue will be very different.

CONFLICTING VIEWS ABOUT COMING OUT AT WORK
As with many things, partners don't always see eye-to-eye on this issue. That's no surprise. Each of us has a different level of comfort with being out. What you consider a perfectly hospitable work environment for being open, your partner may not. For him, perhaps, no environment would be comfortable enough to be open. You can try to gently nudge him into being more open. If he is seriously paranoid and feels negative about being gay, you can encourage him to do some reading on the subject or see a counselor (See Chapter 13, "Health"), but you won't get far if you try to push too hard. Coming out is ultimately his, or your, choice. Neither of you can force the other. For example, if your partner decides to come out at work and you don't like his decision, for whatever reason, you're asking for conflict if you try to force him to live by your rules.

David and Lew have reached a quiet accommodation of each other's views about being out on the job. Lew is a psychologist and senior staff member with a major gay health organization. Almost everyone he works with is gay. David is a typesetter, sealed tightly behind the closet door. While Lew would prefer that David be out on his job—he thinks the deception is ridiculous and a waste of energy—he has given up pushing and is taking a wait-and-see attitude. David told me:

> He has stopped pushing because he knows I'll do it when I'm ready, not when he's ready. I think I've come a long way since I first met him. I no longer make up stories about women. I don't lie. I just don't share the whole reality. I know it's not the healthiest approach, but I'm not prepared for my colleagues to know. I don't really think it will affect my job. But I'm afraid they will think less of me. Besides, it's a relief to have a place to go where people think of me as straight. Coming to terms with being gay has been rough. I think Lew understands that I can't do it all at once.

PLAY

Like work, each of us has different expectations and definitions of play. To some, play is renovating the house or a game of soccer, while to others it may be sitting on the couch reading a book, having friends to dinner, visiting friends or family, or an evening out dancing with friends. With all the choices involved, there's plenty of room for discussion and conflict, many opportunities for compromise, and a tremendous need for the most fundamental relationship skill: communication.

Free Time

Free time is precious. It's a valuable, rare, yet renewable resource. How you spend your time depends on many things, including how much time you have, how much time you like to spend together, how much time you like spending alone, your time commitments outside of work and your relationship, and so forth.

TIME TOGETHER

How much time you spend together depends upon how much time you have and how much you enjoy spending time together. If you have different ideas of how much time you should spend together, with or without friends, you'll have to find a compromise.

How do you make time for each other? How do you avoid letting work, volunteer commitments, and commitments to friends and family consume so much of your time that the only time you have together is when you're asleep? Gary and Mitch were so commited to their volunteer work that they were only seeing each other awake one evening a week. They felt they were beginning to drift apart. Their psychologist suggested they cut back and leave two nights a week for each other, just to be at home together, for dinner, TV, or reading. Each week they now mark out two nights on the calendar when they're not allowed to make outside commitments.

TIME ON YOUR OWN

Spending time alone, without your partner, may not be your idea of a good time, but two people rarely share all of the same interests or all of the same friends. It may be easy at first—during the first months or years—to endure doing things and seeing people you don't like, just to please your partner, but eventually you may find there are days or times of the day when you each need to go your own way. For example, I like to run, and I belong to Front Runners, a gay running club. Scott hates to run. He likes to race-walk. He tried running with me a couple of times and hated it. I've tried race-walking, and I don't like it. I would rather he run with me. A number of times I've been asked by men in my running group whether or not Scott minds that I run without him. He doesn't.

If your partner feels threatened by the time you spend on interests he doesn't share with you, or with friends he doesn't care to spend time with, you have several options. You can encourage him to get used to it, and encourage him to develop his own interests and friends. You can offer to reduce the time you spend on those interests or with those friends. Or you can try a mix of these choices to reach a compromise that accommodates both of your wishes.

For Chet and John, the time Chet spends on his own with friends is one of the biggest sources of conflict in their five-year relationship. John would prefer to spend all his time with Chet, but Chet has many friends and wants to be free to go out with them to movies or dinner on his own every now and then.

Chet: I can't be confined. He has to let me do some things on my own. I'm okay about staying home alone when he goes out with friends.

I realize there's an insecurity when you're just starting out. When you separate, you feel insecure. "What's he doing?" "Who's he with?" "Will he want me tomorrow?" But once you've made a commitment to each other as we have, you can't go the rest of your life with each other seven days a week. You have to trust each other and, because of the commitment, should be able to do things on your own. He doesn't feel that way, even after five years together.

John: The relationship is still new for me. I trust him. I don't ever feel he's going out because he's unhappy in the relationship. I'm not jealous because I think he's attracted to somebody else. The jealousy has to do with my fear that he has a need to go out with other friends because there something missing in our relationship.

Chet: He's just jealous of the time I spend with them instead of with him. I'll tell him I'm going out to dinner with a friend. And John will make it difficult for me. He'll say, "I'm not going to tell you to have a good time."

To try to get John used to his going out with friends, Chet's strategy is to go out more than he otherwise might in the hope that John will become accustomed to it.

John: Chet thinks that if he does it more often, I should get used to it. I'm not getting more used to it.
Chet: But he's getting better. For example, tomorrow night [Friday] I'm going to dinner with a friend. Three years ago that would have been disastrous. He would ask, "Why after a whole week of work aren't you coming home and spending the evening with me?"
John: I would rather we do something together.
Chet: I don't do this every week. He's just concerned I'm going to meet someone.
John: I used to be more social than I am now. I like coming home and the two of us having dinner.

Both John and Chet agree that this is something about which they fundamentally disagree and that, while John may accept Chet spending time with his own friends, it is not something that will ever make him happy.

SCHEDULING
One easy way to keep track of your joint and individual commitments and to make certain that you have enough free time together and alone is to keep a large calendar in a central location that you both use in addition to whatever personal calendars you keep.

From the time we first moved in together, Scott and I overbooked our schedules and we made each other crazy by scheduling two different joint commitments on the same night. After nearly three years, Scott finally got disgusted and posted an oversized "family" calendar in the kitchen. He's primarily responsible for keeping it up-to-date. It helps us see when we've started to overschedule. (We still overschedule, like one month this year when we had more company than we had time for, but at least we knew it was coming.)

Friends

As a couple, you'll probably have three different groups of friends: those you share, his friends, and yours. Don't expect that you will like all of your lover's friends as much as he likes them (you may even dislike them), and be aware that he may not like your friends as much as you do. Just as you won't share all of the same personal interests, you won't share the same interest in each other's friends.

Friendships can be a source of problems as well as pleasure. For example, when you first become a couple, what do you do about friends who take a strong dislike to your new partner, or about friends whom your lover dislikes intensely? And what about straight friends who don't know you're gay and aren't aware of your new relationship? What should you say? How should you act?

PRE-RELATIONSHIP FRIENDS—SHIFTING FROM SINGLE TO COUPLE LIFE

In Fantasyland, when you bring a new lover into your life, all your friends immediately love him and he loves them. And you will have just as much time to spend with your friends as you did before you and your lover moved in together.

So much for fantasy. The odds are much higher that your partner will not love each and every one of your friends, and that you will not love all of his. And there's no question that you won't have as much time to spend with your friends. You may find yourself torn between loyalty to friends and to your lover. You may find that you resent your lover for his failure to share your feelings for your friends. Or you may resent your friends. Again, being aware of potential changes will help defuse tension and resentment if and when it develops. Change is disruption, and some disruption is unavoidable.

When Gary moved to Seattle to live with Mitch, he left all his friends behind. Mitch had a very close network of friends that included a best friend.

Mitch: He was like a brother. We spent all our time together. He and Gary became instant enemies. Since Gary moved here, Rob and I have stopped being best friends.

Gary: Suddenly the best friend became third wheel. There was bad chemistry between us. I felt threatened by their relationship. They were like gingerbread men on a cooling rack.

Mitch: It was devastating to lose my best friend. For a while I resented Gary. Gary really believes that when you get into a relationship you have to sacrifice a good portion of your single life—including some of your friends. I had this fantasy that you incorporate your lover into your single life.

One way to preserve friendships with people your lover doesn't care for is to spend time with those friends without your partner. That is not as easy as it sounds if, as in Mitch's case, your partner is "possessive and extremely protective." It may be hard to convince him you need time with your friends apart from him, particularly early in the relationship.

STRAIGHT FRIENDS

Among all of your friends, it's likely that you have straight friends—single men and women as well as couples. Besides the usual potential problems with any friendships, there may be the added concern of how to—or whether or not to—let friends know that you are gay and that you're a couple. For example, you may have had straight friends who knew you when you were single and, because you weren't involved in any relationship, there seemed to be little reason ever to discuss your sexuality with them. Now that you're in a relationship, there is much to talk about, much that you want to share, and much to hide if you want to keep your homosexuality and your relationship from straight friends who don't know that you're gay. You may also wind up in disagreements with your lover over whether or not to stay in the closet with straight friends.

Even if you have straight friends who "know," there may be much that they don't know about male couple relationships. You should be prepared to answer their questions and anticipate that they may have misconceptions about your relationship based on what they've read or seen on television about male couples. As with family, you may once again find yourself in the role of teacher, having to explain things that seem obvious to you.

COMING OUT TO STRAIGHT FRIENDS

If you decide to tell friends who don't know, you then have to decide how to do it. Should you tell them that you're gay? Should you take the gentle approach Michael and Chris have used with co-workers (see pages 118–120)? The decision, of course, is up to you and your partner.

Peter and Ned let their friends take the initiative, and have accepted the fact that different people deal with their relationship in different ways.

Peter: Our friends are mostly [straight] couples. They run the gamut from people who didn't treat you any different but never talked about it [being a gay couple] to really close friends where you can even joke with the guy about very personal things and can discuss things like AIDS and can be perfectly comfortable.

Ned: I have friends who I've been close to for fifteen years and we never discuss it. If they can't handle it, that's okay. It's no big deal. They come over. We're real good friends in every other way.

I don't want to feel like I'm pushing who I am on anybody. There's no point to that.

Then there's Harry and Jane. Harry asked me once after spending a few days here why we never held hands or kissed or did anything in front of them. He wanted to know if he made us feel uncomfortable. I said it was just the same as they were. I said, "You don't make out in front of us. What we do, we do when we're by ourselves."

There was the time Harry came right out and asked me if Peter and I were gay. Harry and I were in his garage by ourselves and we were talking and out of the blue he said, "There's something I've been wanting to ask you," and he just blurted it out. I said, "Yeah, Harry, we are. I just assumed you knew that." Harry said, "I just wanted you to know it wasn't something we couldn't talk about." I said, "I don't mind talking about it at all." At that point Harry decided he had had enough talking about that issue.

STAYING IN THE CLOSET

If you're comfortable with staying in the closet, fine. But what do you do when you include your partner in an evening with a friend who doesn't know? If he's comfortable playing along with the straight routine, that may be okay, as long as he can remember who he is supposed to be. But what if he objects? And what about mixing friends who know with friends who don't? The "know" and "don't know" game can get awfully complicated. To avoid conflict with your partner, or making your partner or friends uncomfortable by forcing them to watch their words and actions, keep it simple by keeping those worlds separate.

Vacations

Everyone has a different idea of what a vacation should be. It can be a week at home rebuilding the kitchen when you're both off from work; a grand tour of Europe or the Far East; a week backpacking or skiing in the Rockies; a visit home to spend time with family, or an annual vacation to some gentle place where there's nothing to do but just to be together.

For the sake of this discussion, "vacation" means going away. This involves many decisions for any couple, including where to go, how much you want to spend, and what type of vacation you want to take. For a male couple there are additional considerations. For example, will two men traveling together be a problem in the country to which you intend to travel? How do you explain to a reservations clerk that you don't want a room with two single beds?

Because a vacation away already involves so many decisions, it is not always a good idea to take a vacation that involves significantly more decisions if you're not getting along. Conflicts can become magnified when you're suddenly faced with multiple decisions. Even if you're getting along fine, vacations offer plenty of opportunity for conflict. Where are we going to go? Why do we always go there? What will we have for dinner?

CHOOSING WHERE TO GO

Deciding where to go for a vacation is much like making any other decision in which both of you are involved, and both have opinions. You have to talk, maybe argue, and reach a decision. Not only will you have to make a decision about where to go, you will have to decide if you will go alone or with friends, and you will have to decide who will oversee the planning, reservations, and paperwork. Remember, however much you disagree there is always a creative solution to both deciding where to go and how to carry out your plans.

Scott and I don't always agree on where to go. So we trade off. One year we went to Nova Scotia because Scott had always wanted to go there. This past summer one of my dear friends was getting married in Alaska, so we went to Alaska. In theory Scott should get to decide where we go next, but I've just about convinced him that we would be better off spending a week skiing than sitting on a beach.

Not that trading off guarantees smooth planning. By the time we finished planning the trip to Alaska, which also involved two stops in California—one stop was included at the last minute so we could attend the wedding of two of Scott's dear friends—I was ready to kill Scott. I handled all of the reservations, which became a problem when I had to completely rearrange the trip three times because of his changing job obligations and to include that last-minute wedding. I could have told him to make the changes himself, but I prefer to make our travel arrangements. So, unless I'm willing to split or trade off planning responsibilities, I should really stop complaining.

GOING ON VACATION ALONE TOGETHER

A vacation alone together may be just what you need to give you a chance to remember how much you enjoy being together. But such a vacation is not for every couple, particularly if you're not getting along. In that case, time alone together, even vacation time, can be torture.

Every fall, Michael and Chris rent the same room at a rambling Victorian seaside inn for a long weekend or, if time permits, a week, alone. No family. No friends. Alone. It gives them time to talk. Time to get physical.

Michael: I think it's a very good idea to take a vacation together once a year because you get close again.

Chris: Yeah, but when we get back home and go to work it's really cold turkey being apart.

Michael: You just don't have the time to do all those romantic things during the year. When you go away together all those things are regenerated.

COMPLICATIONS OF TRAVELING FOR A GAY COUPLE

Unless you travel to strictly gay resorts or places that you know are "gay friendly," you will have to concern yourselves with at least two critical questions about a travel destination: Will we be welcome? and Will we be comfortable?

Male couples are not welcome at every charming inn, everywhere in North America, and certainly not everywhere in the world. Which does not mean you have to restrict your travel. You just won't be able to ask for a double bed in absolutely every hotel at which you stay. You may even have to do your best not to act like a couple in some places. Beyond considering where you're welcome, you also need to think about where you will feel comfortable. For example, will you be comfortable at a ski resort where it's probable that you will be the only male couple among five hundred families?

Even if you're going someplace where you don't anticipate having problems, what do you say when you call a hotel for a reservation and the reservations clerk asks, "Will that be a room for a couple, or for two men?" And if you've read about a small inn somewhere in the countryside, how do you find out if the people who run it are comfortable accommodating a male couple? I mention this because I know Scott and I wouldn't want to stay at a three-room inn where we weren't welcome. Consciousness-raising is all fine and good, but vacations are not the time we set out to change the world. You may feel differently.

The solutions are relatively simple. You can either do research about travel destinations and make reservations on your own, making certain that you're welcome or you can make travel arrangements with the help of a gay or gay-friendly travel agent. If you do it on your own, you can start your travel research by consulting one of the available gay travel guides (see "Resources"). However, at the time of this writing, there are no truly worldwide gay travel guides. And, of those guides that are available, most only include information about major cities and gay-specific resorts.

When you make reservations to stay at a small inn or a bed and breakfast—or even a large hotel—and you want to make certain that you're given a room with a bed large enough for two, you simply have to ask for it. (Big hotels are usually no problem as most have full-size beds.) Depending on the circumstances, you may also want to ask if the people who run the inn or bed and breakfast have any problem with accommodating a male couple.

On our first vacation together, Scott and I spent half of our week away in a cottage by a river in Nova Scotia. It had a view of the river, a small deck with chairs, and a fireplace. It was perfect except that it had two very narrow single beds. When I had made the reservations, I chickened out asking for one big bed for two men. I've gotten a little better at being bold and for our most recent trip, when the reservations clerk asked, "Will that be a room for a couple or for two men?" I said, "That will be for two men and we are a couple." A small victory.

If you prefer, you can consult with an experienced gay or gay-friendly travel agent. Not everyone is comfortable asking the important questions—and dealing with the possible rejections—or requesting one bed for two men. A travel agent who has experience working with gay couples will know how to find out if the country (or country inn) you're planning to visit is one where you will have to play very straight, and can ask any questions you feel awkward asking.

If you don't have time to plan ahead, simply use common sense. If you're in a part of the country or a part of the world that looks unwelcoming to gay people, and you don't feel like confronting a potentially unpleasant situation, don't make it an issue by asking for one bed. Just pretend that you're two straight friends or roommates traveling together, and act accordingly.

One thought to keep in mind when traveling. Once again, most often if you give people an indication of how they should react, they will react in that way. But use common sense.

STRICTLY GAY VACATIONS

If you travel to a strictly gay resort you don't have to worry about how welcome you will be. In some places you won't even get a second look if you and your sweetheart hold hands. However, one drawback you may find with some of the exclusively gay inns or resorts is that they cater to a young singles crowd. And you may find a strictly gay vacation too limiting.

HOSTILE TERRITORY

When visiting a country, or a part of this country, that you know is hostile to gay people, common sense is the rule. Avoid drawing attention to yourselves. And play single and straight.

For example, if you're traveling to the Soviet Union and you're a couple that likes to get involved with men outside your relationship, before you go, you'd better find out the dos and don'ts from someone who knows, or simply avoid doing anything that can land you in jail. You can generally get this information from an experienced gay travel agent.

SEPARATE VACATIONS

One alternative to arguing about where to go or whether or not to go on a vacation is to take separate vacations. The following are several of the reasons for taking separate vacations given by the couples with whom I've spoken:

1. We don't like to travel to the same places.

2. We can't coordinate time off from work.

3. I need to see my family every year and they don't know that I'm gay and that I have a lover.

4. I can afford to travel, but my lover can't.

5. I love to travel and my partner doesn't.

6. One of us has to stay home to take care of the plants and the dogs.

7. We need a break from each other now and then.

8. We want free time to meet other men.

Not all of these are necessarily good reasons for taking separate vacations. For example, taking a vacation on your own because you have the money to do it and your partner does not can leave the less-affluent partner feeling resentful and the more-affluent partner feeling guilty; hardly emotions that contribute to a healthy relationship. Whatever the reason, you will need to talk about it.

Because of their different interests, Peter and Ned have talked about separate vacations.

Ned: We decided against it. We both realize we have different tastes and there are places that he would want to go that I would think would be totally bizarre, such as Greenland or Antarctica. I want to do more basic things, like New Zealand, the South Pacific.
Peter: Fortunately, there's a lot of common ground.
Ned: I figure that if he can put up with Bora Bora, I can put up with Iceland, Greenland, or whatever.
Peter: So far we've been going places that both of us want to go to.
Ned: And there are plenty of places we can both agree on.

FINDING A TRAVEL AGENT
To find a gay or gay-friendly travel agent, ask your friends, look through the *Gayellow Pages,* or, if one is available, check a local gay periodical.

Going out to Bars, Discos, etc.

Couple life doesn't have to mean the end of going to bars, to dances, dance clubs, or to going out to those places and events with single friends if you choose. For most of the couples I spoke with, these activities tapered off or ended entirely as their relationships deepened. For example, Tony of Tony and Doug says:

Once we became a couple, our friends stopped thinking of us as being gay. If they were going out to bars they wouldn't invite me anymore. If they were planning a dance, obviously I wouldn't want to be involved. Now more of our friends are becoming couples, and as they do we spend more time with them.

Couples gave several reasons for not going out, including lack of time, lack of reason (finding a man) to go out, desire to avoid the temptations offered in the singles scene, and the possible conflicts caused by jealousies and competition for attention.

If you're both comfortable going out together to dance at a club or socialize with friends at a bar, or even to look at or pick up other men, fine. But if either of you is sensitive about the stares or "come-ons" of other men, going out together may be asking for trouble.

Bruce, 33, and Jeff, 22, who are both from New Orleans and now live in Las Vegas, go out together often. They've been together for one year. The attention Bruce gets makes Jeff uncomfortable. Bruce, however, doesn't mind getting the attention.

Bruce: The attention doesn't bother me.

Jeff: That's easy for him to say because everyone always hits on him when we go out. He always gets all the attention.

Bruce: With my prior lover, when we went out and I received more attention than he did, oh my God, poor thing, he just came unglued.

Jeff: We've gone out a lot of times and Bruce gets more attention. About 80 percent of the time I take it as a compliment and think, "He came over here with me and he's gonna leave with me." The other 20 percent of the time I get hurt feelings.

Bruce: All of that attention means something to him. I've been around so long that I know how to make an entrance on a Saturday night. I definitely can get a second look. For me, I just sail through the room and don't give a shit. And Jeff's back there going, "Now what is Bruce up to?" I'm laughing it off saying, "Well, this is a bunch of queers on a Saturday night and they're just staring." And to Jeff it means things. That's what people do. They go out and cruise. I'm a seasoned cruiser. I've been doin' it since I was 17. Jeff's been doing it for a year. He's got a lot to learn.

I knew definitely to wear white across my shoulders and dark across my stomach. I know all of these things. You make your shoulders broader. You know, I'm a sister. And poor Jeff . . . to him the attention is very important because he's young and new. To me, I like the attention, but I'm not going to die if I don't get it.

Bruce is begging for trouble. While the attention may not bother him, the attention he gets makes Jeff feel jealous, resentful, and competitive. Because you're a couple, however you feel, you must be willing to consider your partner's feelings. If you don't you have to deal with the consequences—if not now, later.

RESOURCES

Books

The biggest problem with gay travel guides is that many of the companies that publish them come and go. Another problem is that available guides are often geared to single men.

There are, however, a couple of established companies that publish annually updated guides:

Odysseus USA/International, An Accommodations & Travel Guide for the Gay Community. Odysseus Enterprises, Ltd., PO Box 7605, Flushing, NY 11352, 718–445–2471

> Or you can order through Malibu sales:
>
> 800–533–8567; 800–654–3758 (in California)
>
> This 400-page guide focuses on accommodations for gay men and lesbians in the United States and several countries around the world. The book's appendix lists travel agents, tour operators, cruises, international travel agents, and reservations services.

Ferrari Publications, PO Box 35575, Phoenix, AZ 85069, 602–863–2408

> Ferrari publishes several travel guides including: *Places of Interest—USA, Canada, and the Caribbean, Places in Europe* (Western Europe only), and *Places for Men—USA, Canada, and the Caribbean.*

CHAPTER 8

Sex

"No gay man wants to be the first to admit that he makes love to his partner only once a week or even less."

After reading a few chapters of the average gay pulp "romance" novel by author Gordon Merrick, you're left with the impression that sex is the center of life in a relationship, that physical passion is never ending, that men are constantly erect, capable of one orgasm after the next, they love to bear the pain of being screwed by the biggest cock ever to jump from between two legs, and that all penises start at nine inches. As Bernie Zilbergeld says in *Male Sexuality:* "Penises in fantasyland come in only three sizes—large, gigantic, and so big you can barely get them through the doorway."

Not only are they big, says Zilbergeld "... they also behave peculiarly. They are forever pulsating, throbbing . . . and whenever a man's fly is unzipped, his penis leaps out. . . . Nowhere does a penis merely mosey out for a look at what's happening."

My point is simple. While most men realize that pornography and pulp novels aren't quite reality, many are willing to accept lesser myths and expectations. For example:

1. Men should always be ready and willing to have sex.

2. Sex—and the orgasm thereof—is always incredible.

3. The penis should be rock hard and ready to go with very little attention.

4. Men should be capable of (and want) a second orgasm—or more—in an evening.

5. A man should automatically know what to do, and intuitively know what his partner finds pleasurable.

6. Sex should always be spontaneous.

7. A decline in physical passion means a decline in love.

8. A man has to be in charge of sex.

9. Any physical contact inevitably leads to sex.

10. No erection, no sex.

Sex is physical need, affection, affirmation of attractiveness and desirability. It can be an expression of love and it can also be exciting, pleasurable, and a lot of fun. But sex can also be the source of anger, tension, competition, anxiety, and jealousy. And it can be life threatening. Further, according to many experts, sexual problems—lack of desire in particular—are a leading cause of couple breakups. This chapter deals primarily with these issues: the conflicts, problems, and challenges of maintaining a mutually fulfilling, and safe sexual relationship. It is not, however, a guide to the pleasures of a sexual relationship. For that kind of information, refer to the "Resources" at the end of the chapter.

Lack of desire may be impossible to imagine if you're experiencing the early passion of a new relationship. But in male couple relationships, almost universally (there are exceptions), this passion does not last. Nor, incidentally, does it last in heterosexual relationships. Some men who desire serious long-lasting relationships are victims of their desire for the passionate charge that new conquests bring, and therefore find it impossible to have a long-lasting relationship with one man. Others attempt to satisfy their desire for a long-lasting relationship and new passion by structuring their relationship so they are free to have new sexual contacts in addition to their long-term partner. (See Chapter 3, "Monogamy/Nonmonogamy" for more on the subject of sex outside of the primary relationship.) Still others work on achieving a satisfying erotic relationship with a long-term partner and adjust to declining passion. Ironically, while many gay men know all there is to know about finding good sex with new partners, they know practically nothing about sex in the context of a long-term relationship. Consequently the adjustment to declining physical passion may be very unsettling and difficult.

TOUCHING

Are hugging, touching, and other forms of physical affection important to a relationship? Yes, men need affection. Some more than others. And being physically affectionate does not mean you have to have sex every time you hug or touch each other.

How to Be Affectionate

For those to whom it comes naturally, suggestions about how to be physically affectionate may seem just a statement of the obvious. But there are plenty of men for whom the spontaneous hug or squeeze does not come naturally and will have to make a conscious effort to be physically affectionate.

1. Hugs—You can greet your partner with a hug when he gets home from work or when you get home from work and you can publicly hug each other at just about any airport, train, or bus station without raising eyebrows. At home there are plenty of opportunities to hug your partner besides arrivals and departures. You can put your arms around him from behind while he's cooking, doing the dishes, or just standing in front of the window. You can also hug him in bed before going to sleep and wake him up with a hug in the morning.

2. Kissing—You can show your affection by giving your partner a kiss on the neck. A kiss can also be a way to suggest that you would like to go beyond a kiss, but it doesn't have to be. You can kiss your partner hello when he gets home from work, give him kisses on his face to wake him up, or give him a good-night kiss. The only rule concerns kissing your partner in public. That one is up to you. If you're both comfortable giving each other a kiss in public, go right ahead, as long as you're not in a place where kissing another man can get you in trouble.

3. Holding—You can hold your partner at night while you're sleeping. He can hold you, or if you care to sleep front to front, you can hold each other. Or you can hold your partner while he's sitting on the couch reading, or . . .

4. Touching—Touching possibilities range from a pat on the back to a foot massage to cradling your partner's head in your lap. The range is only as limited as your imagination.

How to Deal with a Discrepancy in Needs for Affection

If you both fill each other's need for affection, great. But what if you want more demonstrations of affection—the spontaneous hug from behind, head in the lap, or a head or neck rub after a long day at work—than you receive? What if your partner isn't very demonstrative or

physical? You have to let him know that you need more physical attention than he's giving. He can't read your mind. If you have a hard time
communicating with your partner, if you can't tell him you need a hug,
for example, you may have to go without. You can try hugging him
more often in the hope that he will reciprocate, but you can't expect
him to connect your increased affection with your need for more affection from him.

Even if you're good at communicating, you won't necessarily get all
the physical attention you want—not if you want your head rubbed
every day for half an hour as soon as you get home from work. But if
you and your partner can talk about it, and you're both willing to make
an effort, you can probably compromise.

SEX TOGETHER

What is there to know? You're both men. You both have the same
equipment. You know what you want. It should be so simple.

Every man brings different sexual needs, expectations, attitudes, and
experience to a relationship. And, as in all other areas of a relationship,
two people rarely match up exactly. So, most likely, accommodating
each other's needs and desires will take some working out. Keep in
mind that achieving and maintaining a mutually satisfying and safer sex
life is not as easy as deciding where to go for vacation, and the efforts
need to be on-going.

Even Fantasyland super-hunks, such as Robbie and Lance in Gordon
Merrick's *The Great Urge Downward*, have sexual problems. For example, Lance's self-hate/homophobia leads him to seek increasingly de-
grading sexual experiences with multiple partners, despite Robbie's
desire for monogamy. And at first, Lance doesn't respond to Robbie—
he can't get it up.

So for both Fantasyland demi-gods and mere mortals, there is much
to talk about when it comes to sex.

Playing Safe Together

Unless both you and your partner never had unsafe sex before you met
each other and have been 100 percent monogamous—not 99 percent,
100 percent—since before the Human Immunodeficiency Virus
(HIV)—the virus experts believe causes AIDS—appeared in the United
States (an unknown date), no discussion about sex that involves more
than one person can begin without a discussion of "safer sex."

AIDS (Acquired Immune Deficiency Syndrome) is a disease that de-
stroys the body's ability to fight off other diseases. HIV (previously

called HTLV-III/LAV) can be transmitted when blood, semen, and vaginal secretions, are passed from one body to another, i.e. through intimate sexual contact or through intravenous drug use where needles are shared. As currently defined, AIDS is believed to be fatal. (See Chapter 13, "Health," for a more detailed discussion of AIDS.)

What if you've both had the HIV antibody test (the only test widely available as of the publication of this book) and tested negative? Is it then safe for you to have unsafe sex with each other? Possibly not. (Because the HIV antibody may remain undetectable from six to fourteen months, you must be tested a second time at a later date.) And definitely not if you and/or your partner continue to have unsafe sex outside of your relationship. The current test, which shows the presence of antibodies, or cells the body produces after exposure to the virus, is not 100 percent accurate. In any case, it is best to discuss your concerns and circumstances with an expert at the location where you have been tested or call one of the safer sex or AIDS resources listed in the "Resources" section of Chapter 13.

The safer sex guidelines outlined in this section were drawn from the most current information at the time this book was published in 1988. No doubt, more accurate testing for the HIV virus will be available not long after this book is printed, and more precise guidelines as to what is classified as safe and unsafe. However, it is unlikely that safer sex will soon become a thing of the past. Even the most optimistic researchers predict that a vaccine is years away. And for those already infected— you can carry and pass along the HIV virus without suffering from any of the symptoms of the disease—safer sex may be something you and your partner(s) will have to live with for a lifetime.

Many foolish men have convinced themselves that they are exempt from the need to practice safer sex. And many such men have already died. Men in couple relationships give all sorts of reasons to defend their exemption from safer sexual practices including: "Neither of us was *that* sexually active before we met each other"; "We've been together since 1983 and we're feeling just fine"; "We've had unsafe sex since we got together a year ago, and anything that could happen, already has."

Wrong, wrong, wrong! You can contract the disease from one exposure. And even if you've been feeling fine since you got together with your partner three years ago, that does not mean you are free of HIV, because the incubation period can be many years long, in some cases perhaps more than a decade. To date, no one really knows. And the risk of contracting HIV increases with the number of exposures. So you may not have passed the virus along to one another even if you've been having unsafe sex for a year or more, but you might with another year of unsafe sex.

However much you love your partner, the tragic reality is that you can kill him. And he can kill you.

In researching this book I was stunned to find couples who continue sexual practices that they know are dangerous, but have dismissed the risk of AIDS as something that doesn't apply to them, even when they've acknowledged that they've engaged in sexual behavior prior to or during the relationship that would put them at risk.

Dennis and Terry are one such couple. When they became lovers in 1983, Terry had little concern that Dennis could infect him with HIV because Dennis had not been involved with men for several years. But Terry *was* concerned about the possibility of passing something on to Dennis.

Terry: I was a little bit concerned because I had played around. I wasn't too worried for me, but I was worried for Dennis. But it didn't stop us from doing any specific sex acts.

Dennis: There have been times over the past three years when we've stopped to discuss whether certain things were dangerous. I think my feeling has always been that I feel very secure in the relationship, that I put my trust in it. We've been together almost three years and I assume Terry is healthy and that I'm healthy. I don't think much about it. It hasn't affected what we do sexually.

Couldn't couples who want to practice unsafe sex take the HIV antibody test to find out if they're truly at great risk? Yes, but there is lots of debate over the advisability of taking the test. (See Chapter 11, "Insurance," and Chapter 13, "Health," for more information on the HIV antibody test.)

During the first two years—beginning in 1983—of our relationship, Scott and I disagreed over safer sex. He couldn't understand my unyielding stand on safer sex. (At first that meant no anal intercourse; oral sex at the time wasn't a risk, to my mind.) As far as Scott was concerned, nice boys didn't get AIDS; he didn't know anyone who had AIDS. But as a volunteer with the Gay Men's Health Crisis in New York City, I had seen first-hand what AIDS could do: Both men I worked with had died. A year before I met Scott I also had had high-risk sex with a man who was diagnosed with AIDS a short time later. I had something to worry about. So despite Scott's wishes, I was not going to risk putting his life in danger.

I also wasn't about to let him put my life at risk. While Scott had only been out for a year before we met, most of his sexual encounters had been in San Francisco—a high-risk city for AIDS.

Scott took a 180-degree about-face in his views on safer sex when a friend and colleague walked into his office, closed the door and told Scott he had AIDS. Scott and I had spent a weekend in the country with Tim and Benjy, his partner of a year, just a few months before. They were very much in love. Scott was in shock. He no longer pressed about unsafe sex. Tim died less than a year later.

Safer sex guidelines are based on the belief that one of the two primary ways in which AIDS is transmitted is through very intimate contact, that is, intimate sexual contact during which bodily fluids are exchanged. Because there is still much to be learned about the transmission of the HIV virus, guidelines are broken down into three categories: unsafe, possibly unsafe, and safe. The guidelines listed below are drawn from several sources. *Because of the rapid pace of research, the guidelines listed are likely to change, so be certain to check with a health organization for the latest detailed information on safer sex.*

SAFER SEX GUIDELINES

UNSAFE

1. Anal Intercourse Without a Condom
Screwing without a condom is a death wish. It is associated with the highest risk of all sexual activities. Both the insertive and the receptive partners are at risk, although the latter is perhaps at greater risk of infection.

2. Oral Sex
All educated experts advise against oral sex entirely, except with the use of a condom. If you have oral sex and don't use a condom, there is the possibility that even if you don't ejaculate, pre-ejaculatory fluid containing the virus could be ingested. Don't ejaculate in your partner's mouth and don't swallow semen.

3. Rimming
Licking the anus is also extremely unsafe, because of AIDS and also because of the many other diseases and intestinal disorders you can expose yourself to when rimming. If HIV is present in fecal residue, it could easily be ingested. (To date, HIV has not been isolated in feces.) Rimming is particularly dangerous if your immune system is already suppressed.

4. Water Sports
Drinking urine is out. Getting urinated on is questionable as well because of the possibility of urine containing HIV coming in contact with a tear in the skin.

5. Sex Toys

Don't share sex toys (dildo, vibrator, butt plug, etc.). If one of you carries the virus, the toy could transmit the virus to your partner.

POSSIBLY UNSAFE

1. Anal and Oral Sex Using a Condom

Latex condoms significantly reduce the risk of exchanging bodily fluids—and HIV—during anal intercourse and oral sex. However, condoms are not 100 percent effective because of improper use during which a condom can slip off or break, and possible product failure even when the condom is used properly. Unfortunately, because no major studies have been conducted on the use of condoms during anal or oral sex there is no way to accurately gauge the failure rate in these circumstances from improper use and product failure.

Studies have been conducted, however, on the reliability of condoms in vaginal intercourse. When condoms are used during vaginal intercourse to prevent pregnancy, some studies show the effectiveness rate to be between 90 and 98 percent. But some researchers think the condom failure rate could be as high as 20 percent over the course of a year.

If you decide to have sex that requires a condom, some experts recommend that when you feel yourself ready to ejaculate, pull out and ejaculate outside of your partner's body. In that way you further reduce the chance that breakage or misuse could result in transfer of semen.

If you're new to using a condom, or uncomfortable about its use, spend some time getting familiar with one. You can practice using one by yourself (masturbation) or with your partner (mutual masturbation) before using one when having oral or anal sex with your partner.

The following guidelines for correct use of a condom were drawn in part from *Safe Sex in the Age of AIDS*, a book prepared by The Institute for the Advancement of Human Sexuality.

    a. Always use latex condoms. Natural condoms may contain microscopic holes that could allow transmission of the HIV virus.

    b. Always use new condoms.

    c. Keep a ready supply of condoms where they cannot be damaged by moisture or heat.

    d. Never "test" a condom by blowing it up.

    e. Put a dab of lubricant into the tip of the condom. This will increase sensation and prevent an air bubble from forming that could cause the condom to break.

f. Put the condom on the fully erect penis, leaving about half an inch slack at the tip to hold the ejaculate, and roll it down all the way to the bottom of the shaft. (If you are not circumcised, retract the foreskin before putting on the condom.)

g. Generously lubricate the anus before entry and lubricate the condom-clad penis.

h. Use only water-soluble lubricant. Oil-based lubricants such as Vaseline or Crisco can damage the condom.

i. Upon withdrawal, hold tightly onto the base of the condom. Make sure it does not slip.

j. After use, dispose of the condom.

Antiseptic lubricants or spermicides are sometimes mentioned (and often advertised in the gay press) as companions for use with a condom during anal intercourse to further reduce the risk of infection with HIV. There is much disagreement about whether these products are safe to use during anal intercourse or effective in reducing the risk of infection with HIV in the event there is an accidental exchange of bodily fluids. However, according to some experts, years of experience with vaginal foams and oral-vaginal contact indicates they are probably safe. And test-tube experiments with a number of spermicides show that in small concentrations they kill HIV. For these reasons some doctors recommend the use of antiseptic lubricants or spermicides as a back-up when using condoms. Others caution against their use during anal intercourse until more is known about the effectiveness and the safety of these products. Check with a national or local health organization for the latest information.

2. Deep Kissing
Although deep kissing appears to be an unlikely way to contract AIDS—HIV has been found in very low concentrations in saliva—as of 1988, doctors are not willing to say deep kissing is safe, which is why it is categorized as possibly unsafe.

SAFE

1. Dry kissing

2. Hugging

3. Massage

4. Body-to-body rubbing
No risk as long as semen does not come in contact with any orifice or cut or break in the skin.

5. Mutual masturbation—with the same provisions as number four.

The Impact of AIDS

AIDS has had a dramatic negative impact on the sex lives of many couples, significantly affecting the things they do together and how often they have sex. There is no good across-the-board remedy for reducing the fear of AIDS, and safer sex is here to stay for the foreseeable future. But time seems to help; and it also helps to know that you are not alone, nor are you crazy if the fear of AIDS has hurt sexual relations between you and your partner and if you find that safer sex is not quite as much fun as was sex in the days before AIDS.

For Gary and Mitch, who have been together for three years, AIDS has "damaged the intensity and frequency" of their sexual relationship. Gary and Mitch ended sexual contacts outside their relationship in part because of a fear of contracting AIDS, and they changed their sexual practices.

Mitch: It scared us terribly. It just started coming too close to home. First the ex-lover of a guy I used to date died of AIDS, then a guy I used to date died, then a close friend died of AIDS. And then I wound up in the hospital with severe diarrhea a year and a half ago. That just threw us into a complete panic.

Mitch did not have AIDS. He tested negative for the HIV test. But he and Gary are still very cautious. Gary has not had the HIV test, and does not plan to:

Now I think we're glad for mutual masturbation and a porno flick. I do get very frustrated and irritated. It took me forty years to appreciate anal sex and now I can't do it.

Anal sex is not necessarily out of the question, but for many of the couples I spoke with, the fears of a broken condom or that one will slip off, is enough to keep them from doing anything that requires the use of one. It's hard to concentrate on having fun when you're worried you might kill each other.

Irwin and Duane, a doctor and nurse couple, did not practice safer sex for the first year of their relationship. During their second year together they became acutely aware of AIDS through their work and began practicing "quasi-safe" sex. They still deep kissed and had oral sex.

Irwin: We were having quasi-safe sex for a year when we decided to go get tested. So we got tested and I ended up being positive and Duane negative, which was a surprise. We still don't understand.
Duane: We were devastated that Irwin was positive. Irwin went into a real funk

over it. Then of course I drew a hard line about sex. "We're gonna have rigid
safe sex."

Irwin: You know, you put on the plastic lunch bags.

Duane: The rigid safe sex went on for a couple of months, which translated into
no sex. It ended our sex life temporarily. It's still not wonderful. We were so
trained with the sex we were all brought up on that it's really difficult to
eroticize safer sex.

Irwin: I'm terrified of transmitting anything to Duane.

Duane: It's like every time you make love, you're risking somebody's life. Even
if you're safe, there's a risk. We've managed some reasonable alternatives that
we find gratifying, but it's not perfect. We do a lot of mutual masturbation,
and there's a lot of physical expression—a lot of kissing, hugging, cuddling,
touching, but less sexual expression.

Bruce, 33, and Jeff, 22, have been a couple for a little more than a
year, but they got together before either knew much about AIDS.

Bruce: Safer sex wasn't all that structured yet in New Orleans. We met at the
bar and went home and carried on like passionate mad dogs. We both had
intercourse with each other before things changed.

Jeff: Then Bruce's best friend called him and told him that he had AIDS. It was
like someone opened the freezer. Bruce wasn't interested; sex repulsed him
for a while.

Bruce: Every time I started to have sex, I thought about my friend being dead.
I was always being turned off. I was always afraid of Jeff popping up and
saying, "I have AIDS." Jeff had had relatively little sexual exposure. I, on the
other hand, had lived with a man for almost eight years. But while I had been
monogamous for six and a half of those years, my lover was very, very promis-
cuous in the seediest kinds of ways—bookstores, baths. He did them all. So
I've had a terrible time reconciling that I might have picked up the bug from
him and given it to Jeff.

Jeff: The changeover has been difficult. When I met Bruce, he showed me there
are lots of things you could do together sexually. And all of a sudden Bruce's
friend gets AIDS and all of this wonderful fantasyland stuff gets pulled out
from under me.

Dangerous Sex

Even without the threat of AIDS there is plenty you can do to harm one
another that falls under the heading of sex. Plain and simple—don't do
anything that draws blood, cuts off circulation, or inhibits breathing. So
if you've always wanted to be tied up, be careful, avoid drugs and
alcohol while you're doing it, and use common sense. The reason I
mention drugs and alcohol is because common sense is one of the first
victims of too much of either.

If you use sex toys, don't insert anything into the rectum that's giant sized, hard plastic, or metal. If you do, you risk a perforated colon and death. Also, don't insert anything into the rectum that could slip into it—that includes the average vibrator or dildo, which is not designed for use in a rectum. If you choose to use a vibrator or dildo, only use one with a large graspable ball, or handle on the end.

This next point is common sense. Fisting (the polite phrase for insertion of the hand and possibly forearm into the rectum and colon) is dangerous and can cause serious injury—even death.

Declining Frequency and Passion

While Scott and I were still experiencing the passion of young love, my cousin Jeanette said, "Enjoy it while it lasts. I've got an example," she said, sounding a lot like the teacher she is. "If you take a jar and the first year that you're living with someone you put one jelly bean in for each time you have relations, at the end of the year you'll have a very full jar. If for the next five years you take out a jelly bean each time you have relations, you'll find at the end of that time you still have jelly beans left. And if you can live with that you can get through." I listened, but I didn't agree. It would be different for us. Our passion would last.

Our love has lasted and grown, but incredible sex six times a week is a nice memory. So is five times, four times, three times, and even two. On our long annual vacation away together, we invariably rediscover weekday sex, even everyday sex, but during the rest of the year, if it's a choice between *The New York Times* and sex, *The New York Times* usually wins.

Why is that a problem? It's not a problem if you don't think it is. I thought it was, because it's not what I expected. It's not what Scott expected. I took note every time there was a drop in frequency—and intensity. I didn't know if Scott did. For close to three years we didn't talk about it. I teased him about it, especially since I seemed to want sex more often than he did. But we never really talked about it, until I got frustrated and began to feel there was something wrong with what was happening. I began to worry that the decline would never level off, that we would wind up one of those couples I had heard about who no longer had sex. Just buddies. Did the decline in interest in sex mean anything more than a decline in interest in sex? Did we love each other any less? Had I become unattractive to him?

When I started speaking to other couples, I discovered we weren't alone. While there are a few couples who have sex every day and twice on Saturday, even after several years together, almost without exception the couples I spoke with experienced a decline in passion and frequency over time. And for many the decline was accompanied by anxiety and concern.

For Chet and John, less interest in sex at first seemed to indicate less general interest in one another. They've been together for five years.

John: We would come home from work. We were tired. We would have dinner and go to sleep. The less sex we had the more it seemed we were drifting apart.
Chet: He complained that we were acting like roommates.
John: I don't feel that way now because we spend a lot more time together now. Especially on weekends.
Chet: We hug each other all the time. He says, "I love you," more than I do. He makes me say it. He'll ask, "Do you love me?"
John: I need to know that. It makes any questions I may have go away.

When they made love several times a week, John didn't need as much verbal reassurance from Chet that he was loved. For John, Chet's desire to have sex was an automatic acknowledgment of love. When sex decreased, he at first thought Chet loved him less.

Gary and Mitch know intellectually that the decline in the frequency of sex in their relationship is not a threat to their life together, but emotionally it's another story.

Gary: The transition is a hard thing to go through because you start doubting the relationship and take it as a personal rejection.
   I realize that sex is not the basis of the relationship. Our life, our family, our friends, our service to the gay and lesbian community—these things have importance to us. Certainly our life together has importance. I don't want to diminish the importance of sex. It's not as important, but it's still important.
Mitch: I don't think that a relationship should be threatened by that decrease in sex. But it's hard not to take it personally. My fear is that I'm not as attractive to Jeff as I used to be—that I don't turn him on.

By the time Scott and I got around to talking, we were not turning each other on as we did in the old days. I was growing ever more resentful, particularly since he seemed less than eager to talk about it. One Friday night, after setting out the candles in the bathroom and luring him into the shower, I cornered him. We sat down in the tub. I told him it was time to talk.

I wasn't exactly eager to talk either. I wasn't sure what he was thinking. Who wants to hear that his lover doesn't find him as sexually desirable as he used to? But I was worried that, if we didn't talk about it, my resentment would continue to grow, which would translate into even less sex, and consequently we would grow apart; eventually we would break up. It was a frightening, yet motivating, scenario. So I cornered him for a talk despite my fears of what he might have to say. I discovered that our feelings really weren't very different, except that I wanted to talk about it and figure out if there wasn't some way we could work on making our sex life more exciting.

Scott was having a hard time adjusting to the changes. He felt sad about the decline in passion. In fact, he was "mourning" the loss of the easy and immediate passion we used to experience together.

The reality wasn't terrible, but it made us feel sad. Scott doesn't turn me on the way he did during our first months together. I love him more, but I don't want to tear off his clothes as soon as he comes through the door—unless one of us has been out of town for a week or two. And I don't turn him on the way I used to. Not that either of us wouldn't be physically capable of making love every day. He told me:

> If you put a new and attractive body in front of me, I could have sex every day. But that's like candy. A long-term relationship has meant giving up some of the sexual excitement of a new involvement. It's worth the trade-off, but sometimes I find it frustrating.

There are many reasons besides familiarity for a decline in the frequency of sex. AIDS is high on the list. But work and life crises can also intervene. For Bruce, concern for his ill father and his job commitments combined with AIDS worries to shut down his sex drive in the early months of his relationship with Jeff:

> All of a sudden my father is unemployed, he's in the hospital every other month, my job is uncertain. The last thing I'm worried about is sex and I have wonderchild over here with a constant hard-on who wants sex every morning, noon, and night, and doesn't care about working as long as he has a daily orgasm.

Greg and Neal have the kind of perspective on the decline in frequency and passion that is a reflection of their twenty-six years together. They are monogamous and don't have sex nearly as frequently as they did when they first met.

Greg: When you first get together, you hump all the time. It's not as frequent now, but it's still good when it happens.
Neal: Other things have taken on depth. It's almost as if sex has taken its proper place in the overall scheme of things. There's a broadening in the relationship where other things now enter in and assume an importance.
Greg: Sex is still important. It may not be as frequent, but I wouldn't want to live in the relationship without it.
Neal: It's still important to make that very, very personal contact.

How Often to Have It

How often is optimal? For some couples, once they settle into the relationship—after the honeymoon—that means once a week, or every other week. For others that means sex every night. My psychological bottom line is once a week. Even if I'm not into it, I feel Scott and I should make the time to have sex at least once a week. I'm not sure how I settled on that number, but that's the number I'm comfortable with. My big fear is that if it declines beyond that we won't be able to maintain a monogamous relationship.

For Scott and me, our sex drives are fairly similar, although I don't think it would bother him if we skipped a week every now and then. For couples where each man has a significantly different sex drive or different ideas about how often the two should have sex, there can be problems.

Differing sex drives can mean a lot of frustration for one partner and pressure for the other to have sex more often than he desires. For example, Patrick and Stan, both in their late twenties, have been together for two years but have yet to work out their sexual relationship in a way that satisfies both of them. Patrick could be quite happy having sex with Stan every day and masturbating during his lunch hour once or twice every day. Stan would be more than satisfied with sex once a week. Their vastly different sexual needs have been a source of tension as they've tried to reach some sort of accommodation.

If you and your partner have different sex drives—assuming your differing interests in sex are not the result of problems in your relationship—you have several alternatives. One approach is to do nothing to accommodate each other, but this will ultimately lead to relationship-threatening tension and/or conflict. Assuming you are the one who desires sex more often, a possible solution is for you to work toward a compromise by trying one of the following alternatives:

1. You can talk to your partner and let him know that you need sex more often and encourage him to try to have a little more interest.

2. You can masturbate alone more often.

3. You can masturbate when you're with your partner.

4. Your partner can bring you to orgasm without getting aroused himself.

5. You can have sex with men outside of the relationship (see Chapter 3, "Monogamy/Nonmonogamy").

Patrick recently started talking with Stan about his frustrations. It wasn't a single conversation, but one that went on over a period of several weeks and months. Stan did his best to show more of an interest in sex and to be the initiator every now and then. They expect the issue will have to be discussed periodically. Patrick decided that masturbating more often wouldn't help because he was already masturbating every day. The third and fourth options on the list they haven't tried yet because Patrick feels uncomfortable about them ("It would be embarrassing"). Patrick doesn't consider number 5 to be an option because he's committed to a monogamous relationship, although Stan has said it would be okay with him if Patrick went outside and had sex with other men. Patrick isn't interested.

The fundamental principle here is communication. If you can effectively communicate your wishes nonverbally—putting your less-interested partner's hand on your very often interested erect penis—and he takes the hint, you won't need to talk about it. Most likely you will need to talk. Communicating can be very difficult for many men, so it may take the help of a professional to get you talking.

Finding the Time

There is always time to have sex as far as the clock goes. But once the spontaneity of sex that characterizes the early part of the relationship has passed, you have to make time—create space—in which you can get in the mood and warm up to each other. If you're one of those lucky few who doesn't need time to separate from work and family responsibilities, anxieties, and daily headaches to warm up to your partner, I envy you.

Gary and Mitch are very involved with work and the local gay community and consequently maintain busy schedules—schedules that don't always allow for time together, let alone sex.

Gary: We're always so busy during the week that if we're going to have sex, it's going to be on a Friday, Saturday, or Sunday. But usually on Friday we're recovering from the week. Saturday we're usually so busy running errands. And on Sunday, in the afternoon, maybe.

For many people, there isn't enough leisure time for sex to be spontaneous, particularly when every other aspect of life is rigidly scheduled. So time often needs to be set aside for sex. If it's your style to schedule your life tightly, maybe you should accept the necessity of penciling in time to be physical together.

The formal approach is not for everyone, however. Scott and I have tried on a couple of occasions to mark out time for sex on a calendar, but neither of us managed to enforce the schedule. So in general we try to leave at least Sunday morning free. By then we've usually had a chance to relax a bit from the work week and catch up on sleep. And we also try to get to bed before 10:30 one night a week just to have some time to be physical.

Terry and Dennis have found that they have to pay attention to making enough time for sex if they want to continue to have sex about twice a week. Neither cares for the idea of a formal schedule.

Terry: The secret is to pay attention to each other.

Dennis: We both notice it, but not necessarily at the same time. Sometimes one of us will become aware that over the past two or three weeks we've only had sex two or three times. One of us will say, "What's going on?" We talk about it. There's often a little bit of defensiveness. We try to figure out if we're overworking.

Terry: We've worked ways around it. We decide we have to get to bed earlier. A lot of times it's just staying up too late and we're too tired.

Dennis: And if we do have sex when we're tired it's qualitatively not so great.

Terry: It isn't that we have to force ourselves to have sex, but we have to put ourselves into situations where we warm up to each other.

Dennis: Don't come home from work so late. Make a little preparation for it.

Terry: Still, once a week we have incredible sex.

Initiating Sex

If you and your partner are competitive, you like to be in charge exclusively, or you partner always likes to be in charge, the question of who initiates sex can result in conflict. Both of you can't always initiate. You can trade off, unless one doesn't mind always initiating and the other doesn't mind waiting until the other does the initiating. If you're unhappy about who initiates when, and your partner hasn't taken your nonverbal hints, you'll have to talk about it with him and try to reach an accommodation.

What to Do

As Dr. Ruth Westheimer says in her book, *Dr. Ruth's Guide to Good Sex:* "In the infinite varieties of sex there are things you will want to do and things you won't. Every human being has boundaries when it comes to sex, and mapping those boundaries with an individual human being can be very complicated. There are things you want to do very much, things you will do to please the other person, and things that— yech! Don't be pressured into doing things you really don't want to do. It may only be something you don't want to do right now. In six months or a year you may feel very differently. . . . You have a right to your boundaries. Stick up for them."

Because you love your partner, you may find yourself willing to do things sexually that you don't find particularly pleasurable. That's fine as long as you don't give in to your partner's wishes so often that you begin to resent him. You can also do an exchange, for example, "Okay, I'll lick your toes if you give me a thigh massage."

Communication is the key—particularly early communication. For example, if you're not fond of anal sex, for whatever reason, better to let your partner know early that you don't like getting screwed, or screwing, than to wait two years, letting resentment build—"He always gets his way"—before exploding one night in bed.

Improving It

There are plenty of self-help books on the shelves, packed with ideas on how to spice up your sex life with your partner. Almost all are geared to the straight reader, but are helpful nonetheless. At their core all of them stress the need for communication and cooperation between partners. If you're interested in working on improving your sex life and your partner has no interest, all the self-help books in the world won't do you much good. Assuming you can convince your partner to take some interest in the subject, there are plenty of alternatives to choose from.

Not all experts agree on what is best for improving your sex life with your partner. The following are ideas—in brief, and sometimes conflicting—gathered from experts, couples, and from my own experience.

1. Talk about your desires with each other—what you like and don't like; your fantasies and ideas.

2. Avoid routine. Try acting out some of the desires and fantasies you learned about from talking with each other. Try sex in the living room once in a while if you always use the bedroom.

3. Schedule time in your week for sex and sex discussions.

4. Save time at the end of the day just to be physical without having sex, i.e., hugging, etc.

5. Learn how to massage each other.

6. Go away for a weekend.

7. Do things together that you find sexually stimulating, for example, dancing or working out together.

8. Use pornography for inspiration if you find that helps; or, if you find it doesn't help, just adds to your frustration, or leads to resentment

from your partner, forget the pornography and concentrate on each other. Some experts believe that pornography leaves the user with unrealistic expectations, and therefore unable to enjoy his partner. These specialists recommend not using pornography.

9. If you find you have little or no desire for your partner and you masturbate and/or have sex outside of your relationship, reduce or eliminate sexual activity with anyone but your partner.

10. There are couples who swear by inviting other men to join them and their partner in bed, or who each go out on their own to have sex with other men. Others find this only hurts their sexual relationship with each other. If this is an option that you and your partner are considering, before you go out and invite your best friend or a stranger to join you in bed, read Chapter 3, "Monogamy/Non-monogamy," to learn about the potential conflicts.

11. Reduce or eliminate reliance on drugs or alcohol. Excessive use of chemicals impairs the senses.

12. There are two schools of thought about fantasy. One school says it's perfectly okay to fantasize about having sex with another man, for example, while you're having sex with your partner. The other school believes it's dishonest or detrimental to a sexual relationship. Common sense seems to be the rule. If an occasional fantasy improves your sex life with your partner, go ahead and enjoy yourself. If you come to rely exclusively on fantasy and find it is not improving your sex life or is just frustrating you, reduce or eliminate fantasizing during sex with your partner. Although, that may be easier said than done.

Not Having Sex

There are couples who no longer have sex together. If you're in such a relationship and both you and your partner are satisfied, then there's really no problem. If you no longer have a sexual relationship and one or both of you wants one, it's time to see a counselor, psychologist, and/or a sex therapist. (See the "Resources" section at the end of this chapter for information on finding help.)

SEX ALONE

Almost without exception, the men I spoke with who are in relationships masturbate. Some talk about it with their partners. Some don't. And almost all agreed that they had no objection to their partner masturbating as long as it didn't interfere with their sexual relationship.

It's simple to keep masturbation from harming your sex life with your partner. If you find that masturbation reduces your interest in sex with your partner, don't do it, or at least don't do it on the same day or within a few days of when you have sex with your partner. If you're not sure what impact masturbation has on your interest in sex with your lover, don't masturbate for several weeks or more and see what happens.

Should you talk about masturbation with your lover? It's up to you and your partner. For some men masturbation is a private matter. They may be very open about their experiences with other men, but when it comes to solo masturbation they prefer to remain private. The whole subject makes many men uncomfortable.

When I interviewed Chet and John, I asked them about masturbation. Chet said, "It never even crosses my mind to do it. If it's not with John, it's not at all." Chet turned to John, I think expecting him to say the same thing. John started laughing. It was obvious they had never talked about it in their six years together. Chet was surprised to hear John's answer:

> There are times when he's not been there and it's been very easy to do it. I can fantasize about him. I've almost felt guilty if I've done it and he wants sex the next night. Will it be as good? It would only be a big issue if that were becoming a major part of my sex life.

Dennis and Terry talk about masturbation now, but they didn't when they first got together.

Dennis: It's sort of a fun little thing we talk about. Sometimes we do it together. Sometimes alone. If one of us is away, we come home and ask how many times the other has done it. "Only nine."
Terry: At first I felt guilty.
Dennis: I never felt guilty. It's a sweet thing.
Terry: If I felt I were taking away from our sex life I wouldn't do it.

SEX WITH OTHERS

As discussed in Chapter 3, sex with others, either ensemble (three-ways) or on your own, is an option individuals in relationships often choose. This section is about the safety of having sex with someone other than your lover.

These days, the specter of AIDS, as well as the long list of other sexually transmitted diseases, should be of concern to all men who choose to have sex outside of their relationships. Most of the couples I spoke with who have sex outside their relationships have cut back on outside contacts. When they do seek sex with someone other than their partners, they mostly practice safer sex. But that doesn't necessarily end the concern about AIDS, particularly when honesty and the definition of safer sex are questions.

Bruce and Jeff have both had sex with men outside their relationship, although Jeff has been the more active of the two.

Bruce: I don't really care if Jeff's monogamous or not as long as he practices safer sex, which really worries me at times because he tends to be very impulsive, and he's not the most honest person this side of the moon. [Turning to Jeff.] Don't get defensive. I know he's been out and that he's done this or that because he tells me, but I wonder about what he doesn't tell me.

Jeff: I know a couple, and when Bruce and I were apart—anytime that I've felt that I had to be with someone—I've stayed with that couple. They practice safer sex with each other. That blew me away. They wear a condom when they have anal intercourse.

Bruce: We never did.

Jeff: Yet I didn't wear one when I screwed them. They didn't seem to mind. I stayed with them a couple of weekends.

Peter and Ned had plenty of time to watch from Hawaii as AIDS spread. Both tested negative for the HIV antibody and intend to keep free from contact with the virus. Although they agreed to an open arrangement from the start of their relationship, they have just about eliminated outside sexual contacts after a friend was diagnosed with AIDS. According to Peter: "Anybody we would have sex with, it would be safer sex."

A final note on sex with others. If you're having problems in your sexual relationship with your partner and think that sex with men outside your relationship might be the solution, forget it. That's called avoiding your problems. First, work on fixing what is wrong with the sexual relationship with your partner. Then you can talk about sex with men outside your relationship. Otherwise you're inviting further deterioration in your sexual relationship, if not in your emotional relationship as well.

SEXUAL PROBLEMS

Sooner or later, all men will experience some problem in their sexual relationship. Sexual problems, some of which have already been discussed in this chapter, range from differences in, or lack of, desire and premature ejaculation to impotence (or erectile dysfunction) and compulsive sexual behavior. Some problems are minor, last only a short time, and can be cured by a little attention, a good book on massage, a bottle of baby oil, or perhaps a book on male sexuality. But if your problems are long-term, persistent, or defy the encouraging words of one of the books recommended in "Resources," it's time to seek professional help. A professional may not have a miracle cure, but he/she can help you unravel the origin of the problem and design a course of action to put you and/or your partner back on track.

If you think it's time for your partner, or for both of you together, to seek the help of a professional—a psychologist, sex therapist, or doctor—and you haven't discussed the possibility with your lover before, there are a number of ways to broach the subject to him. The least constructive way is to say, "You have a problem, you need to see a sex therapist." Even if your partner has the problem (no sex drive, uncooperative penis), you may be part of the cause and will definitely have to participate in the cure. Telling your partner it's his problem will only make him defensive—and probably angry—and won't get either of you anywhere. A more constructive approach is to start by saying, "We have a problem. I think we need to seek professional help." And if your partner refuses? Go on your own, with the hope that the professional you consult can help you to find a way to include your partner.

Compulsive Sexual Behavior

Compulsive sexual behavior takes many forms, including compulsive masturbation and engaging in sex with multiple partners, but the common thread is the inability to control or change that behavior even if you want to. See the "Addiction" section of Chapter 13 for a detailed discussion of compulsive sexual behavior and what you can do about it.

Impotence

According to Eileen MacKenzie, Executive Director of Impotents Anonymous, more than 10 million men of all ages in the United States suffer from chronic impotence—"the inability to gain and maintain an erection satisfactory for intercourse." If such a condition persists for five to six weeks, she recommends that you consult a specialist. The worst thing you can do is wait months or years before seeking treatment. If your partner is the one who is impotent and he's reluctant to seek help, you can find out how you can help him and your relationship by contacting I-ANON, an organization for the partners of men who are impotent. (See the "Resources" at the end of this chapter.)

Impotence *is* treatable. It's caused by many things, including psychological factors, but 60 to 75 percent of impotence is physiologically based.

Causes

The list of possible causes of the sexual conflicts and problems discussed in this chapter is long. The following general list will give you an idea of what could possibly be causing the sexual problems that you may be experiencing.

1. Work tensions/unemployment

2. Depression

3. Relationship problems, such as anger or resentment

4. Money problems

5. Medication

6. Alcoholism or drug abuse

7. Illness or physical limitations

8. Fear—e.g., fear of gagging during oral sex, or of pain during anal sex; fear of giving or becoming infected with the HIV virus

9. Lack of time together

10. Too much masturbation

11. Too much sexual activity outside the relationship

12. Boredom

13. Past sexual or psychological trauma, e.g., incest, rape, impotence with women, etc.

14. Homophobia or other coming out problems such as guilt, religious conflicts, etc.

15. Age—later in life, the penis doesn't respond as quickly, needs direct physical stimulation, and is much slower to recover for another round

16. Habit—being accustomed to having sex with men you don't know; or being accustomed to masturbating and reaching orgasm in three seconds flat

RESOURCES

Finding Professional Help

The help you decide to seek depends upon the problem(s) you're having. You have several choices. If you think the problems you or your partner are having are physiological, you can start with a visit to a doctor who has experience treating sexual disorders. Impotents Anonymous will provide referrals to doctors in your area who are experienced in sexual disorders and are gay sensitive (see "Organizations," below). If the doctor finds the problem to be other than physiological, he can refer you on to a sex therapist or psychologist. If you have serious relationship problems that you think have had an impact on your sex life, a psychologist may be the best person to see.

Finding a reputable sex therapist who is familiar and comfortable with gay couples is relatively easy in metropolitan areas. Typically, the local gay help line or gay health organization can provide a list of potential sex therapists to choose from.

If that approach fails, or you live in a small town or rural area, you can start your search by calling the American Association of Sex Educators, Counselors, and Therapists (AASECT). This group certifies educators, counselors, and sex therapists nationwide and will make a referral to a certified sex therapist in your area.

For more information on how to find a medical doctor or mental health professional, see Chapter 13, "Health."

Organizations

American Association of Sex Educators, Counselors, and Therapists (AASECT), 11 Dupont Circle NW #220, Washington, DC 20036, 202–462–1171

> AASECT will make a referral to a certified sex therapist. However, the organization does not guarantee that the therapists they recommend have experience with, or are comfortable with, treating gay couples. You will have to find that out when you call the therapist. Once you've been given a referral, call the therapist and ask a few questions. For example, you should ask if the therapist has had experience working with gay couples, what his/her views are on homosexuality, etc. If you like what you hear, arrange for an interview to make certain the therapist is someone you and your partner can work with. Discuss the possible treatment and the anticipated cost. If you don't like what you hear during that interview, call another therapist and start the process over again.

Impotents Anonymous (for Impotent Men)
I-ANON (for partners of impotent men)

> These two organizations, both of which are affiliate members of the Impotence Institute of America, a nonprofit educational organization, are dedicated to helping impotent men and their partners. Impotents Anonymous (I.A.) and I-ANON have nearly one hundred chapters nationwide, and while none are specifically for gay men at the present time organization rules require that all chapters be open to gay men and their partners. "We never use the word 'wife.' We always say 'partner.'" Meetings are held regularly at chapters nationwide.
>
> To get printed information on the subject of impotence, send a standard business size, stamped, self-addressed envelope to:

Impotents Anonymous (I.A.) or I-ANON, 119 South Ruth Street, Maryville, TN 37801, 615–983–6064

I.A. and I-ANON prefer that you write, not call. If you write to request information, you will be sent a two-page letter with information on impotence and a brochure that explains what information and services are available (including referrals to local organization chapters and referrals to doctors) and how to make use of those services.

Gay-Specific Books

Remarkably, there are few guides to sex for gay men. Even more remarkably, none are up to date. I am listing the two major books with reservations, primarily because neither sufficiently acknowledges the dangerous reality of AIDS.

The Joy of Gay Sex: An Intimate Guide for Gay Men to the Pleasures of a Gay Lifestyle, by Dr. Charles Silverstein and Edmund White, 1975; reprinted 1986. Pocket Books, 1230 Avenue of the Americas, New York, NY 10020

This is an A (Androgyny) to W (Wrestling) guide to the "Gay Lifestyle." The only reference to AIDS is a notice at the beginning of the book that states: "AIDS may be sexually transmitted. The advice and/or information included in this book should be considered in light of the present understanding of AIDS." Ironically, one of the few things known about Acquired Immune Deficiency Syndrome is that it *is* sexually transmitted. Written during the full flush of 1970s gay liberation, the overall tone of the book is also dated.

Men Loving Men: A Gay Sex Guide and Consciousness Book, by Mitch Walker, 1977. Gay Sunshine Press, PO Box 40397, San Francisco, CA 94140

First published in 1977, and updated in 1985, only the "Gay Health" chapter was revised. You can learn plenty about techniques in this book.

Safer Sex and AIDS Books and Pamphlets

Because information concerning AIDS and safer sex changes so rapidly, I have not listed any books or pamphlets here because they will be out of date even before this book is printed. Your best resource for information is a local health organization. For that information, see the "Resources" section of Chapter 13.

General Books

The Joy of Touch: The Connoisseur's Guide to Touch Techniques for Stimulation, Relaxation, and Healthful Well-Being, by Dr. Russ A. Rueger, 1981. Simon & Schuster, 1230 Avenue of the Americas, New York, NY 10020

While this superb book features photographs of a straight couple, almost all the information it has to offer on touch and massage is just as helpful for gay couples.

Dr. Ruth's Guide to Good Sex, by Dr. Ruth Westheimer, 1983. Warner Books, 666 Fifth Avenue, New York, NY 10103

A frank, fun, and humorous book, written primarily for straight people, about just about anything you want to know about sex, including a section called "Recipe for a Sexual Marriage."

Male Sexuality: The First Book That Tells the Truth About Men, Sex, and Pleasure, by Bernie Zilbergeld, 1978. Bantam Books, 666 Fifth Avenue, New York, NY 10103

This sharp-witted and enlightened guide to sex and men, though written with straight men and women in mind, is the book to read if you read only one book on sex. Zilbergeld works hard to bust popular myths and includes exercises designed to "increase understanding and pleasure."

CHAPTER 9

Legalizing Your Relationship

"If something happens to him, the house should be mine."

You and your lover may manage to spend decades together without realizing that, in the eyes of the law, your relationship is meaningless in most cases. You have the same rights and privileges as do any other two unrelated people who live together. When you want to visit your lover in the hospital, you are just another unrelated friend. When you buy property together, you are simply business partners. If you wind up in court over a legal dispute, more often than not you will be viewed as two unrelated individuals. In the eyes of the law you are not family. However, there fortunately is a lot you can do to make up for the legal blind spots.

In researching this book, time and time again I came across men who didn't take notice, chose to ignore, or simply overlooked the importance of putting together the legal documents necessary to protect their relationship and their personal interests as much as is possible by the force of law. I repeatedly spoke with or heard stories about couples who found they had no legal recourse, or that recourse meant going to court or taking an ex-lover to court. The horror stories ranged from a man who lost his home because it had been in his lover's name and there was no will to a man who could not oversee the medical care of his critically ill lover.

The information provided in this chapter should help you construct a legal framework by which to protect your relationship, each other, and your personal interests should your relationship come to an end or should one of you die. This chapter is *not* a guide to using the court system. All of the information and recommended documents discussed are meant to keep you *out* of court—to save you the expense, trauma, and heartbreak of a legal system that does not generally recognize the legitimacy of male-male relationships.

LEGAL OPTIONS FOR FORMALIZING YOUR RELATIONSHIP

Two men cannot get married. The implications are far more serious than you may realize. Without the legal rights that are granted by a marriage license, no matter how many years you have been together, you do not have the right to make medical or financial decisions for your lover in the event he becomes incapacitated, you may not be allowed access to him if he is in an intensive care unit, you will not automatically inherit his property and, in the event your relationship ends, you are not protected by divorce laws. You can, however, approximate or duplicate many of the rights of a marriage license with several of the documents discussed in this section, including Durable Power of Attorney, Designation of Preference, Will, and Living Together Contract.

You won't want to give each other many of the legal privileges outlined here in the first months of your relationship. You have to have tremendous trust in a partner to give him the legal right to make decisions concerning your life. But if you are together long enough, there will likely come a time when you consider yourselves the equivalent of a "married" couple and will want the legal rights and privileges of a "married" couple.

When you draw up any of the legal documents discussed in this section, do so with the help of a local attorney who is experienced in working with gay couples. You need the help of a professional to guarantee that you are drawing up these documents in accordance with your state's laws.

Durable Power of Attorney and Designation of Preference

The Durable Power of Attorney and the Designation of Preference documents together come as close as is currently possible to duplicating many of the medical and financial decision-making rights and privileges that are automatically granted to legally married couples.

The Durable Power of Attorney permits you and your partner to designate each other as the person you each choose to make medical and financial decisions for one another in the event that one of you cannot make such decisions for himself. In the absence of a Durable Power of Attorney, the courts would appoint someone other than you, probably a parent or sibling, to be a "guardian" or "conservator" to make those decisions for your lover. In most states a Durable Power of Attorney is a legally recognized document. In those states that don't recognize a Durable Power of Attorney, you can use a Designation of Preference—the name some lawyers give to what is essentially a legal letter that is signed by you, two witnesses, and your attorney—as a substitute. Unfortunately, a Designation of Preference does not have the force of law. But while a court is not obligated to recognize a Designation of Preference, it may be enough to convince a court to honor your wishes.

In a Designation of Preference used to substitute for a Durable Power of Attorney, you would name your lover as the person you prefer to have named by the court to oversee your medical care in the event you are unable to make medical decisions yourself. You would also name your lover as the person you prefer to have named by the court to sign your checks, make deposits, handle business affairs, etc., in the event you are unable to handle your own business and financial concerns.

In addition to substituting for a Durable Power of Attorney, you can use a Designation of Preference to name your lover as the person who should have priority to see you if you are hospitalized, and the person who will see that your written instructions for disposition of your body and funeral arrangements are carried out. The Designation of Preference is the appropriate document in which to state your detailed wishes concerning funeral or memorial arrangements from who is to be invited to what music is to be played. Again, this document does not have the force of law behind it, but it may be enough to get you admitted to a hospital intensive care unit to visit your lover.

When drawing up both the Durable Power of Attorney and Designation of Preference documents, some attorneys recommend that you specifically acknowledge family members and then exclude them in order to reduce the chance that they can challenge it. For example, such a passage in a Durable Power of Attorney governing medical care might read:

> I love and respect my mother, brother, sister, uncle, aunt, and my grandparents, and hereby exclude them from making any decisions concerning my medical care in the event I am unable to make those decisions for myself.

It's also advisable to let your family know that you've given your partner the legal authority to make medical and/or financial decisions for you in the event you become seriously ill. By discussing this with them in advance, you reduce the chances your family will challenge your stated wishes.

When you and your partner travel, take copies of your Durable Power of Attorney and Designation of Preference documents. If you

don't have copies of the signed documents with you when you're half
way across the continent on vacation, they will do you no good.

Power of Attorney

There is also a document called a Power of Attorney and it's often
confused with a Durable Power of Attorney. Unlike a Durable Power
of Attorney, a Power of Attorney's legal powers terminate upon in-
capacitation. For example, if your lover signs a standard Power of Attorney giving you the right to sign his checks and make financial decisions
for him and he later becomes incapacitated, the standard Power of
Attorney would no longer be valid. A Durable Power of Attorney would
still be valid. The standard Power of Attorney is commonly used, for
example, to give a friend, attorney, or family member the legal right
to sign your checks and make deposits for a specific period of time. You
might wish to do that if you plan to be out of the country for an
extended period of time.

Will

Without wills, you risk leaving one another in a precarious legal position
if, for example, your lover dies and the house you share is in his name.
Without a will, his family members are legally next in line to inherit his
assets, even if you jointly owned the house. New York attorney Mark
Senak says that, without a will, "A family can come in and strip the
house bare like Sherman attacking Atlanta."

If you and your lover live in a property he owns, or in a rental
apartment whose lease is only in his name, and you don't have a will
that states otherwise, the courts often automatically assume that the
contents of the home belong exclusively to the partner who has title to
the home or whose name appears on the lease.

By both of you spelling out in wills who is to inherit what, you may
be saved the anguish of fighting off relatives who want the bedroom set,
books, your lover's bowling trophy, even his personal letters. If your
intention is to leave one another the bulk of the furnishings and personal possessions, explicitly state in your wills that you leave all of your
furnishings and personal possessions to the other, except for those specifically identified as intended for other individuals. Make certain that
your lawyer includes a provision in your will for the distribution of your
property should your lover predecease (die before) you or in the event
you die simultaneously (in an accident for example). Many states have
statutes that deem that your beneficiary predeceased you in the case of
simultaneous death. Then, in effect, you would each predecease the
other and provisions made in your wills in the event your lover prede-

ceased you would be honored. In these states you won't need an additional provision for simultaneous death because your property will be distributed according to your already stated wishes. A local attorney will be able to advise you as to what is required in your state.

There are plenty of things you can leave to one another without a will. For example, jointly owned property (shared legal title), or joint bank accounts where there is right of survivorship do not require a will for them to be inherited by the surviving partner; insurance passes automatically to beneficiaries; joint trusts can be passed automatically upon death to the survivor.

A will can be as broad—"I leave all personal and real property to my companion-in-life, Rollie Dunbar"—or as detailed—"I leave my silver pen to Uncle Harry, my opera-record collection to my friend Lashe Dejinero . . ."—as you choose. And you can spell out funeral arrangements as well. (See Chapter 15, "Aging and Loss.")

Since you and your lover may want to will significant parts of your estates to someone outside your family—each other—Mark Senak warns that the court could be suspicious. If your lover dies you should be prepared to supply additional affidavits and testimony from witnesses to satisfy the court that your lover was competent and not coerced at the time he signed his will. This may be required before the will is probated (validated by a court).

If you or your lover have any concerns that family members may try to challenge your wills, there is a way to build disincentive into your will. Attorneys vary in their recommended methods but, for example, John could leave his parents $20,000, and each of his two siblings $10,-000, and the rest of his estate to his lover, Paul. He can write in his will, "If any beneficiaries contest the will and lose, they will lose their own bequest as well."

Here again, if you exclude your family from your will, it is advisable to first specifically acknowledge them and then exclude them. This makes a challenge to the will more difficult.

A will is also the document in which you should state your preferences concerning the disposition of your body—cremation or burial—and other preferences, such as disposition of the ashes if you are cremated and burial site, if you are not. Details that are likely to change over time, such as the list of people you want invited to a memorial service, should be stated in a Designation of Preference.

If you and your lover keep your wills in safe deposit boxes and your wills contain instructions for disposition of your body and funeral preferences, keep in mind that following the death of your lover, his safe deposit box is likely to be sealed. In such a case, a court order will be required for you to regain access to it and this could take several weeks—long after your lover has been buried or cremated according to someone else's wishes. Therefore, either make sure the safe deposit box is in both your names, or keep copies of your wills in an easily accessible place—and make certain each of you knows where they are stored.

One final note of caution: Each state has its own laws and customs concerning wills, and the courts can be very exacting. If you don't follow proper procedures according to the laws of your state, you may be wasting your time drawing up a will because it could be invalid. If you're going to write a will, at the very least have it reviewed by a local, experienced lawyer.

Living Together Contract

While marriage vows often include the phrase "till death do us part," marriage laws make certain provisions for the possibility that the relationship may die before the two newlyweds. In a legal marriage you don't have to plan the distribution of property in the event of a divorce unless you want a more specific arrangement than your state's marriage laws provide for. For gay couples, nothing may be assumed; nothing is automatic. As with your wills, you should plan for the possibility that your relationship will end. This is the primary purpose of a "living together" contract.

A living together contract may be as detailed as you and your lover like. It may cover far more than the division of property, including, for example, division of house-cleaning responsibilities. However advisable it is for gay couples to write and sign a living together contract, most couples don't do it. "But they should," notes Mark Senak, speaking from the experience of arguing cases in court on the rubble of decades-long relationships.

In the event you split with your partner, a living together contract is meant to keep you out of court by providing mutually agreed-upon methods for disentangling your financial/property affairs. Without such an agreement you may, according to Mark Senak, "be left with a mess that has no legal guidelines, and you could easily end up in court. And then the only benefitting parties are the respective attorneys for each side."

For example, Jeff and Saul (an imaginary couple based on true stories) have lived together for twenty-five years. The day after celebrating their twenty-fifth anniversary, Jeff told Saul to get out, allowing him to take his clothes and the old sofa bed in the basement. After twenty-five years together they had accumulated three houses and four rental properties. While Jeff made more money than Saul and contributed about

80 percent more toward the purchase of those properties, Saul spent hundreds of hours renovating each of their houses and apartments. Jeff always told Saul that they should keep all the properties in his name for tax purposes. Saul never questioned him about this arrangement. Since they had nothing in writing, Saul was left with no choice but to take his lover to court, where he faced a very difficult and uncertain legal battle. A decision on a similar case is still pending in court.

Eliot and Lloyd drew up an agreement shortly after they moved in together. Lloyd was in his mid-thirties and married with two children when he and Eliot, then in his late thirties, moved in together.

Eliot: We have an agreement apart from our wills should we decide to part company. The disengagement of financial entanglements in which both are involved has been arranged in advance so that there will be fewer skirmishes. We've set in concrete the way our community property will be disposed of.

Lloyd: You always feel a little funny doing this sort of thing because it's acknowledging that this may not work out. You can't be so naive as to think there's no risk of the relationship coming to an unexpected and early conclusion.

Eliot: There's a substantial amount of money involved in our relationship now, so it would be very foolish not to have taken care of it. I think it's very foolish whether or not you have money. It's a manner of reinforcing the relationship when you're willing to make a legal commitment.

I try to let other gay people know that we have such an agreement so that they know there are people who have agreements and that they should think about it.

A lawyer who regularly handles property agreements (most often real estate) between male couples notes that most of them don't have agreements drawn up because they want to avoid the cost of paying a lawyer. But he added, "We make most of our money from people who have not taken precautions and then the thing is on the rocks and then they need us. Then it's a mess. A contract is a cheap form of insurance, but people don't necessarily regard it as such."

CAUTION

If you draw up a contract to clarify your property interests and do it incorrectly, it may be invalid in court, or you may agree to something you don't intend. Don't sign such a contract without the help of a professional. You can certainly do a lot of the preparation yourselves and even write up a contract, but have a lawyer familiar with the laws in your state review what you've written.

Attorneys Hayden Curry and Denis Clifford, authors of *A Legal Guide for Lesbian And Gay Couples,* provide the following warnings should you have to cite your contract in court:

If the contract states (or implies) that a promise was made in exchange for sexual services, it will not be enforced. So never include any statement as to sexual rights and responsibilities in your contract. Identify yourselves as "partners," not "lovers."

There is some risk that in states that still have sodomy, oral copulation, or other antihomosexual laws a judge might refuse to enforce a gay living together contract.

In other words, no matter how you write your living together agreement, it may not be a legally valid document in your locality. But then, the document's primary purpose is to keep you out of court.

Living Will

A living will—or Living Will Declaration—is a document in which you can state your preferences in the event you are hopelessly ill and, for example, don't wish to be force-fed or kept alive on a respirator. In the document you also appoint a proxy—your lover or a friend or family member—to be decision maker if you should become unable to make such decisions for yourself. Alice Mehling, director of the Society for the Right to Die, stresses the importance of this aspect of the living will: "Having someone to stand in your shoes to fight for your written wishes is very important."

Currently thirty-eight states and the District of Columbia have living will laws. In the twelve remaining states, various legal decisions have addressed the issue. And many hospitals and physicians quietly comply with living wills, even if they are in states where there are no living will laws.

Mark Senak recommends completing a living will even "if your jurisdiction doesn't recognize it: The law may change in your jurisdiction; you may be injured in a jurisdiction where a living will is valid; it could be enough to keep you off a respirator." Senak, who has worked with many AIDS patients, notes that it's a lot easier to keep a person off a respirator than to pull a plug, and a living will might just keep you off a respirator if that's your preference. (See the "Resources" section at the end of this chapter for information on how to contact the Society for the Right to Die for more information on living wills.)

Adoption of Your Lover

There are advantages to adopting your lover, some of which can't be achieved with Durable Power of Attorney or a will. Once adopted, the person you adopt is entitled to all the benefits of a family member. You can claim your adopted "son" as a dependent for tax purposes, or your "son" can claim you as a legal dependent. As your adopted son, your lover is eligible for coverage by your company's medical policy if you claim him as a dependent, and vice versa.

Sounds like an interesting possibility—until you consider that you cannot revoke an adoption, not even if the relationship ends. Besides which, most states have laws concerning adoption that make it difficult, and often impossible to adopt one's lover. Some states prevent such adoptions with age restrictions (only minors can be adopted) and other states explicitly forbid adoption of individuals who have a sexual relationship.

One lawyer, who has handled a number of lover-adoption cases in North Carolina, offers this advice if you try the adoption route: "Don't mention the gay issue; otherwise you're just looking for trouble."

LEGAL OPTIONS FOR PURCHASING OR RENTING PROPERTY

Renting Property

What if your lover gives up his own home to move into the place you rent. Before he moves in, review your lease (if you have one), and if you have any doubts about whether or not the lease allows for a "roommate," check with your local housing authority, a broker, or a real estate lawyer. You may have to renegotiate the lease at a higher rent, or you may be in breach of your lease and subject to eviction if your lover moves in, you don't get permission from your landlord, and he later finds out. It depends upon local laws. Whatever the laws in your area, it is most prudent not to mention that your new roommate is your lover unless, of course, you know for certain that it will not be a problem.

Whether or not you are required to add your partner's name to the lease when he moves in, there will come a time in the life of your relationship when you will want to add his name to your lease or want your name added to his lease. This is not just a symbolic move.

A leased apartment or house, unlike a condominium, cooperative apartment, or privately owned house, cannot be willed. If you die and the apartment is in your name, it is likely that your lover will have to leave or go to court to keep the apartment. In a few legal cases involving such circumstances, the live-in partner who was not on the lease succeeded in assuming the lease. But don't count on it, because in other cases the surviving lover has lost the apartment. As always, avoiding the trauma and expense of a legal battle is the best way to go.

If it's not required by law, you may not want your partner's name on your lease, particularly when the relationship is new and/or if you're not confident that the relationship will work out. Because once your lover is on the lease, you may have a hard time convincing him that it's still your apartment if you decide the relationship is not working out and you want him to go. If he's not on the lease, it's legally your apartment and it will be difficult for him to prove otherwise when/if you ask him to move.

Once you are both on the lease, you are both legally responsible for the entire rent. So even if one of you moves out, the remaining tenant is obligated to cover the full amount. That holds true just about everywhere in the country.

Buying Property—Real Estate

There are as many possible configurations for property ownership as there are couples. For example, you may move into a home that your lover already owns and pay rent to him for the first five years before he decides that he will transfer a piece of the property to you or offers to let you buy a percentage of the property. (Consult with your attorney and accountant to figure out the best arrangement for you and your partner.) Or you may live together in a rental apartment for several years and then decide, after reviewing your joint finances, that you would be better off buying an apartment or house. Perhaps you are ten years older than your lover, in a financial position to purchase a house he could not possibly afford, and have no intention of giving him title to any percentage of the house. What it comes down to in the end is whether you purchase the property jointly, or one of you purchases the property alone.

At some point in their relationship many couples choose to purchase property together for financial or legal reasons, for convenience, or as a symbol of their union. This section deals with the legal issues you need to consider when buying property together.

JOINT OWNERSHIP IN ONE NAME

If both of you contribute to the purchase of a home or apartment, but you put the house in one partner's name only, you are at tremendous risk. In the eyes of the law, if only one of you takes title to the property, only one of you owns it. With only your lover's name on the deed, he can sell the house and disappear with all the proceeds from the sale, or he can keep the house and tell you to take a hike. If your lover dies and does not have a will in which he states his wish that you inherit the house, the house will pass to his next of kin. A joint purchase of the property should be reflected on the property deed or equivalent documents.

OPTIONS FOR JOINT OWNERSHIP IN BOTH NAMES

When you buy property jointly, you can take title to property with your lover in one of two ways: as Tenants in Common or as Joint Tenants with Right of Survivorship.

When you take title as Joint Tenants with Right of Survivorship, each of you will inherit your partner's share automatically upon his death. This will happen regardless of whether or not you have a will or a joint ownership agreement. You just have to be certain that clearly written on the deed is that fact that you are taking title to the property as "Joint Tenants with Right of Survivorship." If that is not written on the deed, then it is assumed you are buying as Tenants in Common.

Having to write those words on a public document is one reason some couples choose not to take title as Joint Tenants with Right of Survivorship. The implication of course is that if you buy property with another man and take title as Joint Tenants with Right of Survivorship, you are more than just good friends or business partners. According to one lawyer who handles such transactions for gay couples, "Some men may find it embarrassing. They may not want to give their bank, their lawyer, the seller, or anyone else any reason to believe they are in a lover relationship with another man."

When you take title as Tenants in Common, there is no implication that you have anything more than a business relationship. Each partner has a distinct title to the property and that title depends upon the percentage of the property each of you owns. Your interest does not automatically pass to your lover upon death, but will pass to whomever you choose to leave it as stated in a joint ownership agreement or a will.

Taking title as Tenants in Common is more flexible than taking title as Joint Tenants with Right of Survivorship. If, for example, you are in a new relationship and do not yet want to leave your share of your property to your lover, you can leave it to whomever you choose. But you must back up that flexibility with a joint ownership agreement.

LEGAL REQUIREMENTS

In the eyes of the law, when you and your lover purchase property as Joint Tenants with Right of Survivorship or as Tenants in Common, you are two single men entering into a partnership. Typically, when two unrelated individuals purchase property, they draw up a joint ownership agreement that states what percentage of the property is owned by each of the partners, how costs for maintaining the property are divided, how the property will be divided in the event the partnership is dissolved, what happens upon the death of a partner, what happens if one partner defaults on payments, and so forth.

The joint ownership agreement is meant to cover all of the contingencies that would likely result in a legal dispute without the document.

Legally married couples typically do not need a joint ownership agreement, since they are protected by marriage laws.

To play by the legal rules, and avoid legal hassles if your relationship sours or one of you dies, you need to draw up and sign a joint ownership agreement which is a legally recognized and binding contract between two individuals that pertains specifically to the ownership of property such as a house, apartment, unimproved land, office building, car, sailboat, and so forth.

Besides stating what percentage of the jointly owned property is owned by each partner and how much each has agreed to pay toward monthly costs for maintaining that property, a joint ownership agreement can be used to spell out what will happen in several different circumstances. For example, mechanisms can be built into the agreement for a division of the property and for setting a sales price in the event your relationship ends. If your relationship sours and your lover fails to pay his agreed-upon share of the carrying costs for X months, you can include in the agreement a provision that will force your partner to sell his share of the property to you at a price based on a prearranged formula. You should discuss your specific needs and the necessary provisions with your attorney. And be aware that laws may vary by state.

Plenty of couples end their relationships and divide up jointly owned property without the benefit of a joint ownership agreement. But, without such a document to spell out the division process and other contingencies, there is always the danger that reaching an impass of any kind will force you and/or your ex to take legal action. That can be expensive, time consuming, and may result in a resolution that meets the letter of the law, but is not satisfying to either of you.

What you state in a joint ownership agreement concerning the death of a partner depends on how you purchase the property. If you buy property as Joint Tenants with Right of Survivorship, you don't need to state in a joint ownership agreement that you will each inherit the other's share of the property upon death. That happens automatically. If you buy property as Tenants in Common, you need to specifically state in the joint ownership agreement who is to inherit your share of the property, or you need to state that in a will. If you state that both in a joint ownership agreement and in a will, the joint ownership agreement will take precedence.

A will is the least desirable way of handling the disposition upon death of a home you own as Tenants in Common with your partner. Despite the best of intentions, wills don't always get written, they can be changed, and they can be challenged. For example, if you buy an apartment with your lover, take title to the apartment as Tenants in Common, and agree to use your wills to leave each other your shares of the property upon death, you have no guarantee that he will complete his will, or that he won't later change it, leaving his share of the property to anyone he wants.

Chet and John bought their house in a semirural neighborhood as Tenants in Common. They had planned to sign a joint ownership agreement following the completion of their purchase.

Chet: I had the attorney draw up a contract, but we never signed it. I have no problem with how it stands now. I know his family and I know my family. If anything ever happened to either one of us my family would be understanding. The house would be John's.

John: The agreement he drew up was that his half of the house went to his family. I didn't want that.

Chet: My entire estate goes to my parents and they would divide it up.

John: I don't agree with that. If something happens to him, the house should be mine. My family is not so kind and should something happen to me, I think my family would be in there for blood. I know them.

Chet: I'm too involved in his family for them to do that.

But they could. Because Chet and John couldn't come to an agreement on the terms of the joint ownership agreement, what happens to their shares in their property depends upon what their wills state. As it stands, Chet's will states that his share of the house goes to his family. John doesn't have a will so his share will automatically go to his next of kin. As long as neither dies, they won't have a problem.

The bottom line when it comes to joint ownership is—put it on paper. You can make just about any arrangement you like as long as (1) you both agree to it; (2) the agreement is within the law; and (3) it is stated in the proper formality. Talk it over with each other. Consult a local attorney. Write it down and sign on the dotted line. Otherwise you're asking for trouble.

Buying Property—a Car

Depending upon what state you live in, there are several ways to own a car jointly, the simplest being as Joint Tenants. According to Clifford and Curry, under joint tenancy the signatures of both owners are required to transfer title of the vehicle. If one partner dies, the other may assume full title by acquiring ownership papers from your state's Department of Motor Vehicles, avoiding probate. Laws may vary by state; check with your local Department of Motor Vehicles for details.

Be sure you understand for what form of joint ownership you are opting before registering your car, especially as some forms permit one owner to sell the car without knowledge or permission of the other.

If you buy a car and transfer title to your lover for whatever reason—insurance is a good one, especially if you have several moving violations on your record—keep in mind that if you split up, and your lover decides to keep the car against your wishes, you'll need a good lawyer and a lot of luck to get it back. And if you buy it as a gift for your lover and later split up and want the car back? Forget it. As long as it's registered in his name, it will be difficult, if not impossible, to get it back.

OTHER LEGAL ISSUES

Discrimination

It's perfectly legal to discriminate against homosexuals in employment, housing, and public accommodation, except in those states, localities, and institutions where laws or rules specifically forbid discrimination based on sexual orientation. And even where there are such regulations, it may be very difficult to prove discrimination. Whatever the circumstances, be certain to document your discrimination claim. Keep notes of when and how the discrimination took place; if you have any papers that can be used in a discrimination court case, save them.

If you feel that you and/or your partner have been victims of discrimination because you're gay, contact a local gay helpline to find out what approach to take in your locality. If you don't have a local helpline, contact the American Civil Liberties Union affiliate in your state. (See "Organizations" in the "Resources" section at the end of this chapter.)

Taking Your Lover to Court

Like straight relationships, gay relationships can fail miserably too. In the extreme, that can lead to violence against property or each other and a court case. Lovers may take each other to civil and/or criminal court for all sorts of reasons. But be warned, courts are ruled by laws that may not seem fair. You are better off, for example, depending upon a living together agreement than on a court to decide who gets what in the event you and your lover split up.

Unfortunately, even if you have all the documents mentioned in this chapter that are intended to keep you and your lover out of court, it may be unavoidable. For example, you may need to go to civil court to recover damages if your lover breaks your nose and you need surgery to repair the injury. For another example, to keep him at a safe distance from you, you would have to go to criminal court to get an order of protection.

Time and circumstances permitting, consult a lawyer before going to the police to bring criminal charges against your partner. Once a criminal process begins, it may be difficult to stop.

Getting Arrested for Sodomy

Sodomy laws, while on the books in more states than not, are rarely enforced, so your chances of ever being arrested for sodomy (oral or anal sex) are remote. In the event you are arrested for sodomy—whatever the circumstances of the arrest—attorney Lila Bellar offers simple advice: "Keep your mouth shut and get in touch with a sensitive lawyer." Bellar warns that *anything* you say to *anyone* can later be used against you in court.

RESOURCES

Finding Professional Legal Help

If you can't find a lawyer through a recommendation, the *Gayellow Pages,* or a local gay helpline, or can't find a lawyer who is gay or is comfortable working with gays, there is another route to finding the help you need. While there is no national umbrella organization for legal professionals who can provide phone referrals to a gay or gay-sympathetic lawyer, the Gay & Lesbian Advocates & Defenders in Boston publishes a state-by-state directory of gay and gay-sympathetic lawyers (see "Organizations," below).

Organizations

There are many organizations nationwide that can provide answers to your legal questions, and many can be found in the *Gayellow Pages* (see Appendix). The following are national and regional organizations that may be able to answer your questions or, in the event they can't help you, will refer you to an organization that can:

Lambda Legal Defense & Education Fund, Inc., 666 Broadway, 12th floor, New York, NY 10012, 212–995–8585

> Since 1973, Lambda Legal Defense & Education Fund has pursued litigation to counter discrimination against gay men and lesbians, as well as sponsored education projects to raise public awareness of gay legal rights. Lambda publishes a quarterly newsletter.

GLAD (Gay & Lesbian Advocates & Defenders), PO Box 218, Boston, MA 02112, 617–426–1350

Working primarily in the New England area, GLAD is a public interest law foundation that does educational and litigation work for lesbian and gay civil rights. GLAD publishes a quarterly newsletter—"GLAD Briefs"—and the *National Attorneys' Directory for Lesbian and Gay Rights,* now in its fourth edition.

To order the *National Directory,* call or write GLAD for information.

National Gay Rights Advocates, 540 Castro Street, San Francisco, CA 94114, 415–863–3624

The National Gay Rights Advocates is a public interest law firm that does litigation in the area of gay civil rights. The organization also has an attorney who does work solely on AIDS-discrimination issues. The Advocates publishes a quarterly newsletter and has brochures available on request on security clearances for gay people, a guide to wills for lesbians and gay men called "Wills Give You Power," and a brochure on AIDS and your legal rights.

American Civil Liberties Union (Main Office), 132 West 43rd Street, New York, NY 10036, 212–944–9800

In general, the ACLU defends freedom of inquiry and expression cases; due process of law cases; equal protection of the laws; and privacy. You can check your phone book for your local ACLU office, or you can call or write the main office.

Society for the Right to Die, 250 West 57th Street, Room 323, New York, NY 10107, 212–246–6973

The Society for the Right to Die is a national nonprofit organization whose purpose is "to work for the recognition of the individual's right to die with dignity."

The Society will provide printed information and a Living Will Declaration on request, along with guidelines for completing a living will in the thirty-nine jurisdictions where the living will is legally recognized. For the twelve other states, the Society has a general living will document.

The Society has two staff attorneys who are available to answer questions.

Books

The Rights of Gay People: An American Civil Liberties Union Handbook, Second Edition, by E. Carrington Boggan, Marilyn G. Haft, Charles Lister, John P. Rupp, and, Thomas Stoddard. Bantam Books, 666 Fifth Avenue, New York, NY 10103.

The Rights of Gay People is an A-to-Z question-and-answer resource book on the rights of gay people.

A Legal Guide for Lesbian and Gay Couples, Fourth Edition, by Hayden Curry and Denis Clifford. NOLO Press, 950 Parker Street, Berkeley, CA 94710. In US call: 800-992-NOLO. In California call: 800-445-NOLO

> This is an absolute treasure chest of legal, financial, and insurance information for couples. Often California-specific, it is still a good resource for general information about buying property, banking, writing living together agreements, etc.

CHAPTER 10

Money

"I know how to spend money better.
He knows how to save money better."

"Money" can be a fighting word—especially when there isn't enough, or when one of you has or earns substantially more than the other. Most of the younger couples I spoke with put money way at the top of the list of things they argue about: how much to spend, how much to save, what to spend it on, who pays for what, etc. Competition often plays a role in those arguments since it is likely that one of you will earn more than the other and therefore have greater spending power.

You have many options for how to deal with money in your relationship, from keeping all of your finances strictly separate and splitting all costs 50–50, to merging everything and keeping only one checking and savings account between the two of you.

However you choose to arrange your finances, it is nearly impossible to avoid disagreements and misunderstandings about money, even when you've set up systems to avoid fights. But you can keep the disagreements and misunderstandings from destroying your relationship.

SHARED EXPENSES

How you structure your finances to handle shared expenses requires custom design, as you will see from the examples in this section. The arrangement you choose depends on how each of you feels about money, your individual financial and employment circumstances, how well you each manage money, your personal styles, how long you have been a couple, and how much you trust each other. Don't be surprised if it takes a while for you to develop a system that suits you. And expect the system you choose to modify over time because of fluctuating financial situations, and changes in your relationship.

Strictly Separate

Keeping your finances strictly separate—I pay for my own expenses; we split all joint expenses down the middle—is the most prudent, most advisable, and least complicated approach to take when starting a new relationship.

By keeping separate finances and accounts, you can splurge on an expensive book without talking it over with your partner and he can choose to spend and save as he pleases. Keeping separate accounts also saves you from the grief of arguing over how the records are kept.

Separate finances do not preclude having a joint checking account. You can use a joint checking account as a funnel for joint expenses, as you will see in the section on joint banking later in the chapter.

Separate, But Mixed

Stating that you can take a separate-but-mixed approach to dealing with expenses may sound like a contradiction and may sound confusing. In practice it isn't a contradiction since you can handle some expenses separately and others in more creative ways. It can, however be confusing.

Strictly separate financial arrangements are not always possible, even at the beginning of a relationship, particularly if one of you earns significantly more than the other. For example, if the two of you live in a large home owned by the more financially secure partner, the other partner cannot possibly pay half of the cost of maintaining the house. In that case, the partner with greater earning power will have to pay a larger share of the expenses unless he wants to give up the house and move into something the two partners can afford to support jointly.

For example, because Andrew and Donald live a lifestyle that costs considerably more than Donald could afford if they were to pay equally for everything, Andrew, who earns several times Donald's income, pays a considerably greater portion of the major expenses.

Donald: It was tough for me at first, because I supported myself entirely before I met Andrew. I didn't want anybody to think I couldn't or wouldn't. So it was important for me to share everything. I remember the first few times that he took me to nice restaurants. I used to get really upset because I could not pay.

Andrew: The way we've dealt with this is that whatever he can afford he pays for and he pays exactly what he can afford. He goes right to his limit like anybody would. It happens that I've been able to provide more to make our living situation better.

While Andrew carries the major share of the cost of supporting their apartment and country house, they still split personal expenses such as clothing, and household expenses such as groceries, and they keep separate checking and savings accounts. This is just one of many possible variations on the separate-but-mixed approach.

For the couples I spoke with, the longer they have been together, the less structured they have become in how they handle their money, and the more comfortable they are with differences in income. Distinctions between "his" money and "my" money became less clear over time, especially for general household expenses. Systems for keeping to a strict 50–50 division of shared expenses often fell away. Couples who have been together for several years are also better at understanding and accepting often opposing views about money. They still argue, but they understand why they argue.

The move to a combination of separate and shared expenses can happen for all sorts of reasons, from the example given earlier about Andrew and Donald with their substantially different incomes, to couples where one returns to school for a time while the other temporarily takes over paying for most expenses.

In all of these cases, the method by which expenses are divided takes one of several forms. The following are three of the many possible options:

1. Split all major expenses equally; split all personal expenses; no tracking of household expenses.

2. Pay for major expenses according to what each can afford; split all household and personal expenses.

3. Split some major expenses equally; the partner who earns more pays entirely for some of the major expenses; no tracking of household expenses; split all personal expenses.

I still pay careful attention to *my* money, particularly if *my* money runs out and I'm in a position where I have to borrow money from Scott. It's happened once and made me extremely uncomfortable, at first anyway. For me, the money I earn represents power and a sense of self, and how much I earn has a lot to do with my need to feel that I can take care of myself. Scott and I split all major expenses—more my concern than his—but we've become pretty laid back about accounting for day-to-day expenses.

Duane and Irwin have a difference in income similar to that of Andrew and Donald, except that they live a lifestyle they can afford to pay for equally. But Irwin, who earns considerably more than Duane, will sometimes purchase "family" items, like a microwave oven or stereo, and pay for it entirely. They've been together three years.

Duane: It's something that I have not come to terms with and probably never will.

Irwin: Duane is not at all comfortable with allowing me to pay for things. I guess we go back and forth on this. As the years go by we've developed a sense of marriage, a sense of becoming one. A lot of the money I put in savings I consider to be for us. It's in my name, but it's going to be for us.

Duane: I pay for my own clothes and car. It's just a very fundamental issue— autonomy, and independence. I want to pay my own way.

While there are difficulties with any method of dividing up finances, the separate-but-mixed approach can lead to more misinterpretation and arguments than the better-defined systems like strict separation, or total merging of finances.

For example, Alex, 29, and Brooks, 34, live in San Jose, California. Alex recently started a high-pressure, fast-track job for which he is rewarded with a substantially larger paycheck than he was for his previous job. Brooks is a manager at a small manufacturing company where his moderate commitment to his work is compensated by a modest salary. They have been together for five years and have often traded positions as primary wage earner when one or the other has been out of work or has worked part time. They keep separate checking and savings accounts and, when both are working, basically split costs, although they aren't strict about it.

The conflict started over a bonus Alex received at his job. He has always dreamed of going to Mexico, and decided to spend the bonus on a one-week trip. He wanted Brooks to go too, but Brooks didn't have the money and did not want to put the trip on his already heavily used credit card. Alex's bonus wasn't large enough to pay for both of them.

The plot thickens. Brooks wasn't happy with Alex's plan to spend his bonus on a trip to Mexico because, earlier in the year, Brooks had spent his substantial tax return to overhaul their van—which he viewed as an expense made for both of them despite the fact he owns the van and won't let Alex drive it. He felt Alex's bonus should be used for something they both could do. Alex didn't consider the van overhaul a joint expense, since he doesn't own the van and Brooks won't let him drive it. Alex does not own a car, but depends on Brooks and the van to get around for shopping and for weekend trips.

This is not an unsolvable problem. There are solutions consistent with the way Alex and Brooks have handled their finances and debts in the past. And usually they have compromised. The following are five possible options:

1. Alex can go to Mexico by himself.

2. Brooks can charge the trip on his credit card and join Alex.

3. Alex can offer to pay half the total cost of the trip for the two of them, and then split the debt they incur.

4. Alex can put the bonus money in his savings account and wait until Brooks feels he can spend the money to go with him.

5. They can take a less-expensive trip together.

Alex decided that the bonus was his money to do with as he pleased, and he went to Mexico without Brooks. He was sorry that Brooks didn't see things the way he did and that Brooks was unhappy with his decision, but he would deal with Brooks's resentment when he got back.

Did Alex do the right thing? From his perspective he did what he thought was best for himself, knowing full well that it might not be the best thing for Brooks or for their relationship, and that he would have to deal with the fallout. The moral? If you're going use a system that is separate but mixed, you have to be consistent with, and considerate of, your partner or you're just asking for trouble. If you're not good at being considerate, not consistent, and not willing to compromise, a fluid system of handling expenses is not right for you.

Did Alex think his decision was worth it? No. He had a rotten time in Mexico without Brooks and regretted acting selfishly. If he had to do it again he would have chosen one of the last three options.

Total Merging

Some couples make a conscious effort to physically merge income just months into their relationship by putting all of their money into joint accounts. For most, the process is more gradual. In fact, you can achieve total merging without a single joint account, since total merging is really a mind set more than what appears on a bank statement.

A psychologist who works with gay couples believes that it's important for two men in a relationship to merge finances—to view "his" money and "my" money as "our" money. He believes that merged money is an important symbol of commitment and trust. It's a demonstration that two men are committed to one another for life. By remaining financially independent of one another, he says, male couples keep their distance and feed into the expectation that the relationship won't last. But there are drawbacks to physically merging your finances— major ones. Before you go out and merge your bank accounts, read the next section of this chapter on "Joint Banking and Investments."

Michael and Chris have been a couple for eight years and have lived together full-time for the past five years, since they both finished college. They've viewed their money as shared money and any expenses as shared expenses since they have earned incomes, but they don't maintain joint bank accounts.

When Michael and Chris go to dinner with gay-couple friends, they're always surprised when the two men they're having dinner with each pull out a wallet to pay for his part of the dinner. They just don't separate their money in that way. "It's not separate money, his money or my money. We've always thought of things as our money." But because they each have very different abilities with money, they've developed their own personal system for managing their expenses. You will likely need to work out your own management system to suit your individual needs, although you may not need to develop one that is quite as complex as the one Michael and Chris developed.

Michael: When I was living away at graduate school Chris sent me $100 every now and then. I basically took care of my own finances. That's how I got used to my own way of living. It was very much hand-to-mouth. I never balanced my checkbook. When I moved back home for good and I started working, Chris and I decided this would never work in a relationship.

Chris: We started out with two separate checking accounts and he would never balance his checkbook. Every once in a while a check would bounce and it would piss the hell out of me and I would always try to get him to learn how to balance his checkbook and make all the separate entries.

And he knew nothing about staying on a budget. Michael would do things like say, "Let's go to the movies and go out to eat," and I would say, "Look we don't have the money to go out and also pay our bills." Then we would start arguing.

Michael: There was also the problem of the way Chris spends money. When Chris wants to buy something, he buys it when he wants to and it costs three times as much. I shop. I know how to spend money better. He knows how to save money better. So we divided it that way and Chris takes care of all the paperwork.

So from their experiences with one another, they came up with the "Michael and Chris" method of handling the family money and expenses, a system Chris designed. Because Chris is more responsible with money and bills and is the better saver of the two, he is responsible for taking care of monthly expenses and savings. Michael is better at day-to-day expenses, so that is his responsibility (he pays the dinner check from his account when they go out). To manage their money, they keep two checking accounts (one in each of their names), and one savings account in Chris's name—"It should be in both of our names, but we've neglected to make the change."

Each of them deposits his paycheck into his own checking account. Michael then turns over a percentage of his paycheck to Chris for monthly expenses and the rest is used for day-to-day expenses including groceries, eating out, clothing, etc.

Michael: The point was if my money ran out, it ran out. At least the monthly bills got paid. We just couldn't go out to eat. We ended up keeping exactly the same lifestyles as before. I lived day-to-day and Chris lived month-to-month.

As carefully designed to accommodate each other's personality as their system is, there is still room to argue over money.

Michael: That happens when I run out of money and I say, "Chris I need money."
Chris: And I say "Okay, you can borrow out of my account (the monthly expenses or savings account), but you have to pay it back with the next check."

A warning about confusing total merging for something else. True total merging is not to be mistaken for cosmetic merging. Cosmetic merging comes in a couple of varieties. There is physical merging where each man still acts as if finances are separate, even though their funds are merged on paper. The second major variety occurs when both partners mix all of their finances, but the one who earns substantially more money feels he can make all of the decisions. If you earn more money, or have more money, than your partner, you may feel that you've earned the right to make all the decisions involving your share of the joint money. You don't, or at least your partner won't think that you do. If you want full control of your income and how you spend it, stick to the strictly separate approach to finances and expenses.

JOINT BANKING AND INVESTMENTS—CHECKING, SAVINGS, CREDIT

Joint Checking and Savings

A warning from the experts on joint banking—according to Curry and Clifford in *A Legal Guide for Lesbian and Gay Couples:*

Don't share bank accounts, either checking or savings. If you and your lover each keep your own accounts, there is no possibility of confusion. Sometimes people want to maintain a joint bank account for limited purposes such as household expenses or for a distinct project. Limited joint accounts can be sensible as long as it is clear that they are limited to a specific purpose, and adequate records are kept. That said, let us add that we do know a few lesbian/gay couples who've peacefully maintained joint bank accounts for years. But still, a joint account is a risk, each person has the legal right to spend all the money in the account, no matter who earned it, unless you require joint signatures to disburse any money.

If there is a question of trust, or one of you has a spending, drug, or gambling problem, joint accounts could be an awful idea, although requiring two signatures for a check or withdrawal provides some insurance against unauthorized spending. Curry and Clifford also warn about the confusion that can result if you are both writing checks from a joint account and you don't keep accurate records.

Whether you split or merge your income and expenses, you may find the convenience and symbolism of a joint account appealing. For example, you can use a joint checking account to cover your monthly expenses by each depositing an equal amount of money into the joint account at the start of each month. The amount you deposit would be based on your average monthly expenses plus a cushion amount to avoid an overdraft. If there is anything left over, you can let it accumulate as savings, or reduce the amount you both need to deposit the following month. You can also open a joint savings account to save for joint vacations.

Some men, Scott and me included, consider the two names at the top of the joint checks to be symbolic of their union. Others may consider that implied public statement of their relationship to be too public. As always, do what feels comfortable.

Joint Loans and Credit Cards

In a major city, borrowing money together, particularly for a mortgage, is not a problem as long as you meet the credit requirements. However, if you live someplace where it isn't as common for two unrelated men to buy a house together and to take a joint mortgage, you may have more difficulty finding a willing bank. This is where a real estate broker or lawyer who is gay or has worked with gay couples, comes in handy.

If you take a joint mortgage with your lover or a joint loan of any kind, bear in mind that both of you will be responsible for repayment of that loan—jointly or singly. In other words, if you take a joint loan and your lover decides to walk away from you and the loan, you are responsible for repayment of the full amount of the loan.

Getting a joint credit card is fairly easy in most parts of the country, particularly if you present yourselves as a business partnership—not a gay couple—and as long as one of you has sufficient income and a good credit history. But just a few words of warning about joint credit cards from the experts who have witnessed the legal fallout from credit abuse. According to Clifford and Curry:

> We are no more in favor of joint charge accounts than we are of joint bank accounts. If you want to be generous, be generous with cash, not credit. However, many people do love that magic plastic, and some don't feel good unless they have a pocket full of the stuff. Sometimes lesbian/gay couples have a psychological need to act as if they are married and so they acquire lots of joint cards. Well, as our mothers used to say, "They can't say we didn't warn them."

Problems with joint credit cards arise if one of you is inclined to make impulse purchases and charges up a storm, leaving the other to foot the bill (you're both legally obligated to pay the outstanding bill). If the relationship ends and one of you has run up a bill and then refuses to pay, the other is still responsible for the debt, just like any other kind of joint loan. Failing to pay the bill your lover has run up will get you a black mark on your credit history, whether or not you approved the purchases.

Clearly you and your partner have to have a high level of trust in one another to arrange for joint credit cards or any other type of joint credit. If you have any doubt about how trustworthy your partner is, if your relationship is at all unstable, or if money is a constant source of stress, keep your money and your credit separate.

Investments

If you plan to spend the rest of your lives together, planning your financial future together, including retirement, should be part of that plan.

You can buy real estate, do your taxes, make investments, set up trusts, arrange for your mutual financial future including planning for your retirement, without enlisting the help of a financial advisor. But if neither of you has a keen interest in managing complicated finances, a third, and expert, opinion can be very helpful.

As in all other money matters, you should pay careful attention to how you structure your financial arrangements so that they reflect each of your interests and goals.

CONTRACTUAL ARRANGEMENTS

One way to reduce disagreements and misunderstandings over money, whether it's how much each of you paid into an investment or how much each of you contributes to rent each month, is to formalize your financial arrangements in writing. As discussed in Chapter 9, the options for formalizing a relationship range from a simple living together contract to joint ownership agreements. You can formalize just about any other type of arrangement, from supporting your lover while he goes through school in exchange for his supporting your education later, to exchanging hours committed to the renovation of a house for percentage ownership of the house.

As Clifford and Curry note, "As essential as a written agreement can be, it is no substitute for trust and communication." But they go on to say that, if times do get hard, a written agreement can do wonders to reduce paranoia and confusion and help people deal with one another fairly. You may not feel you need such an agreement now, but you may well regret not having one if you break up with a lover before he meets his promise of paying for your three years of law school after you've just finished paying for his.

MANAGING THE PAPERWORK

Handling the Books and Papers

The goal here is to get the bills paid. As long as you have the money, it's just a matter of finding a system that gets the envelopes opened, the checks written and sent, and the books balanced. The simplest approach is for one of you to be in charge of making sure the joint expenses get paid, and if you have a joint checking account, to keep track of that account. If neither takes particular pleasure in—or you are both equally bad at—keeping the books, you can trade off the responsibility every other month, or every other year.

Even if the bills get paid, the job of keeping track of expenses does not end there. One way to keep track of your family bills, receipts, etc., as well as individual and joint bank statements and joint purchases, is to keep all such papers in an accordian file (the kind with a dozen or more sections), one for each year. Label each section for a different item. For example, "Eric's Bank Statements," "Scott's Bank Statements," "Joint Bank Statements," "Utilities," etc. Keeping the files in order takes some effort and cooperation during the year, but the effort pays off when it comes time to get your papers together for tax season, or when you need to put your hands on a receipt for a piece of furniture you bought two years ago. At the end of each year, store the file and start a new one.

Keeping Track of Household Expenses

For those of you who split household expenses like groceries, toiletries, entertainment, transportation, etc., there are many methods for keeping track of who spends what. Listed below are a few of them. If you find one doesn't work for you and your partner, try another, or make up one that suits your particular idiosyncrasies.

1. *Notepad on Refrigerator*
   Keep a notepad posted on the refrigerator. Divide the notepad in half and put each of your names at the top of a column. Everytime you pay out money for groceries or pick up the tab for both of you at dinner or the movies, list the item on the pad. At the end of the month, add up the amounts and settle accounts.

2. *The Cookie Jar*
   Designate a large-size jar as the repository of receipts. Every time you make a purchase, write your name on the receipt, or on a piece of paper with the amount spent and the date, and deposit it in the jar. At the end of the month, settle accounts.

3. *The Cookie Jar System II*
   Using the same jar as described in option 2, place an agreed-upon amount of cash in the jar every week, two weeks, or month to cover anticipated monthly household expenses. If you run short before the period of time has elapsed, put in an additional agreed-upon amount. This is probably the most labor intensive of the four choices listed.

4. *Trading Off*
   For the less-organized or exacting, you can try trading off. In other words, one of you pays for the groceries this week, the other pays next week. The drawback here is that if one of you likes to keep things even and the other doesn't really care, you leave yourselves open to never-ending arguments. In that case I would recommend one of the more structured approaches so there can be no disagreements about who paid what for the toothpaste and who paid for the movies the last time.

Whichever system you choose for handling everyday household expenses, one of you has to take the lead in tabulating the monthly numbers, or in the case of option 3, you each have to keep an eye on whether or not the funds are lasting.

RESOURCES

Finding the Financial Professional You Need

If your finances or future financial planning are in any way involved with those of your partner, you would be foolish to work with an accountant or financial advisor with whom you couldn't discuss the nature of your relationship. Your job then is to find a professional with whom you can be honest. Since there is no national referral service for gay or gay-sensitive financial advisors or accountants, you'll have to start by asking friends if they know anyone to recommend. If that route fails, look in the *Gayellow Pages* (see Appendix) under business listings for your locality.

Books and Organizations

There are few resources specifically for gay couples that deal with issues concerning money. The three general books on couples listed in the Appendix should be of some help, and Curry and Clifford's *A Legal Guide for Lesbian and Gay Couples* (see "Resources" in Chapter 9), should be of help as well.

CHAPTER 11

Insurance

"He regretted their inability to plan realistically."

This chapter concerns one of those subjects that's easy to put off until it's too late. By the time you discover you need insurance and don't have any, or discover that you have inadequate coverage, it's too late. It may be difficult to think about insurance when you and your lover are in perfect health, but that's the best time to plan for proper coverage and to apply for it.

Several years ago, as I was driving through an intersection in a rented van, I got in the way of a motorcycle. The driver of the motorcycle hit the van broadside, but thankfully was unhurt. His motorcycle was mutilated, however. He was particularly upset because he didn't have insurance. "Why should I?" he said, "I never expected to get in an accident."

No one expects to be in an accident. No one expects to be disabled. No one expects to die young. And if you're foolish enough to believe that you won't ever get in an accident and that your chances of dying of illness or being killed in an accident before your one-hundredth birthday are zero, do exactly as the motorcycle rider did and don't protect yourself. If you're in a long-term committed relationship, that approach is doubly irresponsible because you can leave your partner in financially precarious circumstances.

Your insurance needs—health, disability, and life—may already be met by the company that employs you. But have you ever considered what your insurance needs are? Did you remember to choose long-term disability if that's an option? Did you and your lover remember to make each other the beneficiary of your life insurance policies? Does your lover's company provide enough life insurance to enable you, if he dies, to keep the house that requires both of your incomes to maintain?

I found it easy not to pay attention to the details of my insurance when I left my corporate job and started to work for myself. I figured I would pick up life and disability insurance when I got around to it and thought I had enough medical insurance to cover me if I got very sick or was in an accident. After visiting with an insurance agent, I was stunned to learn I had only chosen to pay for hospitalization insurance and nothing else. I had no coverage for doctor's bills, tests, etc. I had neglected to read the forms that I filled out when I elected to convert my company group coverage to individual medical coverage. Knowing what I do now, I probably still would not read over the forms. But I would have forwarded them to my insurance agent to review, and then to advise me.

You don't have to *be* an expert to make certain you have adequate insurance coverage. You just have to *know* an expert.

WHO NEEDS INSURANCE?

Everyone needs some form of health and disability insurance. And if you and your partner own property, or live in a rental home that requires both of your incomes to support, you need to consider life insurance.

Every couple's insurance needs will differ depending on the age of the partners, the amount of time they have been together, and their assets. If the two of you are both in your early twenties, each making $15,000 a year, and have group coverage at work, that's all you generally need. But needs change as circumstances change. The time to review the insurance you have and to arrange for the various types of insurance you may need is before you leave a corporate job to work for yourself, before you purchase property together, before you invest in a business together, and before you have health problems.

TYPES OF INSURANCE AND WHAT YOU SHOULD KNOW

Medical Insurance

Medical insurance is an absolute necessity if you want to be free to choose the hospital where you will be treated and to protect you and your lover from having to use personal and joint assets to pay hospital bills.

What do you do, then, if you don't have medical coverage, have decided it's time to buy medical insurance, and have a history of medical problems including several sexually transmitted diseases? Hiding the truth is no solution, because insurance companies have access to nationwide databases where records of hospitalizations and serious claims are stored. And on your insurance application you also have to sign a waiver permitting the insurance company to request information from your doctor. If, in its research, an insurance company uncovers evidence that you've provided false information on an application, your application will be denied and the falsification will be noted on your record as well. In that case, not only will your application for insurance be rejected, but you'll have a permanent note on your record that you lied on a prior application. Tell your insurance agent everything about your medical history and let him decide how to handle it.

If, after you get coverage—or later, after making a claim—the insurance company investigates and discovers you failed to disclose information about your medical history, your policy can be canceled.

Disability Insurance

If something happens that disables me for more than a few months and I am unable to earn income, Scott and I would be in financial trouble. Supporting our apartment takes two incomes. Even if it didn't, I wouldn't want to be entirely dependent on Scott to support me. Disability insurance guarantees income for a designated period of time if I become disabled.

Check your company policy to find out what your disability benefits are and then discuss those benefits with the company benefits manager or an outside insurance specialist to find out if the company's benefits are adequate to maintain your standard of living in the event you are permanently disabled. Once you're disabled, it is too late to talk about increasing your benefits.

In many places you can choose a long-term disability option through your company policy. It's an option that extends the length of time you are covered by disability, with only a slight increase in cost. *Call your benefits manager tomorrow to find out if you have that option. If you do, take it.*

If you plan to leave a corporate job to work on your own and want to maintain a disability policy, arrange for that before you leave your corporate job. I always figured I could pick up adequate disability benefits sometime in the future. I was wrong. Once I left my company job to become a freelance writer, I was only able to obtain two years of disability payments, and then only for a relatively small amount. If I had made arrangements before leaving my job, I could have arranged for significantly greater coverage.

Life Insurance

Life insurance is not the absolute necessity that medical insurance is. But if you've invested in property or a business that depends upon both of your incomes, or if you're the primary wage earner, or have children, life insurance is a necessity.

The purpose of life insurance, according to the experts, is to provide after your death, for those whom you choose, in a way you may have provided for them in life. In other words, in life, I will pay for a portion of the mortgage on the apartment I own with Scott, the monthly common charges, and for part of whatever improvements we make. In the event one of us dies, we each want the other to be able to afford to continue to live in our home. We each also have family and most likely will help them financially during our lifetimes, so we have also made provisions for them.

How much insurance you take out depends upon your individual circumstances and is something to discuss with an insurance specialist. Keep in mind that anything you do to call attention to yourself—such as taking out a $500,000 policy on your life when you only make $20,000 a year, own no property, and have no traditional family to support—will result in greater scrutiny of your application. If your medical record is at all shaky, the last thing you want is more scrutiny. But again, consult with your insurance specialist on this issue.

If you work at a job where you don't want anyone to know about your relationship, for whatever reason, you may be reluctant to name your lover as a beneficiary of your company life insurance policy. In that case you will need to take out a private policy, or name your estate as beneficiary and in your will name your lover as the recipient of those funds. But, while naming your estate as the beneficiary gets you past one problem, it creates another, since insurance proceeds are then subject to attack by estate creditors and a will can be challenged. Before adopting this option, check with your local insurance agent and/or lawyer.

Purchasing an individual private policy has its drawbacks. If you name your lover as beneficiary, depending upon your state's law, you may be asked by the insurance company the nature of your relationship with the named beneficiary.

According to Brent Nance, an independent insurance agent in Los Angeles, and founder of CIPHR (Concerned Insurance Professionals for Human Rights), an organization of gay and lesbian insurance industry professionals, insurance companies ask about the nature of the relationship because "an insurance company is looking for an insurable interest (a financial relationship, marriage, dependent, etc.). Naming your lover as a beneficiary does not imply an insurable interest. You can claim there is a financial relationship, i.e., joint bank accounts, jointly owned property, co-ownership of loans, etc. If none of these exist, you may be forced to name a parent, brother, sister, or child as the beneficiary instead of your lover. Once the policy is issued, you're free to change the beneficiary to whomever you want."

In addition, naming another single man as beneficiary may trigger a request for a blood test that includes a test for the HIV antibody. In most states it *is* legal for an insurance company to require an HIV test before issuing a policy. Therefore, if you or your insurance agent are concerned that naming your lover as beneficiary could trigger a request for an HIV antibody test, you can again initially name a close relative as the beneficiary of your policy and later change the person named to your lover. (See the next section for information on HIV antibody testing and discrimination.) Or you can name your estate as beneficiary and in your will name your lover as the recipient of those funds.

If you had an existing life insurance policy when you began your relationship, it's easy to neglect getting around to changing the beneficiary. Tim was 27 and Benjy, 31, and had been together just over two years when Tim was diagnosed with AIDS. He had substantial benefits at his corporate job, including a company-sponsored life insurance plan. It was only after Tim died nine months later that Benjy learned that his lover had neglected to make him beneficiary of even part of his life insurance policy. Even though he was the stronger wage-earner, Benjy was angry that Tim had failed to provide for him, especially since he was suddenly faced with all the living expenses they once shared. He was also upset because he and Tim had depleted Benjy's savings to take Tim to expensive restaurants, on vacation trips, and to buy Tim things he wanted during his illness.

But Benjy also realized that the problem was in part his own fault. He did his best to hide from Tim the reality that he was going to die. Bringing up life insurance would have meant acknowledging the seriousness of Tim's illness, and neither of them could face that possibility. In retrospect, he regretted their inability to plan realistically.

MORTGAGE INSURANCE

Mortgage insurance is little more than a marketing tool for selling life insurance. In fact, mortgage insurance is almost exactly like life insurance, except that, unlike life insurance, the amount of mortgage insurance you have decreases as your mortgage is paid off. If you die before the mortgage has been paid off, mortgage insurance on your home or apartment will cover the balance. Your bank is, in effect, the beneficiary of the policy. If you plan your life insurance correctly, you will not need to take out mortgage insurance. You will instead need enough life insurance to pay off the entire mortgage, or whatever portion you are responsible for, and you can adjust the amount of your coverage periodically as your mortgage decreases.

DISCRIMINATION AND HIV TESTING

Because a male couple is not recognized as a couple in the eyes of the law, and because of AIDS, you face more potential difficulty—and perhaps discrimination—than do straight married couples in applying for and getting life, medical, or disability insurance. You can't buy medical insurance as a couple. You're not covered by your partner's company medical insurance, and insurance companies are reluctant—or refuse—to give joint homeowner, tenant, or auto insurance policies to unrelated couples. An insurance company may also request that you take a blood test that includes the currently available HIV test.

In some places, just being a single male will trigger the request for the HIV antibody test; in others, a single male who lists his beneficiary as another single male will trigger the request for a blood test, as can medical records that show a history of sexually transmitted diseases. If an HIV test isn't requested, or if insurance companies are forbidden by law in your area from ordering an HIV test, then the company may request an immunological study. If the HIV test that is administered is positive or the immunological test results are abnormal, an insurance company is not likely to issue a policy. (If you're leaving a job, consider converting your group insurance to individual coverage, thereby negating the requirement to go through further screening.)

Should you submit to an HIV test if an insurance company requests it? Attorney Mark Senak, who maintains a private practice and works with the Gay Men's Health Crisis in New York City, counsels his clients not to take the HIV antibody test, even if an insurance company requests a blood test as part of its application procedure. He warns that the legal dangers can be extreme if a confidential test turns out to be not so confidential. "If you take the test and you test positive, it can later be used to discriminate against you for insurance and job purposes. Even if you test negative, an insurance company will ask why you took the test in the first place. They'll assume you're in a high risk group and most likely deny your application." (See Chapter 13 for more on the HIV antibody test.)

If an insurance company requests that you take the HIV test, have your broker withdraw the application rather than have it denied. Then apply to another company for the same insurance. If the insurance company you've applied to asks for a blood test, but says it is not doing an HIV test, make certain before you go through with the test that the form on which the requested tests are listed does not include an HIV test. There have been cases where insurance companies have tried to include the test without the knowledge of the applicant.

If you believe you have been the victim of discrimination by an insurance company, contact one of the legal resources listed in the "Resources" of Chapter 9.

WARNING
Don't give your insurance company an excuse to cancel your policy. Pay your policy bills on time!

RESOURCES

Finding an Insurance Professional

Just a few words of caution about insurance brokers are in order before you begin your search for one. If the broker you go to suggests concealing facts about your medical history so that you can avoid being denied life, medical, or disability coverage, don't think it's the insurance company saying it's okay. Most brokers are independent agents. They don't work for the insurance company that issues the policy. They are paid a commission for your policy. And it's not okay to lie or conceal facts. Most brokers are reputable, and would never suggest concealing facts. If the broker you go to suggests concealing facts, find another insurance broker.

When looking for an insurance specialist, start by asking friends if they know anyone to recommend. If that route fails, try the *Gayellow Pages* (see Appendix) business or insurance listings for your locality, or you can try a local gay helpline. If you can't find an insurance professional by using any of these methods, CIPHR (Concerned Insurance Professionals for Human Rights) will lend a hand in finding someone close to where you live. But only contact CIPHR if you've exhausted all of the other suggested methods.

Organizations

CIPHR, PO Box 691006, Los Angeles, CA 90069–9006, 818–247–0426

In San Francisco: 707–762–0107

In New York: 718–225–7597

CIPHR (Concerned Insurance Professionals for Human Rights) was started in 1985 by Brent Nance for gay and lesbian insurance professionals. The organization addresses discrimination within the insurance industry directed at employees as well as insurance customers. While the organization is still new and relatively unstructured, they will try to refer you to a gay insurance agent in your area. Because the organization is so new, the numbers listed may have changed by the time the ink on this page has dried. But at least one of the three numbers should get you in touch with the organization.

Books

See Chapter 9, "Legalizing Your Relationship," for *A Legal Guide for Lesbian and Gay Couples,* which also provides information on insurance.

CHAPTER 12

Rituals and Religion

*"I want a ring for all of the traditional reasons
people have wedding rings; it's an affirmation, a symbol."*

FORMALIZING YOUR RELATIONSHIP

When a man and woman decide to formalize their relationship, there
is generally little debate about how they will do it. They get married.
How they get married is open to discussion and marriage options range
from a secular to a religious ceremony, and from a large formal traditional wedding to a trip to the justice of the peace.

When a gay couple considers formalizing their relationship, there are
no set rules, but there are certainly plenty of options. You can privately
exchange rings or other tokens, sign a living together agreement (see
Chapter 9), have a religious or secular ceremony, plan a traditional
ceremony fashioned after a straight marriage ritual, or design one of
your own, invite everyone you know, or not invite anyone. The possibilities are limited only by your imagination and the law.

You can look at the lack of relationship-formalizing norms for gay
couples as a blessing in that it allows for more choice. But not everyone considers choice a blessing. It's sometimes comforting and less
complicated to follow set traditions, to have some of the decisions
made for you. And in some ways, for gay couples there is less choice
and the planning is more complicated. For example, since two people
of the same sex can't legally marry, you can't choose a civil marriage.
Two men can't choose just any minister or church in which to have a
religious ceremony. And the invitation list, which is often no pleasure
to negotiate for a straight wedding, is likely to be far more difficult to
put together for a gay couple: Which relatives would be comfortable

at such a celebration? Should I ask anyone from the office? And so forth.

Deciding Whether or Not to Formalize
Your Relationship, and How to Formalize It

Only you and your partner can decide if you want to, or feel you need to, formalize your relationship in some way. Some couples do. Some couples don't. If you feel strongly about formalizing your relationship and your partner does not, it may take time to persuade him to go along with your wishes, and remember, you can't force him.

If you and your partner discuss your options, it will help to consider what type of formalization is appropriate for both of you, and to consider the reasons you want to formalize your relationship in the first place. For example, some couples choose to formalize their relationship by exchanging rings because they want a physical, traditional public symbol of their relationship. Others choose a formal and public ceremony because they desire the support and acknowledgment of friends, family, colleagues, church, and God. And some look to the formalizing process as a way to strengthen the bonds of their relationship.

Keep in mind that if you choose to formalize your relationship in some way, whatever the method you choose, it will not work miracles on your relationship. For example, no ring or ceremony will keep your lover faithful, will make your relationship kosher in the eyes of your family if they do not already accept you, or will guarantee that your relationship will survive serious problems. However, a formalization of some kind is very important to many couples and and can serve as a significant step in the deepening of their commitment to each other.

Private Formalization

Many couples who formalize their relationships choose to do so in private, by themselves. Some simply don't like public ceremonies of any kind. Others just don't feel comfortable being that public about their relationship.

If Scott and I ever choose to formalize our relationship, it would be in a private way—just the two of us. Not that I haven't fantasized about something on a grander scale. I had a blast at my brother's wedding last spring, and lamented to Scott that because I'm gay I would never have the opportunity to participate in an ancient tradition that is the Jewish wedding ceremony. And I would never have the big family celebration of my relationship that my brother, sister, and all of my cousins have had. It isn't so much that I wished my family could be accepting enough to handle a Jewish wedding ceremony for two men (not to mention the slight complication that Scott was raised Methodist). The problem is in large part me; I would be extremely uncomfortable. The ceremony was not designed for two men. And the reality is that the "wedding" of two men *would* make my family uncomfortable, which would make *me* uncomfortable. Scott also has strong feelings about not having a public ceremony, so for the two of us there will be no debate over whether to use private or public means should we one day choose to formalize our relationship.

In a private formalization you can exchange rings, traditional gold wedding bands for example, or some other token such as a necklace or even a flower. Some men consider a symbol as recognizable as a gold wedding band to be too much of a public statement, or one that would draw too much attention and questions, particularly if they present themselves as straight and single to their colleagues, friends, or family. Or they may consider the wedding band too symbolic of the straight marriage ritual.

Besides exchanging tokens, you can exchange vows and even add a religious element. You can sign a living together agreement. Or you can go on a vacation with the understanding that this is a special vacation— a honeymoon, one that symbolizes a significant commitment between you.

Irwin and Duane, both in their mid-thirties, have been together for three years. While they have no interest in a public or private ceremony, they have talked about exchanging rings.

Duane: I feel married; I want the symbol. I want to display it. I want people to see it. I want a ring for all of the traditional reasons people have wedding rings—it's an affirmation, a symbol. But I've gone back and forth. Do I want a gold band so that it's a clear message, as opposed to just any ring that means a lot, but won't draw attention?

Irwin: I've thought about one of those interlocking Hebrew letter things. But I also go back and forth. On the one hand it would just be a statement of my commitment, of "marriage." Then I guess there are those deeper coming out issues, like if someone notices the ring and asks me who my wife is. You still have to talk about what that ring is supposed to be to the world. Then there are those vague feelings of, if I wear a gold band, am I really married?

Duane: We've gotten close to doing it. In real sappy moments I think about it, but it's not a preoccupation.

Public

While only a few of the couples I interviewed chose formal public ceremonies, many couples do choose public ceremonies, large and small, both religious and secular. And they do so for many reasons, most of which are the same as those of many straight couples who desire a public celebration of their relationships. For example, they desire public—family, friends, church, God—acknowledgment and support of their commitment and relationship, and the symbolism that such a public statement carries with it.

For Les, who is 26, the public aspect of the religious ceremony he celebrated with his lover, Jonathan, 29, was extremely important to him. According to Les:

> It's important for me to have the outward symbols of what's going on and it's my belief that if you're willing to make that commitment to someone in private, you should be willing to do it in public. Having a ceremony gave us an opportunity to have our relationship supported publicly by our friends and a couple of people in my family, and by the church.

Other couples believe that a public ceremony in which they have involved friends and/or God, will further cement their relationship and help them weather stormy times. Whether a ceremony has that effect depends upon how seriously each of the partners views the ceremony in which they made commitments to one another, and in part on the ceremony itself. For example, the Holy Union ceremony, variations of which are conducted for gay couples at Metropolitan Community Churches across the country, cannot be undone without a formal dissolution of the vows. The Metropolitan Community Church is an interdenominational, primarily gay, church, with congregations nationwide.

If you decide to have a public ceremony, in addition to the many decisions necessary for any party or celebration, you and your partner need to carefully consider three things. First, do you want a traditional ceremony and celebration along the lines of a straight secular or religious wedding, or will you do something different, such as create your own ceremony and celebration? Second, do you want a religious or secular ceremony? Third, whom do you invite?

TRADITIONAL CEREMONY AND CELEBRATION, OR CUSTOM-DESIGNED?

Concern sometimes arises that, by following a traditional ceremony, there is the danger of mimicking straight wedding rituals. Some couples and religious leaders feel very strongly that gay couples should not do this. Others couldn't care less and feel comfortable following society's wedding traditions and rituals.

Larry J. Uhrig, author of *The Two of Us*, notes that in planning a union ceremony, there is the impulse to "mimic heterosexual customs and norms." It is an impulse of which he is critical. "The impulse . . . carries with it a denial of one's selfhood, unique reality, and liberty." Uhrig uses the example of throwing rice, which he notes originated as a fertility rite to express the hope that the couple would bear many children. He states, "To choose every traditional symbol is to deny or diminish our own creativity and ability to symbolize our history in ways that communicate the reality of our relationships."

Ralph and Jerry, who worked with a Unitarian minister to plan their ceremony, were concerned that their ceremony and celebration not resemble a straight wedding. According to Ralph:

> We're two men. We're not a husband and wife. We wanted to affirm that we are two men and not a husband and wife. We felt if we followed a standard wedding format we would wind up not really achieving what we wanted in the first place and just be supporting a stereotype.

While the actual service that Ralph and Jerry planned was pretty much the standard wedding service, including an exchange of vows, which they wrote, and of rings, they tried to avoid the sense that their ceremony was a "wedding" by referring to it as a "service of union" and planned an informal pot-luck party at their apartment following the service, rather than a formal reception.

Les and Jonathan, on the other hand, weren't at all concerned about whether or not they appeared to be mimicking a straight wedding. They wore matching tuxedos, complemented by the tuxedos worn by their four male attendants. The ceremony was the traditional Episcopal wedding ceremony, including the mass, with a few words changed. At the reception there was a three-tiered white cake with two grooms on top. Les notes:

> In some ways it's true that we mimicked a straight wedding. We took our cultural backgrounds and the history of the wedding ceremony and adapted it to our circumstances. We thought about those who might criticize us for the way we did it and decided that if they didn't like it, screw 'em.

The bottom line is, of course, do what feels comfortable and appropriate for you and your partner.

RELIGIOUS OR SECULAR?

Whether you choose a religious ceremony or a secular one, you have many choices to make, from the wording of vows (if vows are to be a part of a ceremony) to planning a party following the ceremony. If you choose to have a secular ceremony, there are really no guidelines. What you decide to do is generally decided exclusively by you and your partner.

Almost all of the couples with whom I spoke who publicly formalized their relationships, did so in a religious union ceremony. Typically, a religious gay union is a formal ceremony—officiated at by a religious leader—during which vows, and often tokens, of commitment are exchanged between two men (or two women) before witnesses. The ceremony is meant to be a process of affirmation, celebration, and symbolization of the relationship.

While such ceremonies have been performed for years by religious leaders, from Catholic priests to Jewish rabbis, few religious institutions—even specifically gay religious institutions—formally endorse, informally endorse, or even have official policies regarding gay union ceremonies. One exception is the United Fellowship of the Metropolitan Community Church (MCC), a primarily gay male and lesbian interdenominational church with more than two hundred congregations nationwide. MCC includes a Holy Union ceremony as part of the regular functioning of the church. While individual members of the clergy at MCC decide on the specifics of the Holy Union, the overall framework has, since the founding of the church in the late sixties, become somewhat standardized.

For those of you who choose to have a religious ceremony, there are several options for you to explore and different arrangements to be made, including deciding which religion or denomination and which religious leader you want, and where you will have the ceremony performed. What you decide depends in large part upon your religion and your circumstances. For example, if you and your lover are active members of a "mainstream" church or synagogue where you are recognized as a couple, you may want to approach your minister or rabbi and ask if he/she will perform a ceremony or knows anyone who will.

That's what Ralph and Jerry did. Ralph had been brought up Catholic, but when he met Jerry he didn't belong to any church. Jerry is music director at their Unitarian church in Lexington, Massachusetts. Shortly after they met, Ralph joined Jerry's church. As far as they know they are the only gay couple in their church. After they had been living together for about nine months, they decided to have a union service and make use of "Unitarian Universalist openness to gays." It helped that their minister, a woman, was very encouraging and willing to perform the service.

Once Ralph and Jerry decided to have the ceremony and discussed with their minister their reasons for wanting a ceremony, they had to decide where to have the ceremony and what form the ceremony would take. Ralph wanted to have their ceremony at the church in Lexington where they were members, but "some of the powers that be at the church were very disturbed by the possibility of having the union there." After their minister let them know there was some opposition, they decided to have the ceremony in Boston at an Episcopal church that they chose primarily because of cost considerations.

With the location decided, Ralph and Jerry began discussing the format of the ceremony with each other and their minister.

Ralph: One of the cornerstones of the Unitarian Universalist church is that the individual has to make his or her own decisions. We were encouraged to write our own service. Our minister helped us with the general format. Jerry is a musician, so we wanted to include more music than most people would.

As mentioned earlier, Ralph and Jerry settled on a fairly traditional service. They started with music at the beginning of the service and ended with music. Their minister made the opening and closing remarks; a friend sang a piece by Handel. And they exchanged vows and rings. Ralph noted that, in comparison to the Metropolitan Community Church Holy Union, their ceremony was light on the religious overtones.

If you're not active members of any church or synagogue, you can contact a gay religious organization of your choice for advice on how to find a religious leader who will perform a union ceremony, or you can contact a local MCC congregation to arrange for a Holy Union ceremony.

According to Reverend Jim Sandmire, one of the pioneers of the Metropolitan Community Church, who performs about twenty Holy Union services a year, the Holy Union ceremony is "to be taken very, very seriously." While there are variations from pastor to pastor, the procedures a couple must go through before a union ceremony and the framework of the ceremony itself are fairly standardized. Before an MCC pastor will conduct a Holy Union, the prospective couple generally has to have lived together in a committed relationship for six months to a year. Reverend Sandmire requires that couples who come to him for a Holy Union live together for at least a year:

The reason for that is that we—gay people—have no social institutions that keep gay people together, so it's important to surround this event with as much caution, care, and concern as we can.

The second rule is that a prospective couple must go through counseling for a prescribed period. Rev. Sandmire requires four to eight sessions over a period of two months.

My requirement is typical of more conservative ministers within the fellowship. The first thing I do is explain the religious significance of what we are doing to make sure they're comfortable with it. We have couples coming to us asking for a Holy Union and they don't really know what they're asking for. Some couples think it's like running off to Reno.

I try to determine whether they have a religious sense and whether they understand that vows taken before God's altar are unique and special.

Then I find out about them. We begin to talk about how they met, and very quickly I can see whether they relate well together, whether they're serious about their relationship. I'll talk to them about communication. I ask what happens when they get mad. We talk about money problems, about role playing, sex, and monogamy.

I don't personally believe a relationship must be monogamous to be successful. I'm at odds with a good many of the other clergy at MCC who are absolutely insistent on monogamy. There is a great difference of opinion. I will say that it is often more difficult to have an open relationship. I think if you're going to have an open relationship you undertake certain kinds of responsibilities for one another that you don't necessarily undertake if you are in a monogamous relationship. What I say to people is, "It is not my business to delve into what kind of relationship you're going to have in that respect. It is my business to make sure that you both understand it." The whole concept is truthfulness.

You would be amazed how many times one person thinks the relationship is monogamous and the other thinks it's open. What I'm asking them to do is say to me that they have discussed this and come to agreement. If they haven't, then they need to go home and work it out before we can go further.

Once I come to the conclusion that this relationship is a healthy one, I explain what kind of planning has to be done. I also make it clear to them that I am dead serious about the Holy Union.

If it doesn't go well, I let them know and suggest that they look seriously at the relationship. They can do that with us or I'll recommend a secular couple counselor. They are always welcome to return to us later.

Part of Reverend Sandmire's counseling includes an admonition to each couple that they must assume the same kind of responsibility for each other that straight couples assume legally by virtue of a marriage certificate. He tells the couples to write or update legally binding wills, draw up Durable Power of Attorney documents, and write letters that will allow them to visit one another should one of them be hospitalized (see Chapter 9), requesting that they be completed before the ceremony.

For couples who choose a Holy Union with MCC, counseling includes a discussion of what happens in the event they decide to have a Holy Union and then later decide to end the relationship.

We indicate to them that if they are going through with this, it is not possible simply to walk away from it. If they get mad at one another, if their relationship appears to be broken, in God's eyes and the eyes of the church they are still joined together, and they need to understand that.

We assume every relationship will have its rocky times. If a couple gets to a point where they feel like the problems are beyond what they can handle, and they're not communicating, part of their Holy Union commitment is to come to us or go to some other counselor before the relationship is beyond repair.

Then, if the couple finds the relationship is still not working, we do understand that there are occasions when a relationship becomes irretrievably broken. While that's very rare for couples who choose a Holy Union, we do make provision for it. If a couple decides to separate, they must come to either the person who joined them in holy union or another minister within our fellowship. The minister investigates, and if convinced that the couple entered into their relationship in good faith and tried to save it in good faith, may decide that it is in the best interest of both parties that the relationship be dissolved.

We will then issue a dissolution of the vows, which simply means that the couple is released from them. The document is signed and the Holy Union is taken off the church records. We point out that if you fail to do that and then enter into another relationship, you have committed adultery in the biblical sense. We get pretty heavy about it. And you will not be joined in a Holy Union ceremony by an MCC minister ever again.

Out of the two hundred or so Holy Unions that Reverend Sandmire has performed, he has issued a half-dozen dissolutions. Reverend Sandmire is careful to note that that low number is probably a result of the strict counseling procedures that couples who choose the Holy Union must complete before being permitted to go through the ceremony. He also recalls several couples who were forced to think twice about ending their relationship because of the commitment they had made in the Holy Union:

I've had people tell me, "There have been times when I've been mad enough I've wanted to leave, and I'd get up ready to go and stop and think, 'I've pledged before God that I was going to stay with this man. Have I given it the very best I can? If I haven't, I had better stay and give it another chance.' " In a moment of crisis the Holy Union can help save a relationship.

Most often Reverend Sandmire performs a standard ceremony in which vows and tokens are exchanged. Most exchange rings.

Gay people are very traditional for the most part. They may rail at society, but they want to have the sense that they have done the things that are "appropriate." The most appropriate way in which you do that is with a ring. The vast majority of the people sitting in our pews look like anybody else. They're bankers, doctors, school teachers. And they're pretty conservative. They want a gold ring.

If not a ring, then a couple may exchange a medallion—often one that is broken in the center. Each wears one half of the medallion. Sometimes I've had people exchange earrings, or just gifts. It's often a piece of writing. I've had people write long and involved messages that are bound and then presented to one another.

In addition to performing a standard ceremony, Reverend Sandmire also permits couples to put together their own ceremony, but those ceremonies must contain certain basic components.

> From my point of view we have to make sure there are specific vows that are repeated to one another on oath and that cover the life situations couples encounter—in sickness and health; for richer, for poorer; for better, for worse. Then there has to be a religious dimension to the ceremony, normally a reading of scripture and prayer.
>
> There's also what I call the pronouncement. In the Christian church, the authority of the clergy to do any of this is based upon the commission that Jesus gave the disciples—to the apostles—in which he specifically said that whatever you bind on earth will be bound in heaven; whatever you loose on earth will be loosed in heaven. It is on the basis of that authority that the clergy makes the pronouncement that, "having presided at this ceremony before God's altar and having heard the couple's vows, then as a commissioned, ordained servant of Christ, I declare that you are. . . ." This pronouncement is followed by a blessing.
>
> The whole thing can be very brief, lasting twelve or thirteen minutes, with just the couple and two witnesses, who may be members of my staff. Or it can be an elaborate ceremony at a church, with the church filled, special dress for the people involved, holy communion, orchestra, organ, and soloists, followed by an enormous reception.

When William, then 37, convinced his lover Martin, 27 at the time, that they should have a union ceremony, they decided to have a Holy Union, in part because the religious aspects of the ceremony appealed to William who has strong religious beliefs. He was raised a Lutheran. Martin was raised a Baptist.

Martin and William made it through the counseling and then met with their pastor to plan the ceremony. They discussed with her their "basic philosophies" and their feelings for one another, which she incorporated into a brief sermon. They each chose a poem, and selected music to be played at the ceremony, including "Somewhere" and "One Hand, One Heart" from *West Side Story*. William says:

> We chose things that were meaningful to us separately. Then we just threw all the ideas together and tried to streamline it. We tried to make sure everybody who wanted to participate had a part.

They invited people from work, friends and family, about fifty in all. Neither of the two men were out to their parents, so they did not invite them. Martin's two brothers were invited, but couldn't make it. But

William's two children, who had lived with him since he had separated from his wife of thirteen years, and his ex-wife attended.

> My children have always been supportive. They were witnesses at our union ceremony. My son was in a tuxedo, and my daughter wore a party dress. My ex-wife wrote a poem, but she started to get very emotional while she was reading it, so my daughter read it. Two other friends read poems as well.

William and Martin exchanged vows and rings.

William: We had rings made. We took all the rings that were special in our lives and had them melted down into two specially designed rings. Each ring has two gold bands separated by a silver braided rope.

They also adopted each other's last names, each adding his partner's last name to his own with a hyphen. William and Martin recently celebrated the seventh anniversary of their Holy Union.

WHOM TO INVITE?

Whether you have a religious or secular ceremony, a public formalization of your relationship means having other people there. Other people can simply mean having a minister or rabbi officiate at the ceremony. Or you can invite a couple of close friends. You may, however, wish to invite more than two close friends and then the question becomes, whom do you invite? Do you invite straight friends as well as gay friends? Colleagues? Family? Much depends on your individual circumstances and personal choice. If you're not out at your job or not out to your parents or straight friends, the decision is simple. You don't invite them. A union ceremony is not the ideal time to come out to friends, family, or colleagues. If you are out to some or all of these people, you have some decisions to make. For example, who among your friends and colleagues would you and your lover be comfortable having as guests. It doesn't hurt to consider whether or not they would be comfortable, but you can still invite them and let them decide whether or not to attend.

Family requires more consideration, and how you handle your families depends primarily on your individual relationships with them and on how well they've come to accept your homosexuality and your relationship with your lover. Remember that families, parents in particular, may know very little about gay relationships. And what they know is likely what you've taught them. However bright or worldly they are, they may not know what to make of an invitation to a union ceremony or what to expect. So while your family may be able to handle your relationship, they may not be open to the idea of a union ceremony and may not attend, no matter how carefully you handle them.

If you are worried about how they will react, or if you think you would be uncomfortable having them attend, one option is not to invite family or even tell them about the union ceremony. But, for many of the men I spoke with, having family attend the union ceremony, when possible, was very important, so they made an effort to invite them. I'll offer only one universal recommendation: It is most prudent to talk with family about a planned union ceremony before sending an invitation.

Ralph and Jerry took different approaches with each of their immediate-family members. Jerry invited a sister from Oklahoma, and made a point to call her to discuss the planned event before he sent an invitation. He decided not to send an invitation to his parents in Arkansas, who knew about his relationship with Ralph, but instead, asked his sister to talk with them about it. Ralph sent invitations to his two sisters, one of whom lived in New Jersey, the other in China. Both were supportive of the event, but were unable to attend. He didn't send an invitation to his brother who lives nearby:

> I've never talked much to him about being gay. So I didn't invite him, although I wish I had. The ceremony was a statement of affirmation that Jerry and I were a couple and, although it would have been touchy to deal with my brother in those terms, that was the time to do it.

Before sending his parents an invitation, Ralph spoke with them:

> My parents had known I was gay for about five years and had been trying to deny it. This was not the type of affirmation they were looking for. Their reasoning for not coming was they felt like this was something they just didn't want their son to be doing. They weren't upset; they just didn't want to be a part of it.
>
> I was both hurt and very angry that they didn't want to attend and I told them so. They didn't want to give up hope that I was straight.
>
> One of the things that led me to believe they would accept the invitation was that they had met Jerry several times before. They had come to dinner here. We had gone to visit them almost every weekend.

In retrospect, Ralph wishes he had put more pressure on his parents to attend. He feels that if they had attended and seen how many of their friends and co-workers were there, they would have been "reassured that what we were doing was okay." But he acknowledges that having them there would have made him uncomfortable.

Rabbi Yoel Kahn, who is the rabbi for Sha-Ar Zahav, a gay Synagogue in San Francisco, believes that it is important to include families in a union ceremony when possible.

The problem is that people are afraid of inviting their relatives because they're afraid they won't take the ceremony seriously. Part of the whole ceremony is to convey the importance of the relationship. For a couple the ceremony symbolizes their striving for legitimacy. But unfortunately, for some families, a ceremony represents ultimate desecration.

For one union ceremony over which Rabbi Kahn officiated—one that I came across pictured on the cover of the New York's *Village Voice* newspaper—the families of both men attended, including parents, siblings (one brother came all the way from London to attend), great uncles and aunts, and cousins. But Rabbi Kahn acknowledges that such broad family support is extremely rare.

One option for helping your parents at least to understand your plans for a religious ceremony is to have them consult with the minister or rabbi who will conduct your ceremony. According to Reverend Sandmire, who has counseled many families:

I think it's helpful. Sometimes they come with their child, sometimes by themselves. Usually their concern has to do with, "Is there any hope that my child can be anything other than gay?" I tell them no. The thing I try to get through to them is that homosexuality is a natural variation of sexuality and that their child can lead a full, useful, and complete life. And most importantly, I tell them that their child isn't condemned to hell. I try to give them some sense that their child is fine with God and that their kid has really been a very strong person.

I explain that their child has now found a partner and that the two of them are going forward with their lives, with stability, and responsibility and that that is a tribute to their strength of character. And that they really need to rejoice about that because the alternative could be lives of emptiness, and drunkenness, and whatever.

CELEBRATING YOUR RELATIONSHIP

Whether or not you formalize your relationship, you can celebrate your relationship in several ways including a hug and a kiss in bed every night before falling asleep; inviting friends over to dinner to celebrate your new home together; or a fifth or twenty-fifth anniversary party to which you invite friends and family. Or you can do nothing. It's up to you.

For the couples I interviewed, the most-often mentioned ways in which they celebrated a relationship was in conjunction with an anniversary or after moving into a new home together.

Anniversary

Before you decide how and if to celebrate the anniversary of your relationship, you have to figure out an anniversary date. That's not always so easy. For a straight married couple there's usually little doubt about the anniversary date, or what that date signifies. For example, when my grandparents celebrated their sixtieth wedding anniversary, the significance of the date was obvious: It was the day on which they were married.

Scott and I mark our relationship by three dates: our first date, the first time we made love, and the day we moved in together. We could have added a fourth—the day we met—but neither of us could quite remember what day that was and it didn't strike either of us as that important. Of the three dates, we consider the first night we spent together to be our "anniversary" date.

You may find you have no difficulty agreeing on what event signifies your anniversary, but you may have difficulty agreeing on the exact date. In that case, if it's important to you, you can choose a date. Marshall and Craig enjoy celebrating their anniversary (of their first date), so choosing a specific day was important, but they couldn't even agree on the month in which they met. "So we celebrate our anniversary on February 14 because it's halfway between what Marshall remembers and what I remember and because it's Valentine's Day."

Chet and John, who consider the day they met to be their anniversary, can't remember exactly what day it was either, although they do remember what month. "It was around the end of February." For Chet and John, their anniversary is no big deal and neither cares much about celebrating the occasion, so they never felt the need to set an exact date. They simply remind one another each year that it's that time of year, again.

Other couples view an anniversary as an accomplishment, a symbol of their successful relationship, something to be marked in a significant way. Greg and Neal decided to celebrate their twenty-fifth anniversary by throwing a party. They sent out simple engraved invitations to friends and family inviting them "to share in the celebration of their twenty-five years together" at their home.

Neal: Twenty-five years is terrific no matter what. I have a brother who barely made fifteen years.

Greg: It was a wonderful party. The joy that people have in seeing people make something work . . .

Neal: People were very happy to be here and celebrate that two human beings can make a life together. We also saw it as an opportunity to do something about the stereotype. Most people see the two-weekers, the one-nighters. They don't know how many people there are like Greg and me.

Greg: In our age group we're not out discoing, so people don't think we exist.
Neal: It was really making a statement that two men who had all the obstacles and all the prejudices to contend with have made it together for twenty-five years.

You don't have to wait until your twenty-fifth anniversary to throw a party. For a new couple, an anniversary party can be a way to say to friends and family that their relationship is more than a casual affair, even after one year. Of course you don't have to do anything as organized as giving a party to celebrate your anniversary. You can exchange gifts, go to dinner, simply acknowledge the date with a hug and a kiss, or you can do nothing. If it's not important to you or your partner, you don't have to do anything. However, if it is important to your partner that you do something special, then make an effort; and if it's important to you and he's not good at taking a hint, tell him. Assuming that you both like to celebrate but run into problems deciding how, there are always options, probably more than you realize. Be creative. For example, Irwin and Duane like to celebrate their anniversary, but they never enjoyed trying to find gifts for one another. After discussing it, they decided to buy one gift together for both of them each year (usually something practical, on the order of a toaster).

Just a note here about parents. If you're out to your parents, it doesn't hurt to let them know that you're celebrating your anniversary. They may not even be aware that male couples celebrate anniversaries. Letting them know can serve several purposes, including serving as a reminder that your homosexuality is not a temporary condition, as a suggestion that your partner is more than just a passing interest, and as an indication that your life is indeed stable, despite what they might have imagined.

But don't expect that by simply letting your parents or friends know when your anniversary is that they will dutifully send an anniversary card every year on the appropriate date. If you feel strongly about it, you may want to let them know how much you would appreciate receiving a card.

Housewarming

One low-key way to celebrate your relationship, and to mark a stage in your life together, is to have a housewarming, inviting friends, family, or colleagues—depending, of course, on whom you and your partner are out to. A housewarming party gives you the opportunity to demonstrate to your guests that you have moved beyond the dating stage to sharing a home together.

RELIGION

A commitment to religious beliefs and membership in a church or other religious organization can be a strong binding force for a couple. For Ralph and Jerry, involvement in their church is a major part of their lives together. Their church is also a source of support and encouragement.

For a so-called subculture that is supposed to be turned off to religion because so many religions reject homosexuality, there are many, many gay religious groups to choose from across the country, including Mormon, Seventh Day Adventist, Lutheran, Christian Scientist, Presbyterian, Quaker, Episcopalian, Mennonite, Methodist, Unitarian, Evangelical, Jewish, and Catholic.

But religion can also complicate a couple's life, whether or not either partner is particularly religious. For Paul, who was raised a Catholic and taught that homosexuality was a sin, that translated into hiding his homosexuality from his parents and hiding his new relationship with Stuart:

> Being Catholic played a major part in not telling my parents. I'm not supposed to be gay. I was taught it was wrong. Even though I don't believe that anymore, it's still a conflict. I love him, I love them. I don't want to hurt them.

Stuart was understanding of Paul's feelings, but when Paul wanted a two-bedroom apartment so that his parents wouldn't be suspicious on visits, Stuart objected—primarily because they couldn't afford a two-bedroom apartment.

For another couple, where one or the other partner comes from a devoutly religious family, extreme guilt about homosexuality can lead to everything from sexual dysfunction and an inability to come to terms with one's homosexuality to low self-esteem and an inability to make a long-term commitment to another man.

If you or your partner recognizes the original source of the problem, one way to work on it is to seek the advice of a gay or gay-sensitive religious leader. If your partner doesn't want to go on his own, offer to accompany him; or go on your own and find out how best you can help him. You can also seek the help of a professional therapist (see Chapter 13 for information on how to find a therapist). Above all, be patient with your partner. It may only take patience, reassurance, and time, as it did with Paul and Stuart, for your partner to get past the negative feelings and guilt about homosexuality that can result from a religious upbringing.

RESOURCES

Finding a Place of Worship or Religious Leader or Counselor

One way to start your search for a place of worship, religious leader, or counselor is by calling your local gay helpline; or check the *Gayellow Pages* (see Appendix), which lists religious resources across the country. The choice of places of worship, for example, ranges from "mainstream" churches that openly welcome gay people, to primarily gay churches and synagogues. You can also contact one of the national religious organizations, such as Dignity and the Universal Fellowship of Metropolitan Community Churches, listed in this section. These organizations can often provide referrals to a local place of worship and a gay or gay-sensitive member of the clergy.

If you decide to have a union ceremony and you live in a metropolitan area, finding a religious leader to perform the ceremony is fairly easy, particularly if you choose a Holy Union ceremony at a local Metropolitan Community Church. If, for example, you're looking for a Catholic priest or a Jewish rabbi, the search becomes a little more difficult, since gay Catholic and Jewish congregations often do not officially recognize a union ceremony. Often, however, they will provide a referral to a member of the clergy who performs union ceremonies.

Religious Organizations

There are hundreds of religious organizations for gay people nationwide. The resources listed here are for a few of the national headquarters of religious groups that have a major presence across the country.

CATHOLIC
Dignity Incorporated, 1500 Massachusetts Avenue NW, Suite 11, Washington, DC 20005–1894, 202–861–0017

EPISCOPAL
Integrity International, 30 North Raymond Street #406, Pasadena, CA 91103

Send a self-addressed, stamped, business-size envelope for information.

INTERDENOMINATIONAL
Universal Fellowship of Metropolitan Community Churches (International/ Main Office), 5300 Santa Monica Boulevard #304, Los Angeles, CA 90029, 213–464–5100

JEWISH
World Congress of Gay and Lesbian Jewish Organizations, PO Box 881272, San Francisco, CA 94188

The organization has no telephone but will refer you to the nearest gay synagogue or rabbi if you write. Enclose a self-addressed, stamped, business-size envelope.

Books

The Church and the Homosexual, by John J. McNeill, S.J., 1985. Next Year Publications, 316 Fifth Avenue, New York, NY 10001

This is an in-depth and highly acclaimed look at the relationship of gay men and lesbians to the Catholic Church.

The Two of Us: Affirming, Celebrating, and Symbolizing Gay and Lesbian Relationships, by Larry J. Uhrig, 1984. Alyson Publications, Inc., PO Box 2783, Boston, MA 02208

Larry Uhrig offers a general discussion of gay couple relationships, with emphasis on the union ceremony. The appendix includes both a "Romantic" and "Legalistic" contract of commitment, and the order of worship taken from the program of the author's Holy Union.

CHAPTER 13

Health

*"Illness is not one of the things you plan for during
the dating period or early years of a relationship."*

The fantasy relationship never includes images of a drunk, abusive
partner, coping with a severely depressed lover, keeping vigil over a
partner's bed in an intensive care unit, or cleaning up a lover debili-
tated by severe chronic diarrhea.

Gary, 39, and Mitch, 29, were faced with serious illness in the second
year of their relationship.

Mitch: I got diarrhea one day and it would not stop. It went on for a week and
the doctor kept trying things and nothing would stop it. Finally I was going
to the doctor just about every other day. I was in his office when I collapsed
from dehydration.

Gary: When we were in the doctor's office and the nurse came out and said
Mitch had collapsed, I thought I would collapse next.

I've always had healthy lovers. When he first got sick, it really got on my
nerves. I had never cared for an ill person. I remember thinking, "I'm not
ready for this." I just don't deal well with illness.

Mitch: You really have to love somebody to put up with shit everywhere.

Gary: I found myself in a position where I had to care for him. When I wasn't
working, I was at the hospital from nine in the morning until ten or eleven
at night. You don't realize the closeness that you develop because of that. I
remember cleaning up after him, bathing him, shampooing Mitch's hair. I
was there constantly, but I really didn't think about it, I just did it.

In a relationship, illness is just not something you think about. Illness is not
one of the things you plan for during the dating period or early years of a
relationship. It's not something we planned for this early in our lives.

Mitch's diarrhea cleared up as mysteriously as it appeared. His doctors were unable to get a positive HIV antibody test out of him and he had no other symptoms. Mitch has been in good health since.

PREVENTION

Much of what is discussed in this chapter is avoidable, and can be prevented if you so choose. But prevention assumes an awareness of danger and an acceptance of the fact that, as human beings, we are all mortal and if we hope to live healthy and long lives we need to pay some degree of attention to the things we do, do to ourselves, and let others do to us. Which isn't to say there aren't those few exceptional specimens who are blessed with genes that let them smoke three packs a day, drink heavily, eat whatever they choose, never exercise, have unsafe sex and live to 95.

For the average mortal, prevention is still the best medicine. But the words out of popular gay culture during the early years of liberation were more like, "What nature dishes out the doctor can cure." The painful lesson many gay men have learned since then is that even when a cure is possible, illness takes its toll on the immune system—the first line of defense for all disease, including AIDS. Also to be considered is what a long list of sexually transmitted diseases will do to an insurance application (see Chapter 11).

A disposition toward prevention, common-sense precautions, and self-education will help guarantee that you can avoid many of the ailments that plague greater numbers of gay men than any other group. Use of condoms, for example, significantly reduces the chance of getting or passing along many sexually transmitted diseases. Following safer sex guidelines (a complete list of safer sex guidelines is found in Chapter 8) will greatly reduce the risk of picking up the HIV virus that is believed to cause AIDS and of passing it on to your lover; and it will reduce the risk of contracting other sexually transmitted diseases as well.

General prevention issues such as diet, sleep, and exercise I'll leave to another book. Just remember that there is a lot you and your partner can do to stay in good health and to improve your health. As a couple, you have the added advantage of having one another to support each other's efforts to stay healthy, whether that means quitting cigarettes, taking regular walks, getting to bed at a reasonable hour, or keeping to a diet that is low in fats.

ADDICTION

Drugs and Alcohol

No matter how you look at the statistics and whatever the causes, drug and alcohol dependency among gay men is a major problem. Most experts suggest that one third or more of all gay men are drug- or alcohol-dependent. Besides the fact that a relationship can hardly flourish when chemicals are at its center, alcohol and drugs are implicated in all sorts of awful statistics from car accidents to physical abuse of a partner. (See Chapter 14, "On the Rocks," for more information on partner abuse.)

HOW CAN YOU RECOGNIZE A PROBLEM?

How can you tell if your partner has or is heading for a drug or alcohol problem? John Whalen is executive director of Pride Institute, a gay-run alcohol- and drug-dependency treatment facility in Eden Prairie, Minnesota. It is one of the only chemical-dependency treatment facilities in the country devoted exclusively to treating gay men and lesbians. The following is a paraphrase of the guidelines he offers for assessing whether or not your partner has a chemical dependency problem:

1. When the life of the couple begins to circle around one partner's usage of drugs or alcohol;

2. A reluctance on the part of a lover to go to social events where chemicals of some sort aren't available;

3. Nothing happens—dinner doesn't get made, you don't go out, he doesn't talk about his day—until after the third cocktail;

4. Increase in tolerance. If he can hold his chemicals, that means his body is becoming accustomed to them and reacting in an addictive way.

5. If your partner has blackouts. A blackout occurs when the mind can't tolerate the chemical as well as the body can, and it simply stops functioning. But the body keeps going. So your partner may start denying things that he's done or remember them differently from the way in which they actually happened. After a while, the spouse who isn't chemical dependent may begin to wonder whose reality is real.

Other possible symptoms include marked personality changes when a partner drinks or uses drugs, continued use of chemicals despite their negative affect on his ability to do his job or to deal with you, friends, or family, and/or the spending of large sums of money either secretively on drugs or on things not consistent with his normal behavior.

WHAT CAN YOU DO?
You alone cannot make your partner end his chemical dependency. *He* must end it. You can, however, seek outside help on how to handle your particular circumstance. This often means seeking help for yourself first, not because you're chemically dependent, but because of the negative impact your partner's dependence is having on you. (That condition is often referred to as co-dependency.) It could mean arranging for an "intervention," in which a third party conveys to the chemical-dependent partner the depth and consequences of his problem and tries to convince him to seek help. Or, if your partner acknowledges his problem and wants help, he may call on you to find that help.

The first thing you should do if you think your partner has a problem—or if you think you have a problem and need advice—is to call the free twenty-four-hour toll-free telephone number at Pride Institute (see "Resources"). Someone there will provide advice by phone and, when appropriate, refer you to resources in your area or region specifically for chemical-dependent gay people—this includes referrals to gay AA and Al-ANON groups nationwide.

Once your partner begins recovering from his dependency on drugs or alcohol, you will likely be asked to reinforce his abstinence by abstaining from alcohol or drugs yourself for a period of time.

WHY SEEK OUT RESOURCES
SPECIFICALLY FOR GAY PEOPLE?
Because a partner must be integrated into the treatment of his chemical-dependent lover, experts agree that the best possible treatment environment for gay people who are chemical dependent and for their lovers is one in which they don't have to worry about hiding who they are. Worrying about hiding, or dealing with homophobic counselors or with fellow patients and their loved ones who are homophobic, can seriously complicate recovery.

John Whalen of Pride Institute—along with other experts who work with chemical-dependent gay people—feels strongly that "you should have a place to go where the realities of the relationship are integrated into the treatment. If the population where the chemical-dependent partner is going for treatment is predominantly straight, the gay patient will not feel free to talk about the relationship and himself. One man I spoke with told me that when he speaks in group therapy sessions he can only refer to his lover as 'this person.' If he talks about his relationship in a realistic way, he gets glares."

**WHAT IF BOTH LOVERS ARE
ALCOHOLICS OR DRUG DEPENDENT?**

If you recognize that you and your lover are both alcoholics or drug dependent, get help for yourself first. If both of you are in similar shape, however, neither one is likely to recognize that you both have a serious problem. In that case, it is most often a family member, a friend, or employer who intervenes. The friend, employer, or family member typically will attempt to convince the partners that they are indeed chemical dependent and need to seek treatment.

WARNING:

Do not attempt an intervention without first consulting an expert or bringing in expert help.

If you prefer to write for information on where to find help, or would like to do more reading on the subject of alcohol- or drug-dependency before calling for help, consult the "Resources" for this chapter.

Sex

At first glance, the notion of being "addicted" to sex may seem funny; unless you happen to be addicted and it's destroying your relationship with your partner, or threatening both your lives, that is. Addiction to sex can take many forms, from compulsive masturbation that leaves you with no desire for sex with your lover, to engaging in unsafe sexual practices that you know are dangerous to you and your lover's physical health. The common thread to all compulsive sexual behavior is the inability to control or change that behavior, even if you want to.

**HOW CAN YOU RECOGNIZE
IF YOU HAVE A PROBLEM?**

It is easier, and I think more effective, to speak of the characteristics most common to people who suffer from sexual compulsion than to speak of symptoms. The following list of characteristics shared by many sexual compulsives is drawn from a pamphlet printed by Sexual Compulsives Anonymous (SCA), a New York City-based self-help organization.

1. As adolescents we used fantasy and compulsive masturbation to escape from feelings and continued this tendency into our adult lives with compulsive sex.

2. We tend to become immobilized by romantic obsessions.

3. We search for some "magical" quality in others to make us feel complete. Other people were idealized and endowed with a power-

ful symbolism, which often disappeared after we had sex with them.

4. Compulsive sex becomes a drug, which we use to escape from feelings such as anxiety, loneliness, anger, rejection, or self-hatred, as well as joy. We sought oblivion in fantasy, masturbation, and compulsive sex. Sex becomes a reward, punishment, distraction, and time-killer.

5. Because of our low self-esteem, we use sex to feel validated and complete.

6. We tend to lose ourselves in sex and romantic obsession, and become addicted to the search for sex. As a result, we neglect our lives.

7. We try to bring intensity and excitement into our lives through sex, but feel ourselves growing steadily emptier.

8. While constantly seeking intimacy with another person, the desperate quality of our need makes true intimacy with anyone impossible. Trying to conceal our dependency from ourselves and from others, we grow more isolated and alienated from ourselves, and from the very people we longed to be close to.

9. We fear relationships, but continually search for them. In a relationship, we fear abandonment and rejection, but out of a relationship, we feel empty and incomplete.

10. We are drawn to people who are not available to us, or who would reject or abuse us.

11. We often develop unhealthy dependency relationships that eventually become unbearable.

12. Even when we get the love of another person, it never seems enough, and we are unable to stop lusting after others.

13. We become addicted to people, and are unable to distinguish between sex, love, and affection.

14. Sex becomes compartmentalized and not integrated into our lives as a healthy element.

SCA is careful to note that the organization does not exist "to repress our God-given sexuality, but to learn how to express it in ways that will not endanger our mental, physical, and spiritual health."

If you recognize yourself in the list above, and feel you want to change and *can't do it on your own,* it may be time to seek help from either a therapist who has experience dealing with compulsive sexual behavior, or from a local self-help organization dedicated to helping people overcome such behavior.

Currently there is no nationwide network of organizations for people seeking help for compulsive sexual behavior, and existing organizations are, for the most part, located only in major cities. To find a group near your community, your best bet is to start with the local gay helpline, listed in your local telephone book or in the *Gayellow Pages*. Or you can call the Sexual Dependency Unit at the Golden Valley Health Center in Minnesota (see "Resources") for a referral to a local support organization or for information.

Cigarettes

As with all addictions, you cannot force your partner to quit smoking. You can encourage him. If your partner decides to quit smoking, you can support him in his effort to stay free from cigarettes. If you both smoke, you can suggest to your partner that you try quitting together. In that way you can encourage each other in your effort.

After twenty-six years together, Greg and Neal don't often argue, but if you want to get them going at each other, just ask Greg about Neal's smoking.

Greg: I worry about Neal's smoking. We've had some unpleasant conversations about it. We probably have more arguments about his smoking than anything else. I yell at him and he tells me to get off his back.

When we first met, I was quite slim, but I've put on a lot of weight since I stopped smoking. I had a scare about four years ago. I had shortness of breath. During that time I stopped smoking and never started again. He holds out because of that fear that he'll put on weight.

Neal: I happen to like smoking. I've cut down. I try not to smoke. I'm just not a "cold turkey" person.

Greg: See, he's rationalized the whole thing.

Neal: Oh, fuck off.

Greg: I'm addicted to smoking. That's why I know that if I have one I'll go back to it. So I don't have one.

Neal: And I'm addicted to chocolate. If I stop smoking I'll overeat. I can blow up in a week.

Greg: I just don't want to lose him.

As the partner of an ex-smoker (he makes a distinction between "ex" and "reformed"), I have a lot of experience saying, "No Scott, you can't have a cigarette." If we're with friends who smoke, he often asks if he can have just one cigarette. He knows I'll say no and that's the end of it. On a couple of occasions when Scott has been away on trips to California without me, and he's spent an evening with old friends who smoke, he has succumbed to temptation. Of course, he never volunteered this information but, as the saying goes, "The truth will out." And it did.

Again, I can't stop Scott from smoking if he really wants to, just as you can't get your partner to stop smoking if he doesn't want to stop. But you can help him if he wants help, and you can certainly get information from the American Cancer Society for him on how to quit smoking.

AIDS (ACQUIRED IMMUNE DEFICIENCY SYNDROME)

The danger in writing anything about AIDS is that the information may very well be obsolete before the ink even has a chance to dry. The pace of research is, by medical standards, awesome. So be sure to check with your doctor, local health organization, or national or local AIDS hotline for the most up-to-date information.

What is not likely to change soon is the fact that AIDS is a sexually transmitted disease, believed to be caused by the Human Immunodeficiency Virus (HIV), which can be passed between partners, no matter how much they love each other. (See Chapter 8 for safer sex guidelines.) AIDS is an infectious disease that attacks the body's ability to fight off some cancers and other diseases.

In its most severe form, AIDS is deadly. In its less-severe form, a condition previously referred to as AIDS Related Complex (ARC), the symptoms can be severe—including significant weight loss and chronic diarrhea—but they are not necessarily fatal. What makes the whole discussion of what is and what isn't AIDS so confusing is that there isn't a test that can determine whether or not you have AIDS. As of 1988 tests can only determine whether you have been exposed to the HIV virus or are carrying the HIV virus. So at the present time, the disease can only be confirmed after a patient has contracted certain illnesses, or "marker" diseases, that are closely associated with AIDS, such as a form of skin cancer called Kaposi's sarcoma (KS), and Pneumocystis carinii pneumonia (PCP), a protozoan infection of the lungs. Because the list of AIDS marker diseases continues to grow, the definition of AIDS will continue to change.

AIDS Anxiety—"The Worried Well"

For most couples, the closest they will get to AIDS is caring for a friend who has contracted the disease. But almost all of the couples I interviewed were affected by AIDS anxiety ranging from mild concern to a devastation of their sex lives. (See Chapter 8, "Sex," for more on the impact of AIDS on sex.)

There are several ways to deal with AIDS anxiety. You can talk about it with each other, seek out a private therapist, join an AIDS-anxiety talk group in your community, or get tested (which can increase anxiety if you test positive). If your partner is having a bout of anxiety, all you can do is reassure him. Don't deny the reality of his fear, which may be well-founded, particularly if a former boyfriend has been diagnosed with the disease, or he has been experiencing symptoms associated with AIDS.

The most important thing to remember is that anxiety is normal. Just as occasional swollen glands is normal. After all, glands are only human.

Getting Tested

There are two sides to the testing debate. There's the "I want to know" school of thought, and the "I'm better off not knowing" school. The current widely available test only confirms *infection* with HIV. The HIV test reveals the presence of antibodies, which the body produces after exposure to the virus. It does not test for the virus itself. And it does not reveal who has AIDS or will ultimately develop AIDS. So there are those who argue that a positive test result only serves to heighten the anxiety without providing any concrete information beyond the fact that you've been exposed. If you take the test and the result is positive, there's not much you can do besides worry. On the other hand, a negative test result (two tests are generally conducted several months apart to confirm a negative result) usually reduces anxiety, provided you're keeping clean by avoiding unsafe sexual practices.

Because of the potential for disruption in your lives in the event the test results come back positive, the decision to take the test is something you should discuss with each other, and possibly with your doctor or with a counselor at the site where you're thinking of getting tested. There are also confidentiality and insurance concerns involved in the test/not-to-test debate. Those issues are discussed in Chapter 11.

Scott and I have discussed at length whether or not we should be tested. We both have reason to believe we may have been exposed, so we figure the chances are 50–50 either way. By not getting tested we can quietly imagine in the backs of our minds that we were not exposed, or that we have successfully fought off the virus. We both agree we would be devastated by a positive test result and consumed by the anxiety of not really knowing what that positive test result could mean. We've chosen the "ignorance is bliss" approach for now. We might change our minds if a test is developed that can predict who will develop AIDS.

Again, the choice is yours. But discuss it with your partner first and discuss the pros and cons with a doctor or health expert. And if you decide to go ahead with testing, be certain you do it anonymously. You don't want a positive test result, or even the fact that you've taken the test, to show up on your medical records.

General Symptoms Associated with AIDS

You should be familiar with the following list of symptoms for your partner, if not yourself. You may recognize symptoms in him that he himself may not recognize. As with any illness—even AIDS—the sooner you are treated the better.

The following list is drawn from "Medical Answers about AIDS," a booklet prepared by Lawrence Mass, M.D., and published by the Gay Men's Health Crisis (GMHC) in New York City. According to GMHC: "Each of the symptoms listed below, it must be emphasized, may be associated with diseases or conditions that have nothing to do with AIDS. When not easily or otherwise explained, however, the development of any of the symptoms listed below should be discussed with a physician or physician-supervised health care provider who is familiar with AIDS."

1. Lymphadenopathy—Enlarged and/or enlarging, hardening, painful, or otherwise prominent lymph nodes (also called lymph glands).

2. Recently appearing or slowly enlarging purplish or discolored nodules, plaques, lumps, rashes, or other new growths on top of, or beneath, the skin or the mucous membranes.

3. Thrush—a thick, persistent, whitish coating on the tongue or in the throat that may be accompanied by soreness.

4. Shingles—an often painful and itchy rash.

5. Weight loss (with or without loss of appetite) of more than ten pounds during a period of less than two months that is clearly unrelated to depression, diet, or activity.

6. Persistent fevers or night sweats.

7. A heavy, persistent, often dry cough that may be accompanied by shortness of breath that is not from smoking and that has lasted too long to be a cold or flu.

8. Persistent diarrhea.

9. Easy bruisability or unexplained bleeding from any orifice or from new growths on the skin or on the mucous membranes.

10. Profound fatigue, which may be accompanied by light-headedness or headache, that is not transient and not explained by physical exertion or by a psychiatric or substance-abuse disorder.

11. Persistent loss of memory, changes in mood, and/or other persistent or frequently recurrent neurologic or psychiatric symptoms that are otherwise unexplained.

Coping with AIDS

If you find yourself faced with the possibility that one or both of you has the disease, you will be in need of far more information than this book can provide. You will need to concern yourselves with many difficult issues from how—*if*—to tell family and co-workers, to getting legal papers in order, dealing with health care providers, dealing with each other, coping with the future. Fortunately, even if you are unable to get support from your family and co-workers for whatever reason, there is an ever-increasing number of resources provided by a remarkable range of organizations. You can start your search for resources by calling one of the telephone numbers listed in the "Resources" section of this chapter. Just remember, this is not something you have to go through alone. There are many people who want to help.

OTHER SEXUALLY TRANSMITTED DISEASES (STDS)

For couples who have sex outside of their relationships, there are plenty of sexually transmitted diseases to worry about besides AIDS. If you use condoms and practice strict safer sex, you greatly diminish your chances of catching many of these diseases.

Even if you are in a monogamous relationship, you should be aware of these diseases—as you may already be if your partner has herpes or is a carrier of the Hepatitis-B Virus. And, you should know how to recognize symptoms of STDs just in case your partner passes on to you a "little gift" that he picked up by accident during that rare—or not so rare—transgression. It happens.

What follows is a partial list of STDs with a very brief description of symptoms for each. The information presented here is only an introduction and is drawn in part from *The Advocate Guide to Gay Health.* For a complete description of the symptoms of the diseases listed, and for more information on sexually transmitted diseases, you can contact your doctor; or a local gay helpline can provide a referral to the appropriate clinic or health agency in your area. You can also contact one of the organizations or consult one of the books listed in the "Resources" section of this chapter.

Gonorrhea is characterized by discharge from the penis and a burning sensation when urinating. Only half of all cases involve the penis, which should come as no relief, since when the penis is involved you can at least tell if you have the disease early on. If your case is anal or in your throat (you can get it from giving or getting a blow job), you may not know you have it until the disease has spread and other symptoms such as fever, chills, loss of appetite, and pain in the knees, wrists, fingers, hands, ankles, or elbows appear. You may also experience a rash. Symptoms usually appear in three to five days—but up to one month—following infection. Using a condom can help prevent the spread of gonorrhea.

Nonspecific Urethritis (NSU) results from one of several different microorganisms that you can pick up from a partner's rectum or mouth. You can get it from having sex with your lover just as easily as from a fling. NSU is not always transmitted sexually. Symptoms can be mistaken for gonorrhea and include discharge accompanied by painful urination. While NSU's symptoms may be similar to gonorrhea, treatment is not, so a careful diagnosis is critical. Use of a condom can help prevent NSU.

Syphilis is not as common as gonorrhea, but is just as nasty and potentially fatal if left untreated. Incubation (the period between infection and onset of symptoms) is nine days to three months—three weeks on average. The disease begins with a solitary chancre at the site where the bacteria entered the body. If that's in your throat or rectum, you probably won't notice it. If left untreated, syphilis develops to a secondary stage, which manifests itself in symptoms that appear, on average, six weeks after the chancre heals. Those symptoms may include a skin rash, sore throat, pains in the bones and joints, loss of appetite, nausea, constipation, and a low fever, and possibly patchy loss of hair. If you miss the disease in this stage you can develop life-threatening complications. If you are HIV positive, make certain you are also checked for syphilis. Your health is severely threatened when both HIV and syphilis are present. Again, condoms can help you avoid catching this disease.

Hepatitis-B is an inflammation of the liver that hampers and/or interrupts liver functions. Symptoms include feeling generally worn out, loss of appetite, nausea, and a sense of pain or fullness in the upper right side of the abdomen. Other symptoms may include flu-like ailments, yellowing of the whites of the eyes and the skin, and dark-colored urine. The virus can be present in fecal matter, saliva, semen, blood, and urine. No treatment or cure exists aside from waiting for the virus to go away, although a vaccine is now available. Two hundred and fifty people die each year from hepatitis-B, and 5 percent of the 200,000 annual cases eventually lead to cirrhosis (scarring) of the liver and early death.

For between 8,000 and 16,000 of the people who get hepatitis-B every year, the disease remains infectious (it can be passed on), even after symptoms disappear. So the only way to tell if you are a chronic carrier is to have a blood test. If you are a carrier, your lover may have to get the hepatitis-B vaccine if he does not already carry antibodies for the disease. Consult with your doctor or local health clinic for more information. Practicing strict safer sex greatly reduces your chances of contracting hepatitis-B.

Amebic Dysentery, Salmonella, and Shigellosis are caused by parasites or bacteria. In all three diseases, bacteria or parasites migrate to the intestines.

Symptoms range from a mildly upset stomach to vomiting, diarrhea, cramps, and excessive gas. But many of those who are afflicted are asymptomatic and are just carriers. Left untreated, these diseases can cause serious damage to the intestinal tract. They can be prevented by abstaining from rimming (anal-oral sex) and by practicing safer sex.

Venereal Warts are warts that appear around the anus and in the rectum or on the shaft of the penis. Venereal warts appear as single or multipe painless fleshy growths around the anus or on the penis. The warts are removed by various methods. The virus is highly contagious. Venereal warts can be prevented by wearing a condom.

Genital Herpes—There are two types of herpes. As a general rule Type 2 appears below the waist and Type 1 above, with a 10 percent crossover. The disease is usually, although not always, transmitted sexually. Symptoms of genital herpes include painful blisters or bumps on the head or shaft of the penis. The blister may appear on the anus, where it may rupture and form soft, extremely painful sores. Herpes can also appear on the thighs or other parts of the body and can be prevented with careful condom use.

MENTAL HEALTH

According to the American Psychiatric Association's Psychiatric Glossary, mental health is "A state of being, relative rather than absolute. The best indices of mental health are simultaneous success at working, loving, and creating, with the capacity for mature and flexible resolution of conflicts between instincts, conscience, important other people, and reality."

In other words, while there will be good days and bad days, if you manage to balance challenges in your day-to-day life, you have a positive state of mental health.

Mental health problems fall into two major categories: mental disorders; and problems of living, coping, and adaptation.

A mental disorder is definable as an illness with psychologic behavior manifestations such as impairment in functioning due to genetic, physiological, social, or psychological disturbance. That would include diagnosable mental disorders such as schizophrenia, major depression, and manic-depressive illness. These disorders are typically treated by a psychiatrist.

Problems of living, coping, and adaptation, such as mild nonclinical depression, grief, sexuality conflicts, homophobia, relationship problems, and difficulties in expressing anger, are typically treated by a psychologist or professional counselor.

Not every problem of living, coping, and adaptation requires professional help. If a bout of depression is the result of the death of an elderly parent, all that may be required is the passage of time and a liberal amount of comforting from a lover, friends, and family. Self-hate in the form of homophobia may be helped by peer counseling. You can also seek the advice of a member of the clergy.

The difference between a mental disorder and a problem of living, coping, and adaptation is in the severity of the symptoms. If you or your partner suffer from depression or an inability to function for more than six to eight weeks, you should seek a workup and diagnosis by a *medically oriented* psychiatrist. The reason I make this recommendation is that it's simple logic to rule out the more serious disorders first.

If you choose to seek the help of a professional counselor or therapist, shop around and be careful. Mixed in with qualified and able therapists are plenty of unqualified therapists. Don't feel you have to settle for the first therapist you meet. Try to find someone with whom you feel you can work, someone who expresses values that make sense to you. It may take several sessions with different counselors before you find one with whom you're happy.

If you think your partner needs help, you may first need to consult a professional yourself to find out how to go about letting your partner know that he needs help. If you think you can "cure" what ails your partner, forget it. There is no way you can be both lover and mental health professional.

KEEPING PHYSICALLY FIT

My definition of fitness is "the ability to live a life that gives you the vitality to do what you set out to do, without borrowing against your future vitality." By borrowing against future vitality I mean abusing drugs, smoking, eating fatty foods, and not getting fifteen to thirty minutes of brisk, sustained exercise three times a week.

Then there are more specific characterizations of fitness, such as a definition of cardio-vascular fitness that appeared in an article in the *Los Angeles Times*—one that was endorsed by the chairman of the American Heart Association subcommittee on exercise: "Cardio-vascular fitness is a state of body function that enables a person to exercise vigorously for long periods without undue fatigue, and to respond to sudden physical or emotional demands more readily and with less strain."

To stay physically fit, the basic and common recommended regimen—also endorsed by the American Heart Association—is to exercise briskly for at least fifteen to thirty minutes three times a week. Brisk exercise includes brisk walking, swimming, running, and so forth.

The word fitness, however, can mean many different things to many people. Your definition of fitness may mean being able to run five miles three days a week, or just a hard body with plenty of muscle definition. In popular gay culture, and in our society in general, the hard body symbolizes the epitome of fitness, whether or not that hard body can run up a hill without suffering cardiac arrest. The popular myth about gay men would have you believe that every gay man has a membership to a gym or keeps a set of weights stored under his bed. Some do. Most of the couples I interviewed don't. In fact, very few of the couples I spoke with do any exercise at all beyond getting in and out of a car.

You and your partner will not necessarily agree on what constitutes fitness or how much, if any, effort you want to put into it. If you're a running enthusiast, for example, you can encourage your partner to join you in your efforts, but don't think you will be able to make him over if he is not so inclined. You can't count on getting him to join you for 5:30 A.M. runs five days a week or expect him to change his diet because you've decided to run the New York Marathon and have given up red meat. You can encourage him, but pushing too hard may just set the stage for tension, arguments, and rebellion.

A few words of caution: If you decide you're interested in getting more fit by means of an exercise program and you haven't exercised much before, do some serious reading on the subject and consult an exercise professional and/or doctor before buying a set of weights or pair of running shoes. If you're not careful, you can seriously injure yourself, or die, particularly if you have undiagnosed high blood pressure or heart problems.

RESOURCES

Finding the Professional You Need

When choosing a doctor or mental health professional, you should look for someone who is good at his or her job, someone who is comfortable and experienced working with gay people, *and* someone with whom you feel you can be completely honest. That doesn't mean you *have* to find a gay doctor or shrink, or that a gay doctor or mental health professional is any better at his or her job than a straight person. There are many heterosexual health professionals who are perfectly competent to treat gay men.

To find a doctor or mental health professional you can get recommendations from friends, or call a respected hospital or mental health clinic in your area and ask for a referral. If you specifically want a doctor or mental health professional who is gay or gay-sensitive, you can call your local gay helpline, consult the *Gayellow Pages*, or call a local gay health clinic or gay mental health organization. If you live in a part of the country with few resources for gay people, or you are part of a group medical plan at your company and haven't the foggiest idea how to find out if one of the doctors who is part of the plan is gay or has ever worked with gay people, these methods may get you nowhere. In that case, the two groups listed below should be able to lend a hand in finding a gay or gay-sensitive professional.

Don't forget. When you ask for a referral, get at least a couple of names if possible, and interview the prospective doctor, psychiatrist, or psychologist on the phone or in person. You're buying a service. It's your right to shop around for someone with whom you feel confident working.

DOCTOR OR PSYCHIATRIST REFERRAL:
American Association of Physicians for Human Rights (AAPHR), PO Box 14366, San Francisco, CA 94114, 415–558–9353
415–673–3189 in the nine counties in the San Francisco Bay area

> AAPHR is a national organization with approximately five hundred members who are at least gay-sensitive. The organization will make referrals to gay and gay-sensitive doctors and psychiatrists in the U.S., Canada, and Europe.

PSYCHOLOGIST REFERRAL:
The American Psychological Association (APA) has a Committee on Lesbian and Gay Concerns that will provide referrals to psychologists who have expressed interest in, and have experience working with, gay people. The list does not yet include psychologists in every state. The APA does not guarantee that the referral it makes is to a psychologist who has an affirmative view of homosexuality, although it is unlikely there are many on the Committee roster who take the "cure" approach to homosexuality. The Committee may also be able to provide referrals to other counseling resources in your area.

Again, it is important to interview the referrals you are given to be certain that the psychologist has an affirmative view of homosexuality and is someone with whom you feel you can work.

You can write to:

Staff Liaison to Committee on Lesbian and Gay Concerns, American Psychological Association (Central Office), Committee on Lesbian and Gay Concerns, 1200 17th Street NW, Washington, DC 20036
Or call: 202–955–7727

> That number will get you to the American Psychological Association Office of Social and Ethical Responsibility. Ask to speak to the person who is Staff Liaison to the Committee on Lesbian and Gay Concerns and he or she will take it from there.

Organizations

American Cancer Society

> To get information about cigarette smoking and how to quit, contact your local unit of the American Cancer Society (check your phone book). The

Society has several pamphlets available including: "Quitter's Guide—7-Day Plan to Help You Stop Smoking Cigarettes," "How to Stay Quit over the Holidays," "How to Quit Cigarettes," "Facts and Figures on Smoking," and "Dangers of Smoking, Benefits of Quitting."

National Association of Lesbian and Gay Alcoholism Professionals (NALGAP), 204 West 20th Street, New York, NY 10011, 212–807–0634

1208 East State Boulevard, Fort Wayne, IN 46805, 219–483–8280

NALGAP is primarily an organization of and for professionals, but the organization also publishes a national directory of professional and peer-level services—such as AA—for gay people who are alcohol dependent. The organization also publishes an annotated bibliography of articles and books on the subject.

To order the directory, write to NALGAP at the New York address, for information. If you are interested in ordering the bibliography, you must write to the New York address as well. As of the publication of this book, NALGAP had not yet arranged for printing or sale of the bibliography.

NALGAP will accept phone calls, but it only provides information about the organization itself by phone. Do *not* call to order either the directory or bibliography or for referrals.

ADDICTION:
Pride Institute, 14400 Martin Drive, Eden Prairie, MN 55344, 800–54–PRIDE. In Minnesota: 612–934–7554

Pride Institute is a thirty-six-bed in-patient facility that treats alcohol- and drug-dependent lesbians and gay man. It is staffed by professionals who are experienced in both the alcohol- and drug-dependency fields as well as in mental health. It's 800 number is available twenty-four-hours a day (a real person, not a machine) for information and advice on alcohol- and drug-dependency as well as referrals to local organizations and treatment facilities for gay people.

SCA (Sexual Compulsives Anonymous), PO Box 1585, Old Chelsea Station, New York, NY 10011

SCA "is a fellowship of men and women who share their experience, strength, and hope with each other, that they may solve their common problem and help others to recover from sexual compulsion." SCA is not a national organization, but will send information on its organization and on compulsive sexual behavior if you contact the organization by mail.

Sexual Dependency Unit, Golden Valley Health Center, 4101 Golden Valley Road, Golden Valley, MN 55422, 612–588–2771 (ask for the Sexual Dependency Unit, or extension 5300)

The Golden Valley Health Center Sexual Dependency Unit offers a four-to-six week in-patient program based on the twelve-step method of AA for people (straight and gay) who have sexual dependency (compulsive sexual behavior) problems. The Unit also offers information on sexual dependency and makes referrals to local self-help organizations, as well as doctors and therapists. If you seek a gay or gay-sensitive doctor or therapist, ask for a referral to a support group in your area and then contact that group for a referral.

AIDS/SAFER SEX/SEXUALLY TRANSMITTED DISEASES:
National Gay/Lesbian Crisis Line, 800–221–7044. 212–529–1604 in New York, Alaska, Hawaii, and outside the U.S. 3:00 P.M.–9:00 P.M. (Eastern Standard Time), Monday–Friday

The Crisis Line is run by the Fund For Human Dignity, the education arm of the National Gay and Lesbian Task Force. Callers can get information on AIDS, safer sex, and sexually transmitted diseases, as well as referrals to health services in their area.

Gay Men's Health Crisis Hotline, 212–807–6655, 10:30 A.M.–9:00 P.M. (Eastern Standard Time) Monday through Friday, Saturday 12:00-3:00 pm. At other times, an answering service will take your call.

GMHC is a not-for-profit corporation founded to serve the public as a social service and education agency. Among the many services it provides, GMHC makes nationwide referrals to organizations or hospitals in your area that are involved with treatment of AIDS and organizations that offer counseling and support groups. It will also provide information over the phone about safer sex.

You can also call or write to request printed information on AIDS and safer sex:

GMHC, Education Department, Box 274, 132 West 24th Street, New York, NY 10011, 212–807–7517

National AIDS Hotline, 800–342–AIDS (Calls accepted from all fifty states and Puerto Rico)

The national hotline is staffed around the clock by operators who answer questions about AIDS. Information is provided on everything from basic facts about AIDS to referrals for treatment and counseling centers. Your call will be answered automatically by a taped message. If you need more information, an operator will assist you.

San Francisco AIDS Foundation, 333 Valencia Street, Fourth Floor, San Francisco, CA 94103, 415–864–4376

Since 1982, the San Francisco AIDS Foundation has been a pioneer in the field of AIDS education. The foundation currently publishes a catalog of its available booklets, brochures, fact sheets, posters, reports, and videos. Call or write for the catalog.

VD National Hotline, 260 Sheridan Avenue, Palo Alto, CA 94302, 800–227–8922, 800–982–5883 in California, 8 A.M.–8 P.M (Pacific Time), Monday–Friday

Trained volunteer operators give information on sexually transmitted diseases and refer callers to public clinics and private doctors. If you specifically want a gay-sensitive clinic or doctor, tell the operator that is what you prefer. Because the hotline is always short-staffed, you may have to wait a while before your call is answered.

You can request literature on any sexually transmitted disease by phone, or you can write.

FITNESS:
Contact your local chapter of the American Heart Association for a copy of its booklet, "Exercise and Your Heart."

Or write for information: American Heart Association, National Center, 7320 Greenville Avenue, Dallas, TX 75231

Books

AIDS AND SAFER SEX:
I have not listed information-oriented books on AIDS and safer sex because books, this one included, quickly become outdated. For the latest printed information on AIDS and safer sex, it is best to check with a local AIDS organization or call one of the AIDS organizations listed in this section.

CHEMICAL DEPENDENCY:
The Way Back: The Stories of Gay and Lesbian Alcoholics, 1981. Published by the Whitman Walker Alcoholism Services

To order the book, write to: Whitman Walker Alcoholism Services, 1638 R Street NW #21, Washington, DC 20008
Or call: 202–462–4232

Dual Identities: Counseling Chemically Dependent Gay Men and Lesbians, by Dana G. Finnegan and Emily B. McNally, 1987. Hazelden Publications, Box 176, Center City, MN 55012, 800–328–9000

This book is primarily about counseling, but the information should be of value to those who have questions concerning chemical dependency.

Hazelden Catalog

The Hazelden Catalog lists more than 2,000 books, pamphlets, audio and visual tapes, etc. on alcoholism, drug and chemical dependency, eating disorders—you name it. The catalog is free and can be ordered by mail or phone.
Write to: Hazelden Publications, Box 176, Center City, MN 55012
Or Call: 800–328–9000, 800–257–0070 in Minnesota, 612–257–4010 outside the continental U.S. (ask for Telemarketing)

HEALTH:

The Advocate Guide to Gay Health, by R. D. Fenwich, 1982. Alyson Publications, PO Box 2783, Boston, MA 02208

Informative general guide, but because parts are dated and the book is not always accurate, and information on AIDS is incomplete and inaccurate I do *not* recommend this book as a primary source for health information. For example, about cocaine the books says, "As long as it's coke and not something else, it is, as uppers go, relatively harmless." Such information is dangerous and obsolete. In another passage, the author notes, "[Marijuana] is approaching social acceptability and may soon become legal."

Strategies for Survival: A Gay Man's Health Manual for the Age of Aids, by Martin Delaney and Peter Goldblum with Joe Brewer, 1987. St. Martin's Press, 175 Fifth Avenue, New York, NY 10011

CHAPTER 14

On the Rocks

"Confrontation may be the kindest way
of telling our partners we are unhappy."

Almost all couples have problems. And almost everyone is dissatisfied with his relationship at one time or another and even fantasizes about ending it. Most problems don't lead to the end of a relationship but, if left unresolved, even relatively minor problems may lead to the beginning of the end.

If you're facing serious problems in your relationship and are considering perhaps ending your relationship, I urge you to read the information in other chapters of this book that address many of the problems discussed in brief in this chapter, and then to pursue the many available resources listed throughout the book.

WHAT'S THE PROBLEM?

Before you can face a relationship problem and attempt to resolve it, you have to recognize it. Recognizing the problem, even with the list of problems that follows, may be difficult for three reasons. First, you may not be aware that the symptoms you're experiencing, depression or sleeplessness for example, are due to specific relationship problems. (It may take a therapist to unravel your symptoms.) Second, your lover may not be letting you know in a way that you can understand that there are problems in the relationship. He may be dropping indecipherable hints. Third, you and/or your partner may be suffering from denial—the inability or unwillingness to accept that there could possibly be something amiss.

The following list of problems is divided into two parts: "Chronic" problems, which potentially you can work out on your own or with help of a counselor; and "Catastrophic" problems, those that can't possibly be resolved without professional help. None of these problems *have* to result in the end of your relationship if you recognize and deal with them early.

Chronic Problems

1. Getting Along/Compatibility

As the months and years pass, you and your lover will inevitably get to know each other. And as you get to know each other you may discover you're having trouble getting along. For example, now that the physical passion has cooled, it doesn't seem like much else has been holding the relationship together. Or you and your lover compete with each other in a destructive way. Either or both of you is jealous of the other's looks, power to attract other men, earning ability, etc. You may discover you are fundamentally incompatible, that your priorities conflict (one devotes too much time to work, too little to the relationship, for example); or you may have different attitudes toward money. You may simply be too different to survive— to thrive—together in a long-term relationship.

2. Sexuality

For numerous reasons, many men have difficulty coming to terms with the fact that they are homosexual. They may feel negative about who they are, and perhaps feel negative toward other gay people, including a partner. Because coming to terms with one's own sexuality and the "coming out" process are different for each man, you may be years ahead of your partner in that process, and this can cause conflicts over how to deal with colleagues, friends, and family.

3. Sexual Incompatibility/Dysfunction

Over the lifetime of a long-term relationship, you will likely experience at least periods of incompatibility. And it's likely that one or both of you will experience some form of sexual dysfunction, whether it's one-time impotence or a temporary decrease in desire. But compatibility and sexual dysfunction can also be extreme. For example, one partner prefers sex twice a month and the other prefers sex five times a week; one partner may be experiencing chronic impotence; or, you're no longer having sex and are unhappy about it.

4. Diminishment of Passion

Decrease in frequency and intensity of lovemaking or of spontaneous demonstrations of affection may lead to doubt by one or both of you about the other's interest in and commitment to the relationship.

5. *Monogamy/Nonmonogamy/Infidelity*

Many problems and tensions can result from whatever arrangement you and your partner work out. For a monogamous couple these problems can range from a conflict over a real or suspected infidelity or difficulties adjusting to a monogamous arrangement, to compulsive sexual behavior that leads one partner to seek multiple outside sexual contacts. For a nonmonogamous couple the potential problems range from jealousy and insecurity to the breaking of agreed-upon guidelines.

6. *Family Interference*

Families have disapproved of chosen partners for as long as there have been families and relationships. As a male couple there's the added potential of family hostility or rejection because the chosen partner is another man. Interference can be relatively minor, such as offhand remarks about your partner, and not cause any problem between you and your lover. But in extreme cases, where a man has had to choose between a partner and his family, there is great potential for resentment and tension between partners.

7. *Serious Illness*

While serious illness can draw a couple together, it can also put tremendous strain on the relationship.

Catastrophic Problems

1. *Drug or Alcohol Dependency*

One or both of you can suffer from dependency, or you can suffer from the effects of a partner's dependency. Before you can help your partner or your relationship, you have to seek help for yourself—even if you are not substance dependent. The best help is the advice of a professional.

2. *Mental Disorder*

Mental disorders are not something either you or your partner can realistically expect to cope with on your own. Professional help is essential.

3. *Domestic Violence*

Domestic violence within gay relationships is just now being recognized as a problem. To determine if you are the victim of domestic violence (as defined by one social worker who counsels men in couple relationships), ask yourself the following questions: Does your lover try to control you through violence or threat of violence? When you're with your lover are you afraid for your safety? Does your lover destroy your personal property? Are you sexually abused or coerced in your relationship?

If you can answer yes to any of these questions then you may be the victim of domestic violence. Violence in your relationship, whether you are the abuser or the abused, is not something you have to accept. You may think you're the only person in the world with an abusive lover, or the only person who is physically abusive. That's not the case. There are people who are eager to help you. It may not be easy for you to ask for help. You may feel embarrassed about your circumstances, but pick up the phone and call the National Gay Crisis Line (see Appendix) for information on how you can get help in your area. You can also call or write the New York City Gay and Lesbian Anti-Violence Project for information on domestic violence (see "Resources" at the end of this chapter).

RESOLVING/NOT RESOLVING PROBLEMS

After you've acknowledged either chronic or catastrophic problems in your relationship, you have essentially two choices: to face them, or to ignore them and let them slowly, or sometimes abruptly, destroy your relationship.

In the case of catastrophic problems, facing the problem means seeking professional help. If your problems fall into the "chronic" category, however, you can attempt to work them out by talking about them openly with your partner and trying to come to some sort of accommodation or resolution, or you can seek the help of a professional.

Because it is often so difficult to talk openly about problems with a partner, lovers typically bring up a problem by dropping hints that something is bothering them. Unfortunately, dropping hints is usually no more effective than ignoring the problem altogether. Unless you find a way to communicate to your partner the seriousness of the problem, you cannot work to change the situation. Short of walking out, a solution that assumes your commitment has dissipated, there can probably be no solution without communication.

If you know there are serious problems in your relationship and you choose not to find a way to resolve them, you may be condemning yourself and your partner to a continuous outward drift that can last years before your relationship actually comes to an end.

If you decide to work on a problem, *it must be a joint effort.* One method is to seek the help of a counselor. Little good will come of one partner bundling off to the therapist, with the other assuming the attitude, "It's *your* problem. *You* need the help." Nor will it do much good if your partner suggests that the two of you should go to couple counseling, and you go just to humor him, or you drop out after a couple of sessions. *You have to—absolutely must without exception—accept that any problem within the relationship is a mutual problem, not just "his" problem or "your" problem.* Because you are a couple, any problem in the relationship affects both of you and any solution must be the result of a joint effort.

Confronting your problems does not mean there is no risk of bringing the relationship to an end. There is always such a possibility, even if you resolve the problem(s). For example, if you're both drug dependent, once you are both drug-free you may find that the only binding force in your relationship was your shared dependence on drugs and that without shared addiction nothing holds you together. Or you may find that your problem is symptomatic of your basic incompatibility, which you feel you cannot resolve except by ending the relationship.

THE BREAKDOWN OF A RELATIONSHIP

The process by which a relationship ends—the "uncoupling" process—is very complex and is described in detail in a book by sociologist Diane Vaughan, appropriately titled *Uncoupling*. What follows is a brief summary of the uncoupling process in the hope that familiarity with it will put you in a better position to make an effort to either save your relationship or avoid prolonging the agony of its dissolution.

DYNAMICS OF DECLINE
According to Diane Vaughan:

> Uncoupling is primarily a tale of two transitions: one that begins before the other. Most often, one person wants out while the other person wants the relationship to continue. Although both partners must go through all the same stages of the transition in order to uncouple, the transition begins and ends at different times for each. By the time the still-loving partner realizes the relationship is in serious trouble, the other person is already gone in a number of ways. The rejected partner then embarks on a transition that the other person began long before. Admittedly, identifying who is the initiator and who is being left behind is not so easy in some cases. Over the course of a long relationship, these roles may be passed back and forth, with one person assuming the role of initiator at one time and the other acting to end the relationship at another.

The uncoupling process begins with a secret. According to Vaughan, that secret may simply be an uncomfortable feeling in the relationship.

The secret dissatisfaction is unarticulated or poorly articulated through unrelated complaints or hinting at a problem. The real problem never gets resolved and the "initiator" begins to distance himself from his partner; over time he begins severing ties with his partner and making new ones outside of the relationship. That could mean no longer sharing friends, or perhaps having an affair. Eventually the initiator makes the partner aware of the severity of the problem, but by that time he has so separated himself from the relationship that reconciliation is extremely difficult if not impossible.

ENDING A RELATIONSHIP

This is not a book about ending relationships. The fact remains, however, that many relationships don't last. There are no numbers on just what percentage of long-term male-couple relationships come to an end but, like heterosexual relationships, many male couples ultimately separate. And, like heterosexual relationships, the process of ending a relationship is likely to be difficult and painful for both partners, no matter who is initiating the breakup and whether both are in agreement or not that the time has come to end the relationship.

Making the Decision

Assuming you are the one who wants to initiate the end of the relationship, no one can make the decision for you. You have to feel ready emotionally, and if your partner has been supporting you financially or contributing significantly to your support or the support of your shared household, you must be financially prepared for the split as well.

If you're in a relationship that makes you unhappy and you want to end it, you may find yourself nagged by good arguments for staying in the relationship nonetheless. This is normal. You may be reluctant to risk the unknown. You may be haunted by the fear of AIDS, or the fear that you will never find another man. You may feel that it's better to have an unsatisfying relationship than no relationship. Or you may feel that you've made a commitment, that you're not a quitter, you don't want to be thought of as a failure, or that you're out to prove to the world that a long-term relationship is possible between two men. If you're unhappy in your relationship, these are not good reasons to stay there. However, these are good reasons to seek the help of friends, family, and/or a professional in sorting out your feelings about ending the relationship.

The Right and Wrong Ways to End a Relationship

No two couples are the same, nor are two circumstances the same, but there are right and wrong ways to end a relationship. Both cause pain, but one causes more pain than the other.

Assuming you are the one who wants out of the relationship, the wrong approach is the indirect one where you force your partner—who is not aware of your discontent—to end the relationship. You can do this by making him so unhappy with you and/or your behavior that you leave him with little choice but to end the relationship. Diane Vaughan calls this "shifting the burden." This process is one with which I am quite familiar. I remember in college praying that a long-term boyfriend toward whom I had been relentlessly mean would end the relationship and spare me the unpleasant task of telling him I wanted out. I remember rationalizing that it would be better for his self-esteem if he were the one to initiate the breakup. Of course, in retrospect I realize that it would have been far kinder if I had spared him the months of cruel assault on his self-esteem by summoning the courage to end the relationship myself. In the end I had to end the relationship anyway because I couldn't bring myself to be quite cruel enough to push him over the edge.

Diane Vaughn breaks the indirect methods into three categories: the fatal mistake, decreased interaction, and rule violation. (Remember, these are the methods to avoid.) With the fatal mistake approach . . .

> the partner responds to the initiator's escalating display of discontent by committing some grievous error. The initiator seizes on it, confronts the partner with the wish to terminate, and points to the partner's behavior as the reason for all the ills in the relationship. The initiator confronts, but the partner's failure is the reason the relationship has come to crisis.

Decreased interaction involves withdrawing from your partner "psychologically while in the home and to disappear more and more into the outside world." As the disaffected partner's unhappiness increases, his absences from home become more prolonged.

"Rule violation" describes a whole range of behavior, from having an affair even though you originally committed to a monogamous relationship to being nasty, violent, and/or abusive.

With all of these methods you can fool yourself into believing that it was all your partner's doing.

The right way—ultimately the least painful for all concerned—is direct confrontation. Putting all the cards on the table. Telling him it's over. According to Vaughan:

Since there is no painless way of letting the other person know we no longer want to be with them, in the long run direct confrontation may be the kindest way of telling our partners we are unhappy. Direct confrontation lets the partner participate. . . . It allows the two people to negotiate with each other and try. It creates the possibility of transforming the relationship into one that may be better for both. And if trying does not work, the experience clarifies the situation. It enables the partner to come to grips with this turn of events as soon as possible. It frees the partner from the paralysis of hope and ignorance, opening the way for the construction of a new life.

If confrontation sounds like an incredibly unpleasant approach, that's because, in general, it is. No one likes a confrontation. But in the long run, as Vaughan states, it is the least painful approach.

You may need help telling your partner you want to end the relationship. You may not have the confidence to tell your partner you want out, you may be afraid of his reaction, or you may not know how. You can seek the help of a friend, a family member—if they are supportive of you and your relationship—or the help of a professional therapist. (See Chapter 13 for information on how to find a therapist or counselor.) You may find that the only way you can tell your partner that you want to end the relationship is in the presence of a couples counselor.

RESOURCES

Finding a Couples Counselor

How do you find a counselor who specializes in couples counseling and has experience with male couples? Like any other professional, you start by asking friends. If you're unable to find a counselor by that route, refer to the "Resources" section of Chapter 13. One warning about couples counselors: Once you find one, speak with the counselor and make certain that he or she is someone whose values make sense to you. For example, if you and your partner have been having problems over infidelity and you strongly believe in a monogamous relationship, don't choose a therapist who believes an open relationship should be the goal of all couples.

Organizations

There is only a handful of organizations that concern themselves with the problems of domestic violence in gay relationships. Call your local gay helpline or the National Gay Crisis Line, listed in the Appendix, for information about resources and information available in your area.

You can also write or call the New York City Gay and Lesbian Anti-Violence Project for information:

New York City Gay and Lesbian Anti-Violence Project, 208 West 13th Street, New York, NY 10011, 212–807–0197

Books

Uncoupling: Turning Points in Intimate Relationships, by Diane Vaughan, 1986. Oxford University Press, 200 Madison Avenue, New York, NY 10016

This is an interesting, sometimes fascinating (although also sometimes sociologically dense), look at the process of how relationships dissolve. The anecdotes and information provided may help readers recognize problems in their own relationships and perhaps stop the drift toward uncoupling if, in fact, such a process is at work in their relationships.

Diane Vaughan uses anecdotes from straight and gay couples, and specifically discusses gay couples on a number of occasions. I found some of her generalizations about gay couples troubling. For example, she states: "The situation of gays in relation to their parents differs from that of heterosexual couples because gays who uncouple do not usually risk the loss of support from family members—since that typically disappeared when the individual came out. Families may be unaware of their gay members' couplings and, if they are aware, they seldom qualify as 'friends of the relationship.' They tend to see the breakup as a return to traditional values and therefore applaud it."

For the men with whom I spoke, family members were often friends of the relationship and had strong positive relationships with a son's partner. One parent I interviewed was heartbroken by the breakup of her son and his lover. I feel certain that in many cases Vaughan is right, but without having interviewed that ever-elusive "representative" group of male couples, I don't believe it is possible to say that the loss of family support is typical or that family members seldom qualify as friends of the relationship.

CHAPTER 15

Aging and Loss

"I have a much keener awareness
than Greg of being old and poor."

There are several significant differences between gay and straight couples when it comes to growing older. For one thing, straight couples enjoy certain legal guarantees automatically. Gay couples can take measures to parallel many of these guarantees (as discussed in Chapter 9), but more subtle than the lack of automatic legal guarantees for gay couples is the frequent absence of certain life assumptions. Most straight couples, for example, assume the eventuality of children. For straight married couples this creates a climate in which the need to plan for the future together is often self-evident. While many gay couples also perceive and act on such a need, many do not. Never having to ask themselves, "What would become of the children if I die or my spouse dies, or we die?" and for other reasons, they neglect to plan for the eventuality of illness, loss of income, and death. By not planning for the possibility of illness and the inevitability of death, many gay couples fail to consider the possibility of family interference, and neglect making arrangements that would go far to eliminate interference. Unfortunately, by the time the need becomes apparent, it's too late.

Responsible gay couples in long-term relationships, regardless of their age, income, or physical well-being, should plan ahead and make the necessary legal, financial, and insurance arrangements. And gay couples need to plan for what will happen after they die. For older couples, who are more likely to make use of the health care system and are closer to facing the eventuality of death, as well as for all couples facing serious illness, the need for complete planning is even more critical.

To make certain you have made adequate plans, you must be sure that the lawyer, accountant, insurance agent, doctor, etc. you use are all aware of your couple relationship. Unless each professional is aware of the relationship between the two of you, he cannot help you plan properly. If the professionals you currently work with aren't aware of your relationship, you can tell them about it or, if you don't want to do that for whatever reason, you must find new professionals—straight or gay—with whom you can be completely honest. (Refer to Chapters 9, "Legalizing Your Relationship"; 10, "Money"; 11, "Insurance"; and 13, "Health" for information on how to find the professionals you need and with whom you can be honest about your relationship.)

GROWING OLDER

In popular gay culture, gay and gray generally don't mix. (I like to think that's changing.) The anti-age bias is not exclusive to gay life of course. But popular gay culture has been especially effective at promoting the image of youth; many readily forget that, of the tens of millions of middle-aged and elderly people across the country, millions are gay.

Many of the fears and concerns of growing older are universal, such as the physical changes that occur with aging, the possible loss of independence, and the potential lack of adequate financial resources.

For example, Greg and Neal, both in their fifties, have planned their finances so that they can remain independent and financially secure if and when they retire.

Neal: I have a much keener awareness than Greg of being old and poor. We don't have families, and families aren't interested in caring for old people anyway. There is nothing at all wrong with being old. It's being old and having to be dependent on people who really don't give a shit about you.

Greg: That's one of the first things I remember you saying. That's an awareness you've always had.

Neal: I am much more plugged into the idea that if Greg and I decide to stop working we can call the shots for our own lives.

Other concerns, such as physical changes and the fear of isolation, while universal, are intensified for gay people. Still other concerns, such as the lack of adequate social services and sensitive care providers for older gay people and couples are things straight older people don't have to worry as much about.

Physical Changes

Rationally, you should expect changes in appearance and body functioning. In real life, we're usually surprised and often self-denying about physical changes due to aging. Scott recalls shopping several years ago for pants and getting into an exchange with the salesman about waist size. "My waist size will never go up," he declared impetuously. "It's not going to happen to me." That was eight years and three inches ago. The fact is, your body won't be as cooperative as you grow older, and you will have to work harder as you grow older just to *maintain* its flexibility and endurance. Sex drive is likely to diminish (diminish, not disappear), your penis will need more physical stimulation to get going, and it will likely take longer to reach orgasm. If you're accustomed to having two orgasms in a row, the time needed to get an erection again after an orgasm will increase.

About the extra attention your penis is likely to need to become erect after a certain age, Dr. Ruth Westheimer explains in *Dr. Ruth's Guide to Good Sex,* as men grow older they lose the ability to get erections stimulated solely by the mind (psychogenic erections): "With the passage of time, the penis may get tired of all those messages from the brain and say, 'Come on, stop all the talk and show me how you love me. Pat me, play with me.' . . . Erotic thoughts are no longer enough." If you've always physically stimulated each other's penises in foreplay, you may not even notice the change from psychogenic erections to physically stimulated ones.

Older gay people *do* have sex and, unfortunately, the AIDS statistics prove it. One social worker noted that many older gay men think they don't have to worry about AIDS simply because they are old and most of those who have gotten the disease are young. Older people are every bit as, if not more, susceptible to infection by the HIV virus. They need to take the same precautions as young gay men. (See Chapter 8 for more information on AIDS and safer sex.)

In both the straight and gay world, appearances—youthful looks—are very, very important. In couple relationships this translates into concern over whether or not you're still attractive to your partner. For most of the couples I interviewed where one partner was significantly older than the other, diminishing attractiveness was of particular concern—but just to the older partner. One man, who at 40 is ten years older than his lover, said, "When I'm 50, will my lover still be hot to trot?" His lover gave him a look that said, "You're being stupid."

Andrew and Donald have been together for five years and are close to ten years apart in age.

Andrew: I'm concerned about the differences in age for Donald's sake.
Donald: I think as we get older the gap gets smaller.
Andrew: I want to make sure that he's not left with an old fart.
Donald: I'm going to be one, too. Maybe not quite as old, but . . .

As one couple fourteen years apart in age, and seventeen years together, said, "In the high plateau of middle age, there's really no difference physically or emotionally."

Isolation

Many senior citizens experience isolation as they grow older and spouses, friends, and family members die. But there are still many opportunities for straight older people to socialize with their peers. The same is not so true for older gay people. There is only a handful of organizations that provide places for older gay people and couples to socialize and feel comfortable talking openly about their lives (see "Resources").

Isolation can be particularly intense for today's older gay people, who grew up in a world where "the secret" was kept until death. After the loss of a spouse, there may be no one else in the world who knows their secret. If they were rejected by family, or pulled away from family because of a fear of being found out, they may lack a family support network as well.

Those who work with older gay people speak of the great lengths to which they go to to reach out to the gay elderly and to guarantee their confidentiality.

Dealing with Care Providers

The unfortunate reality is that those who provide care for the elderly—social workers, nursing homes, hospitals, etc.—are woefully uninformed about gay seniors. When one social worker, who is involved in educating social service providers about the needs of the gay elderly, called a major Jewish social service agency to discuss developing a workshop for its care providers, the administrator on the other end of the phone said, "This is a Jewish agency," as if to say that being Jewish had nothing to do with being gay. To that administrator, it simply was beyond possibility that any of the Jewish elderly people his agency cares for are also gay and terribly isolated.

The lack of care providers familiar with gay couples becomes critical when, for example, your 80-year-old lover's health has deteriorated to the point where he needs to be cared for in a nursing home. How do you find a nursing home that will be sensitive to the fact that you are a couple? Is there such a place? Can you even admit him to a nursing home? In the eyes of most, you are not spouses or next-of-kin. You're just two unrelated friends.

You can get answers to some of these difficult questions and advice on how to approach your particular circumstances by calling SAGE, an organization for gay seniors, listed in the "Resources" section.

ELDERLY PARENTS

Parents grow old. And, often, this means that they grow more dependent. Typically the biggest part of the responsibility for dealing with their dependency falls on the adult child (or children) who lives closest. But, unless they're completely estranged, all adult children of elderly parents, near or far, gay or straight, should share the responsibility, even if unequally. This may mean visiting regularly (or having them come visit), providing financial support or, in the extreme, moving them into a retirement home or having an elderly parent move in. It could also mean having the moral courage—mixed, one hopes, with compassion—to take away a driving license. Several of the couples I interviewed have a parent living with them and others anticipate caring for an older parent some time in the future.

As a gay couple, it may not occur to you that the care of parents could become your responsibility. It certainly didn't occur to Craig and Marshall in the six years they've been together, until a recent extended visit by Craig's mother.

Craig: My mother is getting older now and she talks about retiring. After examining all of her children she has decided our relationship is the one she prefers. She has problems with my brothers and my sisters. So she decided that she wants to live with us.

Marshall: No way in hell!

Craig: There are a lot of problems to consider when a mother-in-law comes to live with you—a lot of problems we never thought about. If you're a heterosexual couple, it's one thing. You think about it, you talk about it, read about it, or you've heard about it from a million other couples. As a gay couple we never considered this a possibility, so no bells went off until the day she showed up for a long visit.

Marshall: We had major brawls. Dorothy has very set ideas about how she's going to organize her life and she went to it with the house. And I finally put my foot down.

Craig: When she realized that the room on the third floor might be her room— she had some very definite ideas about how the room should be decorated.

Marshall: And of course I also have very definite ideas of how it should be decorated. And the two sets of definite ideas did not coincide.

Craig: I came home one day from work and found them both going at it: "I don't care what she says, the walls are not coming down." "I don't care what he says, I will not live with a bathroom in that corner."

Marshall: And there's Craig, being a son, saying, "Yes, yes, yes," which is how he deals with her. So now I've got two of them to fight with, not one. When she started in about the circular staircase that was going to come down into the study, I said no way in hell. I blew up.

She may move in ultimately, but I feel that if she moved in on a temporary status and understood that she was a guest and nothing more, that would be the best. I do not want her to move in on a long-term basis.

Craig disagrees, but I would like her to move nearby, or create an apartment for her in another building we hope to own, but not in our own home. Ultimately she would be frustrated living with us. She's been her own woman for many years and would hate to have to live with someone else's rules.

Craig: This is a major thing to be thought about, discussed, considered, in the same way a heterosexual couple would do it.

If you're faced with the possibility of a parent moving in, first talk about it and consider the issues that specifically concern you, your lover, and the parent. For example, if your parent needs financial support as well as a place to live, will you carry that burden alone, or will your lover share the cost? Can you all get along in the same house? Will your parent need to be cared for while you're both at work?

If you're in a position to do it and have the resources, first try extended visits as Marshall and Craig did. They were able to anticipate the problems of having Craig's mother live with them before she moved in and now feel that they understand their options better, including having Craig's mother live nearby, under their wing if not under their roof.

In a couple relationship money and move-in decisions about elderly parents are shared decisions. They should be discussed thoroughly with each other as well as with siblings. Siblings and extended family may be concerned about a parent living with a gay couple, but more likely than not they will be relieved that the parent is not moving in with them.

For couples who have a good relationship with an older parent, and who share the same values concerning caring for an elderly parent, it may be easy to reach a decision. Consider Greg and Neal. Greg's mother is reaching an age where she may no longer be able to live alone.

Neal: We talked about it a long time ago. One thing I said was that it's better to experience inconvenience now than regret later. If worse came to worst we would take in Greg's mother as opposed to putting her in a nursing home. Whatever arrangements we have to make, we make, and she comes to live with us.

Greg: God knows, no one else will offer to take care of her.

Neal: [with a smile] Anthropologically, that's why there are gay men, so we can take care of our elderly parents, while our heterosexual siblings can have their children.

Greg: And straight brothers or sisters expect you to do it because you don't have the responsibilities of your own family.

AND THEN THERE WAS ONE

Assuming you keep your relationship on track, sooner or later one of you will die and leave the other behind. Unless one of you dies after a long illness, it is difficult to prepare emotionally in advance, and even then it may be difficult to face the loss until after your lover has died. But, while you can wait until after your lover has died to deal with the emotional impact of the loss of your beloved, there are some things that cannot wait until after one of you dies. If, for example, you want to honor your lover's wishes for cremation or burial arrangements following his death, you must make certain that his legal papers are in order and that his wishes are clearly stated in those papers and that the executor—most often the surviving partner—is someone who will carry out the stated wishes. And the same goes for you.

Making Funeral, Burial, or Cremation Arrangements

Some people think it's ghoulish to talk about planning for a death in advance, particularly if they're young and in good health. The spectre of AIDS has led many young gay men and couples to think about their mortality, if only in the abstract. If you're a couple and have specific wishes about arrangements following your death, you can't afford to think about mortality only in the abstract, particularly if you think there is even a remote possibility that members of either of your families may try to interfere with your wishes. Traditionally, next-of-kin has the right to decide everything, from identifying the body to what goes on a tombstone.

In any case, it is best to protect yourselves and your plans by discussing and making plans in advance and stating those plans, such as a desire to be cremated or buried, in a will. It won't hurt to also state those plans in a Designation of Preference. Specific details, such as who is to be contacted in the event of death, or what you would like to be said at a memorial service, should be stated in a Designation of Preference, not a will, which should not contain details that are likely to change over time. (See Chapter 9 for more information on drawing up a will and Designation of Preference.)

Through a will, your lover can grant you or anyone else he wishes to name as executor, the legal right to carry out his wishes after death—including cremation—over the wishes of next-of-kin. (Laws vary, but in general only next-of-kin can authorize cremation unless it's designated in a will.) If your partner wants to be cremated, he should state that wish loud and clear in black and white and state explicitly what he wants done with his ashes. Greg and Neal have stated in their wills that when both are deceased they wish to be "urnmates." "We stated that we were together while we were alive and we wanted to be urnmates after we died."

To plan in advance, you will have to talk about it. And realistically, if your lover is terminally ill, particularly if he is young, you may be reluctant to even acknowledge to yourself or to suggest to him that he is dying. But again, if you don't prepare in advance and his family interferes, you will not have the force of law behind you to carry out his wishes and your joint wishes. *Without the force of law behind you, his family will likely prevail.*

One funeral director in New York City, who has completed arrangements for hundreds of people who have died from AIDS, noted, "I had a man who made out a will and designated his lover as the executor of his will and stated in his will that he wished to be cremated. The deceased man's mother called from Utah and objected to the cremation. I told her that because of the legal will, she didn't have a leg to stand on. I informed her that she should speak to an attorney in her town and that I would wait a day if she wanted me to. She decided not to challenge the will. Without the will, she could have stopped the cremation."

In addition to stating plans in legal documents, you should, if possible, make certain that relatives, particularly your parents, are aware of the existence of the documents and have learned to live with the decisions you and your partner have made. According to Tom Stoddard, executive director of the Lambda Legal Defense and Education Fund, an organization that handles test cases involving gay rights, "In almost every circumstance where there has been a fight, it has occurred when the in-laws were surprised."

If you decide to talk about it in advance and make plans, you need to discuss burial vs. cremation, type of memorial service if any, disposition of the ashes, costs, etc. Besides stating these wishes in a will and Designation of Preference document, you can also make advance arrangements with a mortuary service or funeral home. You can even pay for the arrangements in advance (the money should be held by the funeral home or mortuary service in an interest-bearing escrow account until death), or the estate, through a will, can be directed to pay for the prearranged funeral costs.

Costs for burial or cremation range from $500 for a beginning-to-end cremation (pick-up, transportation, paperwork, cremation, burial of ashes at sea) to $2,000 and up for a funeral that includes burial and all the trimmings.

Depending upon circumstances, there are benefits available from state social service agencies (check with a local agency), Social Security, and the Veterans Administration to help defray cremation, burial, and funeral costs.

If your partner dies from AIDS, there are additional concerns when making funeral arrangements. The public is still naive about AIDS, funeral directors included. Some funeral homes and cremation services impose unnecessary restrictions and/or add special handling fees to their regular charges when handling someone who has died from AIDS. According to one funeral director, "A funeral home may try to make extra money by imposing *unnecessary* restrictions on how the body can be handled. They try to charge extra for those services and take advantage of people."

Some states and counties require special handling of people who have died from AIDS (just as they do for people who have died of hepatitis-B, for example), and some funeral homes and cremation services choose to pass along the costs of special handling.

Before calling around to funeral homes or cremation services, you can try to get a referral from the hospital where your partner was treated, or call the local gay helpline for a referral to a funeral home that is experienced in dealing with people who have died from AIDS. If you're unable to get a referral, you may have to call several funeral homes before finding the right one, keeping in mind that if the funeral home or cremation service you've reached requires what sound like unusual restrictions and extra charges, you should call another one.

The bottom line: Protect yourselves, plan in advance, and get the force of law behind you.

Life After Loss

After my Uncle David died I asked my Aunt Terri what it was like to be without the man with whom she had happily shared her life for decades. She said she didn't know how she would get through it. The emptiness that his death left was so great. How, she wondered, would she ever fill that void. I couldn't help but wonder what it would be like to be without Scott. I couldn't imagine.

Losing a lover, especially a long-term lover, is often devastating and can even be life-threatening for the surviving spouse. According to Sister Patrice Murphy, coordinator of the Supportive Care Program (bereavement counseling), at St. Vincent's Hospital and Medical Center in New York City's Greenwich Village, "Studies have shown that there is fairly high morbidity and mortality among spouses who lose a partner of many years with whom they had a positive relationship. People die of broken hearts."

Sister Patrice spends much of her time counseling gay men who have lost their lovers to AIDS, and she has led workshops for bereft lovers in conjunction with the Gay Men's Health Crisis. I met Sister Patrice three years ago when I was on a reporting assignment for graduate school. I was struck by her caring, warmth, and concern for the people she counsels. Much of the information presented in this section is drawn from discussions with Sister Patrice and is applicable both to men who have lost young partners and men who have lost partners after many years together.

Emotional Responses Following Death

In the first months following the death of your lover, you are likely to feel a paralyzing sense of loss, the feeling that your experience is unreal—that it couldn't possibly have happened. You will feel disorganized and may find it difficult to think and concentrate. Depression after the death of a lover is common and may be accompanied by a real temptation to commit suicide—not to end personal pain but out of a desperate hope of being with your lover again. You will feel angry—at God, at your lover for dying, at the people who didn't help while your lover was dying (if he died from a long-term illness), or at people who have not given emotional support since your lover died. You may feel guilt—guilt that you didn't do enough, or guilt that you weren't there at the moment your lover died—that is likely unwarranted. These are all normal feelings, and over time they will diminish.

These negative feelings come early. When a little time passes and you begin to feel better, you are likely to have positive feelings that you have grown as a result of your loss, that you are now able to face your own mortality, that you may have a better sense of the priorities of life. In time you will begin to think about how you can make a new life for yourself.

Grief can last for several years and still not be considered pathological. The degree to which you experience grief and mourning has a great deal to do with the intensity and length of the relationship. The norm is probably somewhere around fifteen to eighteen months.

If you've lost a partner after a long illness, the grieving process may have started before his death. Having been realistic about his approaching death and not in a state of denial, you can have experienced "anticipatory grieving." People with strong denial mechanisms are shocked regardless of the length of the illness preceding death, and recovery is slower. The more realistic you are, the better. And the more you express your grief before your partner's death the less painful it will be after his death.

For men who have lost a lover to AIDS, the grief issues can be complicated by extreme anger, fear of developing AIDS themselves and of having no one to care for them, and difficulties with the former lover's family.

If you feel you have sufficient support from family and friends, or you can draw strength from your faith or church and community, that may be all you need in addition to time to get through your grief. However, if you don't have those supports and your body, mind, and spirit tell you that you need outside assistance, or after a year and a half you are still feeling undiminished despair at your loss, you can, and probably should, seek the help of a counselor who has experience with bereavement. In the case of a loss of a lover to AIDS, you can also seek the help of a local organization that provides appropriate counseling or support groups.

Check the "Resources" section of Chapter 13 for information on how to find a therapist or counselor, or call one of the AIDS-specific organizations in that section for information on where to seek such counseling or support groups. In addition to following the recommendations provided in Chapter 13, you can ask a social worker at the hospital where your lover was treated for a referral to a professional with experience in bereavement counseling.

The key to recovering from the loss of a lover is to avoid isolating yourself. Isolation may come automatically with the loss of your lover if you are older and no longer have family or friends, or if you and your partner were completely in the closet and were each other's only intimate friends. If you're a gay senior, and unable to find support from friends, family, and/or don't feel comfortable seeking out social services provided in your area, contact SAGE, which is listed under "Resources."

One final note on grief. According to Judy Tatelbaum, in her book *The Courage to Grieve*, "The only grief that does not end is grief that has not been fully faced. Grief unexpressed is like a powder keg waiting to be ignited." If you find that you're unable to express grief for the loss of your partner, or for that matter, the loss of anyone else who is close to you, don't wait twelve years, as I did following my father's death, before getting help. From personal experience I can tell you Judy Tatelbaum is right on target.

RESOURCES

Organizations

In the *Directory of Homosexual Organizations and Publications*, there are more listings for gay prisoners (two) than there are for senior groups (zero). However there are a couple dozen groups specifically for senior gays (a population some define as gays over 50 and others define as those over 60 or 65), but most organizations are concentrated in California, New York, and Massachusetts. The largest and most prominent is SAGE—Senior Action in a Gay Environment—in New York City. SAGE provides services for older lesbians and gay men who are homebound or confined to nursing homes or hospitals. For healthy and independent older gay people, SAGE serves as a social and educational center, as well as providing education to social service providers, gay people of all ages, and the general public.

While SAGE has a national profile, it is not a national organization, but if you call or write, SAGE will provide referrals to the local group or community center nearest where you live. SAGE also has a nationwide pen-pal service, through which it will link you with another senior gay person.

SAGE—Senior Action in a Gay Environment, 208 West 13th Street, New York, NY 10011, 212–741–2247

Books

GAY SENIORS:
Gay and Gray: The Older Homosexual Man, by Raymond M. Berger, 1982. Alyson Publications, PO Box 2783, Boston, MA 02208

> In *Gay and Gray* the author profiles ten older gay men and reviews information gathered from 112 responses to a questionnaire.

Quiet Fires: Memoirs of Older Gay Men, by Keith Vacha, 1985. The Crossing Press, Trumansburg, NY 14886

> Keith Vacha offers the stories of seventeen older gay men, drawn from more than one hundred interviews.

GRIEVING AND LOSS:
On Death and Dying: What the Dying Have to Teach Doctors, Nurses, Clergy and Their Own Families, by Elisabeth Kübler-Ross, 1969. Collier Books, Macmillan Publishing Company, 866 Third Avenue, New York, NY 10022

> Through the stories of her patients, the author sensitively analyzes the different stages of dying. Kübler-Ross also discusses the role of a patient's loved ones.

Recovery from Bereavement, by Colin Murray Parkes and Robert S. Weiss, 1983. Basic Books, 10 East 53rd Street, New York, NY 10022

> This book is an in-depth analysis of the bereavement process, oriented toward those who work with people suffering from a loss. The book includes anecdotes from widows and widowers. While it is about straight people, the insights offered are applicable to all people.

The Courage to Grieve: Creative Living, Recovery, and Growth Through Grief, by Judy Tatelbaum, 1980. Lippincott & Crowell, at Harper & Row, Publishers, Inc., 10 East 53rd Street, New York, NY 10022

> This is a positive, optimistic, self-help book about surviving grief.

PHYSICALLY AGING:

How a Man Ages—Growing Older: What to Expect and What You Can Do About It, by Curtis Pesmen and the Editors of Esquire, 1984. Ballantine Books, 400 Hahn Road, Westminster, MD 21157

> *How a Man Ages* explains what changes to expect in your body and your emotions as you grow older. The book provides practical advice on everything from hair to heart, lungs, and muscles.

CHAPTER 16

Two Couples

There's no such thing as a typical male couple. The more couples I interviewed, the more this became apparent. Male couples are as varied in their backgrounds, goals, problems, habits, work, income, division of labor, family relations, sexual practices, and long-term prospects as heterosexual couples. Every couple I interviewed told an interesting story. They were remarkably candid, and many made discoveries about each other as they described to me their lives, accomplishments, and anxieties.

Two couples particularly intrigued me for different reasons. One, Mark and Dale, live as close to the heart of Bible-belt redneck country in the rural south as you can get. Their lives are very ordinary, and for this reason, exceptional and inspiring. The other couple, Len and Eric, are young, inexperienced, earnest urban professionals learning by trial and error what works in a relationship and what doesn't. What keeps them together is commitment and desire.

LEN AND ERIC

Len and Eric are yuppies—young, urban, and professional. They have no problem with the label, but they reject its negative connotations for they lack neither conscience nor do they live extravagantly. Len is 27, an investment banker, earns a healthy income, went to Yale, then Harvard for an MBA, and knows the rules of squash. Eric is 29, attended a no-name state university and prefers going to a Mets baseball game to a game of squash (he refuses to play). He's an avid runner, and writes software and installs new computer equipment for a major national bank. He lives in a modest, one-bedroom duplex apartment with Len on Manhattan's still tattered but fast gentrifying Upper West Side.

Their apartment, which is just across the hall from the studio apartment Eric lived in when he met Len, is small by any standard other than New York's. The comfortable living room is neat and modestly furnished with a well-worn modular couch and a glass coffee table. A television and VCR are on one wall. The living room windows look out onto a narrow courtyard and other apartments. Adjacent to the living room, the small, fully stocked kitchen suggests that someone does a lot of cooking. Up a narrow flight of stairs is Len and Eric's bedroom. Len proudly gave me a tour of all the trophies and awards Eric has won over the years for his racing. And then there are the "children"—about a half dozen stuffed animals, each with its own name and personality. All but one, Len tells me, is gay or lesbian.

After a year and a half together, Len and Eric are determined to make their relationship work; despite their different backgrounds and a recent falling out—Len broke their ironclad agreement to be monogamous—they both look forward to a life together. It's a life that so far does not include their families. Len has two younger sisters and a younger brother. His parents live in Denver. Eric has three older brothers. His parents, whom he visits about once a month, live on Long Island. Both Len and Eric have never spoken to their parents about being gay. Len has met Eric's parents once. Eric has never met Len's parents, which is something of a sore point with Eric.

Both Len and Eric had relationships with other men before they met, but neither had ever lived with a lover. And for both of them, the other is untypical of past boyfriends. Len, who was in his last year of business school, was in New York City interviewing with major banks for a job when he met Eric. He was staying with friends, when Eric, who lived down the hall, dropped by.

Eric: I went down the hall to visit my friends because I was a little depressed that day. I was lonely. There was this nerd—Len—there who was interviewing with the Exxon Corporation and who had also been interviewing with Bank of America. He asked me for my card so he could find out more about Bank of America where I also happened to be working at the time. I thought he was pretentious. He went to Yale and got his MBA at Harvard and wanted everyone to know that. I also did not find him physically or emotionally attractive. I didn't find him interesting at all.

Len: I thought Eric had beautiful blue eyes, but "boy, is he dumb." My friends had already told me about him, that he was the "Belle of the Ball," that everybody was in love with him. I just imagined that if he was that beautiful and everybody was in love with him, he had to be dumb.

Eric, at least six feet tall, and indeed graced by beautiful blue eyes, has a winning smile to match. But despite Eric's eyes, handsome face, and lean body, and Len's Ivy League credentials and warm sense of humor, they were so mutually unimpressed that they quickly forgot about each other until a year later when they happened to meet again. It wasn't until the second time they met—at a birthday party at the same apartment where they had met the year before—that they made a date to have lunch together.

Len: Eric worked right across the street from where I ended up getting a job. I thought it would be nice to have someone who did not work for the same company to go to lunch with.

Eric: Len said he would call me for lunch and I said, "I'm going to be away for a few weeks, so don't bother."

Len: He didn't put it quite that rudely. Actually he's very polite, until you marry him.

Eric: I stayed much too late at the birthday party and got up early to catch a flight the next morning to Buffalo. I got back to work three weeks later, and there was a message that Len had called. I said to myself, "Oh no, I don't want to go to lunch," so I didn't return his call. The next time he called I happened to pick up the phone myself.

Len: I knew he was avoiding my call. I also knew he was going to have lunch with me whether he wanted to or not. He told me he never got the first message.

Eric: Len finally got me to agree to a day to meet for lunch. That's when my opinion changed. When we had lunch, I found Len very interesting to talk to. I thought he was fun. And I think I was getting tired of going out with a lot of pretty boys that . . .

Len: Watch it.

Eric: . . . a lot of pretty boys that I really didn't find interesting to be with or talk to. I realized that Len was interesting to talk to. I admit, most of the men I had gone out with before, I had been physically attracted to immediately. No doubt about it. I'd see a man and know that's what I wanted. But that was not the case with Len. [To Len] "Sorry, but that's the truth."

Len is not unattractive, but his looks are ordinary. When they walk together in their Manhattan neighborhood, it's Eric who gets the second glances.

Len: It doesn't bother me.

Eric: It doesn't?

Len: No, I'm pleased. It's like jewelry—ostentatious conspicuous consumption.

It doesn't bother me that he's the belle of the ball. His being attractive doesn't have much to do with me being jealous, because he's very faithful. I would probably be much more jealous with somebody else.

Eric: Impossible. Impossible for him to be more jealous. He's jealous of the attention I get, the attention I give others, my time. All of those. He gets upset if I spend time with a friend rather than with him. He gets upset if someone shows me attention. He gets upset if I show someone attention. I assume he thinks I'm trying to flirt.

Len: I have to admit I did get upset once when this little blond thing was literally hanging off of him. It was disgusting. It was a little waiter who had a crush on Eric and made no bones about showing it. He yapped behind Eric like a little dog. Nonetheless, it's fun to look at Eric. I wouldn't have it any other way.

A week after that first lunch, Len invited Eric to dinner.

Eric: I was all set for this big romantic dinner . . . I'm not sure I was interested yet, but I thought he was. When he invited me over for dinner I expected dinner, not tacos and his roommate.

Len: All he got was tacos on a bare table; my roommate was there, and the TV was blaring. It was not romantic at all.

Eric: I wasn't used to that kind of treatment.

Len: Usually they fawn and swoon. I had always been a student up until that point so I never had to entertain more formally.

The following week, Eric reciprocated and invited Len to dinner. By then they were both definitely interested.

Eric: I wanted to show him how you're supposed to entertain people.

Len: When I came over he had the whole table set with wine glasses and flowers and napkins all folded up neatly in front of the plates. Dinner was practically prepared by the time I got there. He was so sweet and so kind. I have never, never had a date where somebody treated me so nicely.

Eric: It wasn't an unusual event for me. It was the kind of dinner I would have made for any date. But by then I was interested. I guess I was trying to nab him. I thought he was "H.M." (husband material). After dinner we smooched for the first time. That was three weeks after we started dating.

Len: I felt very uncomfortable because he wanted me to spend the night, and I hadn't really intended to. But after that I was madly in love with him.

Eric: Was it the sex or the dinner?

Len: It was definitely the dinner. We had fun together. We laughed a lot and we entertained each other.

Eric: I still thought he was a nerd, though. He didn't like any of the things I liked.

Eric and Len are, in fact, quite different.

Len: Eric likes baseball, running, and rock-and-roll music. I hated all of them.
Eric: He smoked.
Len: I smoked. I stopped soon after we met. For him.
Eric: Len took up running, too. We started going to movies. But there's a difference in the kinds of schools we went to. We have different types of jobs.

During the months following that first romantic dinner, Eric and Len started spending more time together. First, just weekends, then weekends and one night a week. Then two nights a week.

Eric: Len kept leaving his clothes. First a suit, then a shirt . . .
Len: Well it got to be annoying having to stop at home to change. I was getting to work late. So I started leaving clothes there. And of course, I was very insecure so I'd always ask, "Should we see less of each other? Should I not stay over?" I told Eric, "Whenever you don't want me to stay over, let me know." He said, "Don't worry, if I don't want you to stay I'll let you know." Over the next three months we grew into living together. We didn't talk about living together. It just happened.
Eric: I think if we planned it, it wouldn't have happened.
Len: I wouldn't have wanted to move in with him because that would have been too risky at that point, and he wouldn't have wanted me to move in because he liked the independence of having his own apartment. What if I had moved in all my stuff and a week later he broke up with me? In New York you can't just walk out and find another apartment.

Within a few months, Len was spending every night at Eric's studio apartment. They still hadn't talked about moving in together, so when Len had to move out of his apartment downtown, he looked for one just for himself. He found a one-bedroom duplex—by coincidence, he says—right across the hall from Eric.

Len: I talked to Eric about it to find out if it was okay with him.
Eric: I was hesitant to say yes, because if our relationship didn't work out he would still be across the hall. But I thought it would work out. My feeling going into the relationship was that I was going to work much harder than ever before to maintain this relationship. I had had enough short-term relationships before. I was tired of them.
  Having Eric move across the hall was a big step, but at least he would have his own apartment, and I knew I could tell him to leave my apartment if I needed to. He went ahead and rented the apartment, but didn't move into it for over a year. He just lived with me.

Eric liked his one-room apartment and wanted to stay there. But Len had the larger, more comfortable apartment, and it was just across the hall. With a bit of a push from Len, Eric gave up his place and moved in with Len.

Both Eric's and Len's parents know their sons share an apartment, but neither Eric nor Len has ever discussed with his parents the fact that he is gay. Len's told his two sisters, but no one else, although he suspects that his mother knows. Len has yet to make the trip home with Eric, who has made it clear to Len that he would like to visit Len's family in Colorado. Len has met Eric's parents, but says it was only a quick visit and dinner.

Eric: There was more to the day than just a quick visit and dinner. I took Len out to Long Island and showed him where I went to school and where I went to work and where I grew up. In one day he found out more about me and my experiences than I know about him.

Len: That's because I'm interested, and I made Eric take me out.

Eric: [To Len] Haven't I asked you to introduce me to your mother and father?

Len: [To Eric] Yes, and I said when we go out to Colorado we can meet my mother and father. It's easy for Eric because all he has to do is rent a car and say, "My good buddy Joe, he came out with me in the car. It's boring driving out by myself. So I brought him out. Is it okay if we have dinner?" We have dinner and then drive home. But if Eric flew home with me it would be a big to-do, because I've never brought anybody home with me. Bringing Eric home would be a huge statement.

I'm pretty sure my mother would accept Eric, but my father wouldn't. My father doesn't even know what a homosexual is. The thought of two men living together in a marriage would be completely foreign to him. He just would never understand. It wouldn't even be worth telling him. My mother would understand.

Eric: By not bringing me home he's saying he's ashamed of me, maybe? That he doesn't feel the relationship is worth doing that? That he doesn't feel it's long term? For me, meeting his family has to do with security. It's a way of knowing how serious he is in terms of the relationship and where he thinks it's going. If he's willing to introduce me to his mother and father, then I know he's serious.

Len: The first step was to introduce him to my friends. He thought at first that I wouldn't. He seems to have gotten over that, and now he's on to my family.

Eric: In my family, bringing home anyone is a big deal as well—for all of us. My brother, who is straight, is having quite a time with that. The one time he brought a girlfriend home there was a big argument between her and my father at the dinner table. You have to understand my family. They're very unaffectionate, very closed, very WASPish. They don't discuss sex. They haven't made a practice of expressing their love for their children, though they're improving. It's been difficult growing up in that kind of situation.

I think my father would probably not like to know. With my mother, I just don't know, which is probably keeping me from discussing it with her. In some ways I know she wants to.

I don't know if my mother could accept Len. I'd like her to accept him very much. I want my parents to know more about my life. I want them to know when I'm happy or upset. I feel they just don't know me. As long as they don't know me, I don't really know them. I don't think this is healthy for my relationship with Len or for my life.

For Len, commitment is measured not only by a willingness to introduce Eric to his family.

Len: For me, the biggest thing so far has been subsidizing Eric's rent.
Eric: Huh?
Len: See, he doesn't think much of it. [To Eric] How many boys' rent do you subsidize? I subsidize the rent, and I see that as symbolic of my commitment to the relationship.
Eric: I don't see it that way. Len makes substantially more money than I do. And just about everything in this apartment is mine. And it was part of the . . .
Len: . . . pacifier I had to throw him to make him a little less uneasy about leaving his old apartment and living here. I see the subsidy as symbolic of my commitment to the relationship. I've never lived with anybody before.
Eric: This is the first time I've been aware that Len feels that way.
Len: The fact that I'm willing to live with him and subsidize his rent is fairly significant.

If all goes according to plan, Len will assume full responsibility for paying the rent when Eric returns to school next year to get a law degree. The financial arrangement is Eric's idea. Eric's decision to seek a law degree was encouraged by Len.

Eric: The whole fact that I'm going to law school is due to . . .
Len: Due to me? How in the world did he get that? I never said he should go to law school.
Eric: Of course he did.
Len: No I didn't. I encouraged Eric once he decided to go.
Eric: Len helped me decide that I needed to do something more. I've never really been satisfied in the work I've been doing and Len was aware of that. We began discussing how I could become more satisfied. And really the only way to do that, I think, would be to go back to school. We thought about what type of school. I studied landscape architecture, but that's a difficult major to use in Manhattan. So we thought about business school, but I couldn't think of a satisfying way to use a business degree.
Len: Eric has something of a social conscience. Eric decided he would like to do some sort of gay advocacy work. Something not dealing with corporate America, where he would have to wear a little blue suit and deal with yuppies and guppies.
Eric: I don't mind wearing a blue suit. I dislike making money for wealthy people who don't care about anyone but themselves.
Len: So we determined that even though his skills were less geared to law

school, that that's what he should really do long term considering his larger goals.

Eric: I would not have seriously thought about going to law school before. It would have been a fantasy for me. Len was, in part, responsible for the increase in my confidence about becoming a lawyer. He helped me realize that my lack of interest in work and/or inability to accomplish or succeed at work probably had more to do with not being challenged than a lack of ability.

Len: Eric says that when he starts school I'm going to pay for everything. I say, "No, you're going to get a parttime job and still pay your share of the rent."

Eric: I'm not going to pay my share of the rent. And Len is not paying for everything. I'm taking care of my tuition.

Len: We still have some ground to cover. He's still going to pay his share of the rent.

Eric: My parents are willing to help me, and I have some money saved. So I think I'll be able to make it, but I don't want to work. We've discussed this. I don't want to work while I'm going to school because that's what I did while I was going to college, and it had a very bad effect on my grades. I don't want to do that again.

Len: I worked my way through college. But I might pay a little bit more of the rent.

Eric: I'll pay you back.

Len: We'll work something out. I really do want Eric to go back to school because he would be happier. I think that going back to school would give him self-confidence. It turns out that although he is beautiful, he's quite bright. In fact, he's very bright. And he's sort of depressed about his situation, and I'm sure that has a bad affect on our relationship. So I think things would be better overall if he went back to school. He'd be happier, I'd be happier. He'd lead a richer life.

Eric: And some of your wishes and needs to help society would . . .

Len: . . . be met vicariously by sending him out into the world to be the gay advocate instead of me, because I can't really assume that role and keep my position at work.

Eric: Then he doesn't have to march in a gay pride parade. Still he surprises me. When I first met him I didn't think he was out at all, but he gets involved in quite a few organizations, which I didn't expect. Sometimes I wish he were more out. Sometimes I'd like to take the back seat. Len's need to be involved is fulfilled through my going to law school and doing what I want to do. Sometimes I feel I would rather be in that position. Or if I had someone who was more vocal, I would assume an even more vocal position myself.

Len: I'm vocal, just not on gay issues.

Eric and Len have had other disagreements as well. They are the first to admit that they argue.

Eric: It was ten minutes into our relationship before we had the first argument. We fight a lot.

Len: A lot. We have very different personalities. I'm aggressive and have a terrible temper. When he makes me mad I jump all over him. He's very stubborn, so instead of backing off and saying, "You're right," which would take the wind out of my sails, he sticks his chest out and fights back, which of course makes me all the more mad. The arguments tend to get fairly spicy. The argument ends in the same way a firecracker finishes—in a huge explosion. Finally one of us has to break down before the relationship crumbles apart. Until recently, I was always the one who has backed down. He finally backed down once because he was in danger of losing me.

I asked Len what that argument was about.

Len: We don't want to go into that.
Eric: No, we do. I think we should. But I'll let Len explain.
Len: Eric said that I was unfaithful to him.
Eric: [To Len] I said? Or you *were?* Which one?
Len: I wanted to make Eric mad. And I did make him very mad by going out into the park and meeting a nice boy.
Eric: And so why did we have a fight?
Len: When I came back from the park, Eric asked me if I had done anything. I said "Yeah, I masturbated in the park (we each did our own thing)." Eric got very upset and he ran out and disappeared. When he came back the next day I insisted that he had to tell me where he had been all night long before I would even think about reconciling.

Eric and Len had agreed to be monogamous from the start of their relationship. This was the first time anything like this had happened. The fight that sent Len in the direction of Central Park began just after Len and Eric returned from a baseball game. (They go to every Sunday home game.)

Len: He cheated on me.
Eric: [To Len] In what way?
Len: Eric had gone out running, and I went out running after he did. So he got home before I did. When I came upstairs, he was lying in bed with all the things you need to do "hoochy-koo" with me. But I had stepped in dog poop on my run without realizing it, and he immediately smelled it and went into a tizzy, yelling and screaming and telling me how stupid I was and how could I walk into the house with dog poop on my shoe? I immediately went into the bathtub and washed off the bottom of my shoe. I thought I'd come out and see him still there lying on the bed waiting for me. But in the meantime he had gotten up and gone downstairs and futzed around and came back up and took a shower. He told me that when he was in the shower he did "hoochy-koo" by himself. Well, I thought that if was going to deny me the pleasure I was going to deny him the pleasure.
Eric: He went out to the park immediately without any discussion whatsoever. Neither of us had ever done that before.

Len: We had an agreement: No hoochy-koo with anybody.

Eric: Or?

Len: We break up.

Eric: It was just not permitted in this relationship. Len was the one who was really insistent on that. I don't think I would have discussed it. He was the one who initiated that discussion. I think I assumed that that was the case. It's just the way I was brought up I guess. And that's the way a relationship should be. Just because.

Len: I don't think that's the way people are naturally. You have to work very hard to be that way. But I knew monogamy was very important to Eric, and all I did was bring it out into the open and discuss it and say this is our agreement, right?

   Anyway, I didn't really think about what I was doing. I just thought about it as a way to make him angry. I never even saw it as a breaking of our agreement until later when I calmed down and Eric calmed down and we discussed it a little bit. It was quite clear that it was breaking the agreement and that I never should have done it. But when you're furious at one another you don't always sit down and analyze the situation. I never intended to go out and find a new boyfriend. All I wanted to do was to be able to come back and say, "I did the same thing to you as you did to me. How does it feel?" I probably went overboard.

Eric: It was days before I would tell him where I stayed. I decided I would tell him. But in the meantime things got really, really nasty. Len threatened to lock me out.

Len: We were very close to breaking up. I wouldn't even speak to him until he told me where he was. He would call me on the phone. He would aggravate me at work and I would just hang up on him.

Eric: I was trying to resolve the situation and point out to him how ridiculous it was for him to have to know where I was, that he should trust me. But there was no way to convince him of that.

Len: Nope. I didn't want to encourage him to go out all night and not tell me where he was. That's not anything that I would have settled for. So I wasn't about to let him get away with it this time. We had been trying to make some progress in terms of communication and I wanted to see that he was able to sit down with me and tell me something like that, like where he was. Whether it was good or bad I wanted him to be able to tell me. I thought it was good.

Eric: Liar.

Len: He thinks I believed he had done something that was bad, but I was pretty sure he had been faithful because even afterwards he said that he had not done anything. We generally have an honest relationship. For example, I had to tell him the truth about what happened in the park.

Eric: I think Len had to tell me because he was feeling guilty about it.

Len: I was feeling very guilty about it. Well, eventually Eric gave in and told me where he had been (with friends) and everything was better.

Eric: That's what I don't understand. I don't understand how someone's feelings could change so quickly. I don't understand how Len can threaten to lock me out of the apartment one minute and be loving and caring the next. I just don't understand that. I'm still having problems with that fight. One positive aspect of the whole situation is that we will try to get some counseling to help us deal with some of the problems in our relationship. Len's jealousy, his temper, my inability to really open up as much as he would like, to express affection . . .

Neither Len nor Eric wants to end their relationship despite their initial agreement to break up if one of them ever broke their agreement to be monogamous. I asked them why they're still together.

Eric: I'm not sure. I guess my commitment to the relationship is still very strong. I think it's caused some damage to the relationship but I don't think it's beyond repair. As long as Len is willing to try to change things, change his personality in some ways, then it's worth continuing.

Len: The rent would be too much if he weren't here.

Eric: [To Len] Truth.

Len: He's a nice guy.

Eric: Who's having trouble expressing his feelings now?

Len: I like him. I would be miserable without him.

Eric: For how long?

Len: For three weeks?

Eric: How long?

Len: Maybe three years. Besides I don't have time to go shopping for a new husband. And I don't think I would find someone like Eric that easily.

Because of Eric I totally changed the way I lived. I went from a typical yuppie with engagements every night for dinner or drinks or something like that to being a typical homebody who never sees anybody but his husband because Eric just makes the perfect home. The house always looks nice. It's very warm.

It's very homey. He has all the little gizmos you need to make a nice dinner at home. Whereas I had just the bare necessities. He keeps the refrigerator stocked with food all the time. I was lucky if I had eggs in there. It was just so nice to have a nice dinner together and maybe watch TV for an hour or go out for a walk or watch a movie or whatever. But it was just so nice to have a married life and do things together and understand what that whole side was about. And that's what I would miss if he were to go, because my entire life would go away too and my little homemaker and my little home. Everything would disappear.

Eric: I have hope about the future. That we're still together. That we're both still alive. [Eric chokes up and pauses before going on.] I hope that maybe we live somewhere in the country and have an apartment here in the city. That we are madly in love with each other.

Len: I feel pretty much the same way except for the house in the country. Maybe a house in France.

In this day and age you have to worry about not being alive in five years. Both of us have friends who are kicking off all the time. And when you see people you went to school with or used to run with getting sick you begin to worry about yourself.

We haven't been tested. We've talked about it. My doctor is encouraging us to because he feels that if you are tested then you will be smart enough to make wise decisions. And if you come out positive you won't do dangerous things. Right now we don't do dangerous things. The doctor knows we've been together a long time. We probably won't get tested. If it comes, it comes. If it doesn't, it doesn't.

MARK AND DALE

Mark and Dale's story seemed remarkable because, in some ways, they are so unremarkable. Except for the fact they are two men, their way of life is, by any standard, unexceptional and conventional. But they *are* two men living on a family farm in the heart of what they describe as Ku Klux Klan country, with Dale's 15-year-old son and 80-year-old mother. Within the scope of my research, their circumstances challenged my expectations. I also had a lot of fun visiting with them, their family, and friends during a summer weekend.

Mark and Dale would be the first to tell you that the way of life they now have, and the relationships they have built, have taken years of work and commitment. There have been plenty of tears, frustrations, illnesses, and arguments along the way. In many respects, they're like any other family. That wasn't what I expected to find on their farm in rural Tennessee.

Mark and Dale live on a large piece of property they share with several members of Dale's family, about thirty miles outside a small Tennessee city. The drive out from the city took me through small towns, past farms and many, many churches. Turning off a main paved road onto the dirt road that leads to the entrance of Mark and Dale's corner of the family property, I passed the small stone house where Dale's parents used to live, a field of fruit trees, a fenced-in area filled with boisterous white turkeys, and the stable where Precious, their beautiful sand-colored horse, lives. The entrance to the property is blocked by a gate, one of Dale's imaginative Rube Goldberg-like mechanical wonders made of weights, an old bicycle wheel, rope, and an electronic keypad. Punching the right numbers sets the whole contraption in motion, clearing the way to the house.

Despite a recent drought, the road to their house was lined with flowers. Dale has slowly been landscaping the property. Already there's a small sitting area nestled into a hillside surrounded by shrubs, flowers, and trees. A little fountain sends water splashing over a pile of rocks near the stone patio.

Their house is down a few stone steps from the patio and across a dirt driveway, its front facing a pasture. Dale has finished the roof and his son's room, but except for this and the mobile home around which the house is being built, the rest of the structure is just a shell. Until it's finished, living arrangements are tight. The main room of the mobile home is a combined kitchen and living room. It's filled with furniture, dozens of flowering African violets, and a pair of parakeets. There's a special chair set aside for Dale's frail 80-year-old mother, who lives with them as well.

Jimmy's room is a hint of how wonderful the house will be. It's ceiling is about twelve feet high, topped by a skylight. There's a loft bed reached by a ladder, and a "Hobbit" door that leads out to a small balcony overlooking the field—complete with tranquil-looking cows— in front of the house. The walls and ceiling are painted white, the wood trim and carpeting are blue. Jimmy's weightlifting equipment fills the middle of the room.

Dale is 39. He's the youngest of nine children and grew up on the land where he and Mark now live. When he was 17 he was briefly involved with the KKK. At 18 he was married, and at 19, left for Viet Nam. He's a tall, quiet, solid-looking man who used to drive trucks and carry one hundred-pound bags of flour on and off his truck. He barely reads or writes. He quit his trucking job about a half-year ago because of back problems and now splits his time between working on the house and working in a cleaning business Mark owns. Dale separated from his wife in 1976. By then he and his wife had had two children:

> We had a pretty good marriage but it faded away. I've always been gay and just not known it. When I went to Nam I found out there was a different life. She didn't accept it right off and had a hard time, but she realized that separating was for the best and realized that I wasn't going to change. Now she's made friends with both of us.

Mark is articulate, sandy blond, blue-eyed, and looks older than his 28 years, which isn't surprising given the hard time he had growing up, coping with being gay and living with an alcoholic mother.

> I tried the suicide routine in high school. I felt worthless and useless. At one point I committed myself to a mental hospital.

Mark made it through college, but wasn't managing his life much better than before when he met Dale.

> My friends were all eager for me to settle down and stay on one track. I was doing lots of drugs, drinking, and tricking. The way the world is now with AIDS, I wouldn't be alive.

Mark and Dale met in 1979 through Dale's trucking partner and on-again, off-again lover.

Mark: I was living with friends at the time. I was in a foul mood one night and didn't feel like hitting the bars or bookstores, and a roommate and some of his friends suggested we go to a bar in a nearby town. I met a fellow down there, Ray. He looked like an easy mark. I went home with him but found out he was awful and got up to leave. I found Dale in the living room. Dale was driving a truck then. Ray was his partner. I wound up spending the night with Dale instead.

Dale: I was really attracted to Mark because I was into young men and Mark was a real young guy. That started it and then I found out about his personality. I discovered that he was a lot like me. He was easy to be with.

Mark: Dale fascinated me. I was real lonely up to that point. I had been running around a lot and wasn't getting any satisfaction from it. I found Dale very interesting and very strong, dependable, supportive. He flattered me. He made me feel good about myself—at ease and very protected.

Over the next few months Mark and Dale got to know each other · between Dale's long-haul driving assignments. Around Halloween, Dale moved in with Mark.

Mark: We didn't discuss it or plan it. It was just the thing to do. We had a lot of people living in the apartment then. Mark was home two days out of the month so it was more of a telephone relationship for the first year. We talked every day.

Dale: I missed him a lot.

For two and a half years Mark and Dale lived in the city. Dale had wanted to move up to his family's property and Mark eventually gave in.

Mark: I was very nervous about it because I didn't know his mother well at that time or his brother or his other brother. After we moved to the country and were in the middle of family land that Dale's family had had for years and years, I just knew that the minute Dale left for the road, the lynch mob was going to come for me. But the family met us the first day with apple pies.

Dale: I wasn't worried. I didn't care what other people thought of my life. They didn't give me any reason to be worried about it. I didn't know how they would accept it. We didn't talk about it. The subject's come up since then. I had one brother in Texas who had some negative things to say about us living up here and Grandma living with us and it took Charlie, my brother who lives next door to us, all of five minutes to put him in his place. My brothers here and my sister in Baltimore are the most open-minded.

Mark: Now I don't see us as any different than any other family up here because they don't make us feel any different. Even Dale's siblings' children have been respectful. They give us the same kind of respect they would give any other married couple that was their neighbor or family.

Dale: Since Jimmy [Dale's son] has lived up here and is going to school here, more friends come in from outside who we haven't known before and they're all just as respectful and abiding as everyone else. I don't know it for a fact, but I feel sure they've had to defend us to outsiders, maybe people in the church asking questions or making comments. I know my family and I'm sure they have defended us and supported us.

Mark's parents were not supportive at first, but since his mother's death four years ago, he and his father have gotten along fairly well.

Mark: My mother spit in my face when she found out I was gay. We never talked about it again. My father took her negative view of me and our relationship until Momma was gone. Then he changed entirely. He met Dale the day after she died. I talk to my dad weekly. I don't feel real comfortable there. Maybe because of his new wife.

Mark and Dale lived together for a short while before Dale's mother, who's in ill health, came to live with them. She's a long-time fan of evangelist Jimmy Swaggart but turns off the TV whenever he starts in about homosexuality.

Dale: If she weren't living with us she wouldn't be alive.
Mark: It was the thing to do. She needed us.
Dale: We needed her too.
Mark: She goes to the doctor two or three times a month. Last summer her left knee was replaced. She had to have somebody with her at all times. We can't go anywhere without making sure she's taken care of.
Dale: For any couple having to care for an ill parent it would put a strain on their relationship. It can make tensions high, but we're thankful we can do something for her.
Mark: We get mad at her sometimes. Senility can make you angry. But she's not a burden. She's a lot of trouble sometimes, but she's not a burden. She's been through a lot in her lifetime. We get a lot of pleasure out of caring for her.

Dale and I put a lot of value on our family. You don't turn your back on your family.
Dale: My mother has adopted Mark. She tells everyone that Mark is a part of the family. She wouldn't know what to do without Mark.

A couple of years after Dale's mother came to live with them, Dale's son Jimmy, now 15, moved in full-time. After Dale left his marriage, he never expected either his daughter or son would live with him.

Mark: Dale felt the road he had taken would take him away from his kids.

Dale: I wasn't going to push any of the kids to live with me, even if I could take care of them. I felt my life wasn't right for raising kids, but everything changed around. Before I met Mark I wasn't much at all. I didn't have a life, let alone a life for children. It was a lot of empty space.

Mark: At first I saw the kids as a hindrance to me being with Dale. But the more you're around them, the more you love them. We talked about the possibility of Jimmy moving in for years, because we knew Jimmy would eventually want to move in.

Dale: He stayed the summer with us every year.

Mark: He wasn't happy living in the city. It became obvious that he needed to be with his daddy more than we needed to keep together the brother and sister.

When it comes to raising Jimmy, we both jump right in there feet first.

Dale: It's everybody's job to keep him in line.

Mark: Dale's never called me for being out of line. I've never been told that he wasn't my kid or it wasn't any of my business. We disagree sometimes, but no one has ever questioned my authority.

Dale: He's a lot stricter than I am, but he can also be very wishy-washy. All Jimmy has to do is act right and he gets his way with Mark.

Mark: I've asked him if any of his friends have ripped him about his dad being gay and he's told me no. It doesn't seem to bother him or embarrass him to talk about it. We let him know that we're here to talk about it if he wants to. I've always been paranoid and so scared that someone was going to give him a hard time, but no one has.

Mark is credited by their friends for pulling Jimmy together scholastically.

Mark: We just let him know we expected that from him. We put a lot of time into doing homework. I'm strict and Dale doesn't put up with laziness either. We all get our jobs done.

When Mark and Dale first got together, they never imagined they would be living on the family property, taking care of Dale's mother, and raising Jimmy together. They never even imagined their relationship would last.

Mark: I didn't think those relationships lasted. I had that same stereotyped belief that gay couples never lasted. I figured that two years was a record.

Dale: One of my biggest questions at first was why Mark was staying with me. I thought that these gay relationships didn't last. But it's good and it's better than when we first met. We have more and more roots tied down.

Mark: At first we clinged desperately to each other. We were desperate for love and someone to love. It felt good so we hung onto it.

Dale: I was worried that it might not be there tomorrow.

Mark: We weren't sure at first that it would last. I'm sure it was a couple of years before we realized that it was something that could last. Now we can't imagine anything different.

I also thought that if I did find someone, that I would have to withdraw from society, but you don't have to. We don't scream from the rooftops or throw it in anyone's face. We just approach it honestly.

After seven years together, Mark and Dale view their relationship as rock-solid and permanent.

Mark: I see what we have as above marriage. What we've got is more binding than a ceremony or paper. It's a commitment.

Dale: It's more binding than the marriage I had with my wife. I feel like Mark was the one I was meant to be with. It's everything I always wanted.

Mark: It's love and commitment that makes it what it is. It's an unspoken commitment. There are no rules or anything to tell you when you've run afoul of it. We support each other, look out for each other, draw strength from each other. That keeps us pretty glued together.

It helps that we agree for the most part on everything that rolls by on the six-o'clock news. We feel very strongly about things in the same direction— viewpoints on world affairs, religion, raising children. Our goals are things that drive us. It was not this way with me at first. At first when we got together the kids were a nuisance to me, but it was just something that had to be dealt with. There was not a lot of pleasure around the issue of kids at first. Now I love them. I would fight anyone tooth and nail who said they weren't mine. And I guess that's probably one of the biggest motivators for why we work so hard to make sure our relationship works well. We enjoy it and we have our kids and family to look out for. We see ourselves as being right here on this dirt until we die and we see the kids taking it after we're gone and enjoying what we've built for them. It's just the same good old red-blooded American dream that any family would have for their kids. That's why we get up and go to work. It isn't to take vacations and to buy big-screen TVs. It's to build a home for our kids. We hope that when we get old they'll take care of us like we take care of Grandma now.

Mark and Dale also share a common view about fooling around with other men outside of their relationship.

Mark: We gave it a try once, a year into the relationship, and pretty much threw him out of bed and didn't go through with it. At the last minute we realized we did not want to do this, that it would be detrimental to the relationship. It would disgrace and discredit the relationship. He gives me what I need. We look. We're not above looking at a cute guy, but that's as far as it goes.

Dale: It made us feel bad later that we had shared something that belonged to each other. It's not only sex, but the commitment and feelings we have for each other, the love we have for each other.

Mark: We've been approached and had people make offers. We let them know

it's just something we never do. Now with the health issues, we're so thankful
we never did. It makes it an even more secure and safe relationship. We were
both tested for the HIV antibody, and we tested negative.

Although they share values and beliefs about most issues, Mark and
Dale are quick to note that they don't always agree and sometimes
argue.

Dale: We've had our fusses, but never knockdown fights. We've never struck
each other.
Mark: We've had our ups and downs, but we've never stopped loving each
other. The problems are over the usual things. Making ends meet. Tensions
run high when you're short on cash. Sometimes we disagree on how to raise
kids. And we've had our problems here with constructing the house.
Dale: I'm building the house, so things go where I want them to go.
Mark: I can bring up the idea and draw it, but I wouldn't know how to begin
to start building it. It just comes out of Dale's head. None of this came from
blueprints. We get rough ideas. From that point I'm the carpenter's helper.
We dream it up. He tells me what he's seeing in his mind. Then I get it on
paper. He corrects it. Once he's finished building, the painting and furniture
is up to me.
Dale: I'm worst at that.
Mark: I'm not wild about painting either. And even though Dale says he's not
into painting or decorating we still have arguments about paint color.

Mark took out a loan in his name to finance the cost of construction
and the mortgage on the mobile home is in his name as well. Where
they live, Mark feels it would be a hassle to get the mortgage and loan
in both names. They own the land together.

Mark: Sometimes when people combine those things they think it will force
them to think twice before splitting. We don't see it that way. If it weren't
a hassle, everything would be in both names.
   When we've worked separate jobs, our paychecks went straight into the
same bank account. You get out there and do the best you can do and bring
home as much as you can bring home and put it all together and make it go
as far as it can go. We've got friends where one charges the other rent. We
can't comprehend doing things that way. We feel like you've got a commitment to each other and you do it together.

At the end of the interview, I asked Mark and Dale if they had any
advice for men who were looking to be in a relationship or for men who
were just starting a relationship. Mark responded:

You just have to find someone that you're comfortable with, can be at ease
with, that you can be yourself with, that you don't have to play games with.

Sure, on your first date or encounter you're gonna play games and put up some fronts.

You've got to become friends first, and be comfortable and honest. And when you get over the infatuation and you're not having sex six times a day, and you settle down a bit, that's when you have to put the effort into it. You have to decide if this is the right relationship, if this relationship is worth working for. And then you have to get in there and work every day, all the time.

Don't go into a relationship and expect things. You've got to go in and do things. You have to show your love and show your commitment. That's what will get into someone's heart and make the relationship. Then you find somebody else who's willing to put the equal into it. Then you've got a relationship.

When I left Mark and Dale early Sunday afternoon to return home, Mark was preparing a roast for Sunday dinner. Dale's ex-wife and daughter were expected any minute. When they arrived, Mark, Dale, Jimmy, Grandma, Dale's former wife, and his daughter all planned to head up to Dale's older brother's house on the hill to join several other family members at the swimming pool. I was sorry I hadn't planned to stay longer.

General Resources

ORGANIZATIONS

National Gay/Lesbian Crisis Line, 800–221–7044
212–529–1604 in New York, Alaska, Hawaii, and outside the U.S.
3:00–9:00 P.M. (Eastern Standard Time) Monday–Friday

> The Crisis Line will provide information, referrals, and crisis counseling concerning coming out, domestic violence, relationship crises, youth counseling, custody, AIDS, substance abuse, assistance for disabled gay/lesbian people, discrimination, anti-gay/lesbian violence, prisoner assistance.
>
> The Crisis Line is a program of the Fund for Human Dignity, established in 1974 to "combat ignorance and antigay bigotry through education." Printed information is also available from the Fund for Human Dignity on a variety of subjects, including AIDS, coming out, and gay/lesbian seniors.

For printed information, write or call:

The Fund for Human Dignity, National Gay/Lesbian Clearing House, 666 Broadway—4th Floor, New York, NY 10012, 212–529–1600

Couples National Network, Inc., 343 Orizaba Avenue #C, Long Beach, CA 90184, 213–433–3518

> Couples is an international social/informational organization for gay male and lesbian couples. The organization is careful to note that is has no religious or political affiliations. Couples publishes a monthly newsletter.

Homosexual Information Center, 6758 Hollywood Boulevard #208, Hollywood, CA 90028, 213–464–8431

The Homosexual Information Center provides general information on homosexuality as well as specialized in-depth analyses for scholars and students. It assists in the preparation of papers and research projects. The Center maintains a circulating library and publishes bibliographies, reading lists, a directory of homosexual organizations (see "Books/Publications"), and a newsletter.

National Gay and Lesbian Task Force (NGLTF), 1517 U Street, NW, Washington, DC 20009, 202–332–6483

NGLTF, founded in 1973, is a private nonprofit organization dedicated to public education and civil rights advocacy. It has publications available on a wide variety of topics related to homosexuality, including discrimination and violence. NGLTF is funded by more than seven thousand members.

BOOKS/PUBLICATIONS

General

Directory of Homosexual Organizations and Publications: A Field Guide to the Homosexual Movement in the United States and Canada

Published by the Homosexual Information Center, the *Directory* lists hundreds of gay organizations across the U.S. and Canada, from social organizations to religious groups. (See "Organizations" for address and phone number of the Center.)

Gayellow Pages. National (USA and Canada) and regional editions. Renaissance House, Box 292, Village Station, New York, NY 10014, 212–674–0120

The *Gayellow Pages* is packed with information about how to find everything from doctors, lawyers, and dentists to helplines, travel agents, religious groups, and AA groups. Write or call for information and current prices.

Twenty Questions About Homosexuality

This pamphlet is published by the National Gay and Lesbian Task Force (NGLTF) and is available through the organization. (See "Organizations" for information on how to contact NGLTF.)

Couples

American Couples: Money—Work—Sex, by Philip Blumstein and Pepper Schwartz, 1983. Pocket Books, 1230 Avenue of the Americas, New York, NY 10020

This is a detailed study of American couples—straight and gay—packed with statistics, graphs, and charts. The book focuses on money, work, and sex. Unfortunately the conclusions drawn about gay male couples and casual sex seem naive. Included in the book are five profiles of male couples. Regrettably, the authors chose five nonmonogamous couples, which only serves to perpetuate the myth that monogamous male couples are as rare as hen's teeth.

The Male Couple: How Relationships Develop, by David P. McWhirter and Andrew M. Mattison, 1984. Prentice-Hall, Route 9W, Englewood Cliffs, NJ 07632

The authors have drawn together a great mass of information about male couples and they present a compelling thesis about the development of male couple relationships. They base their conclusions on interviews with 156 couples in San Diego, California. They are careful to note in the introduction to their book that "the very nature of our research sample, its size, its narrow geographic location, and the natural selectiveness of the participants prevent the findings from being applicable and generalizable to the entire gay male community." It is important when reading this book to keep these limitations in mind when comparing the authors' findings with your own experiences.

The Mendola Report—A New Look at Gay Couples, by Mary Mendola, 1980. Crown Publishers, 34 Engelhard Avenue, Avenel, NJ 07001

The Mendola Report is based on a nationwide study and personal interviews of gay male and lesbian couples. Relying primarily on anecdotes and the results of the survey, Mary Mendola discusses a broad range of couple issues from everyday living together, sex, and financial partnerships to families, gay widowhood, and retirement.

Man to Man, by Charles Silverstein, 1981. Quill, 105 Madison Avenue, New York, NY 10016

Drawing from his experience as a psychologist and interviews with 190 gay men across the country, Silverstein writes on a variety of topics concerning couple relationships.

Partners—The Newsletter for Gay & Lesbian Couples, PO Box 9685, Seattle, WA 98109, 206–329–9140

First published in December 1986, this monthly newsletter is written by a male couple who intend to develop *Partners* into a resource and forum for gay and lesbian couples.

BOOK MAIL ORDER SERVICES

Note: Only those services that publish a catalog are listed. Call or write for information on how to order a catalog.

A Different Light, 548 Hudson Street, New York, NY 10014, 212–989–4850
 4014 Santa Monica Boulevard, Hollywood, CA 90029, 213–668–0629

Chosen Books, 940 West McNichols, Detroit, MI 48203, 313–864–0485

Deskins & Greene, Box 1092, Atlantic City, NJ 08404, 609–646–6920

Elysian Fields Booksellers, 80–50 Baxter Avenue #339, Elmhurst, NY 11373, 718–424–2789

Giovanni's Room, 345 South 12th Street, Philadelphia, PA 19107, 215–923–2960

Lambda Rising, 1625 Connecticut Avenue NW, Washington, DC 20009, 202–462–6969 (Lambda Rising publishes "The Whole Gay Catalog," which lists videos, music, as well as books.)

Oscar Wilde Memorial Bookshop, 15 Christopher Street, New York, NY 10014, 212–255–8097

Paths Untrodden Book Service, PO Box 459, Village Station, New York, NY 10014, 212–924–5421

Index